BASIC CON

in the metho

of the social sciences

3.25
/14

HSRC SERIES IN METHODOLOGY

Series Editor: Johann Mouton

[Incorporating the HSRC Investigation into Research Methodology's Research Reports Series (REPORTS) and the HSRC Studies in Research Methodology (STUDIES)]

Published titles

1. Norval, AJ. 1984. 'n Teoretiese studie van die metodologie van kruiskulturele houdinsmeting [Reports No. 1]
2. Joubert, Dian. 1986. Waardes: Navorsing, metodologie en teorie. [Reports No. 2]
3. Mouton, Johann (ed) Social science, society and power [Reports No. 3]
4. Mauer, KF & Retief, AI (eds). 1987. Psychology in context: Cross-cultural research trends in South Africa [Reports No. 4]
5. Van Straaten, Z (ed). 1987. Ideological beliefs in the social sciences [Reports No. 5]
6. Retief, Alexis 1988. Method and theory in cross-cultural psychological assessment [Reports No. 6]
7. Kruger, Dryer. 1988. The problem of interpretation in psychotherapy [Reports No. 7]
8. Strauss, DFM 1988. Die grondbegrippe van die sosiologie as wetenskap [Reports No. 8]
9. Mouton, J. et al. 1988. Essays in social theorizing [Reports No. 9]
10. Mouton, J. 1988. The methodology and philosophy of the social sciences: A selective bibliography of anthologies [Reports No. 10]
11. Mouton, J & Marais, HC. 1985. Metodologie van die geesteswetenskappe: Basiese begrippe [Studies No. 1]
12. Van Huyssteen, JWV. 1986. Teologie as kritiese geloofsverantwoording [Studies No. 2]
13. Snyman, JJ & Du Plessis, PGW (reds). 1989. Wetenskapbeelde in die geesteswetenskappe [Studies No. 3]
14. Mouton, J & Marais, HC 1988. Basic concepts in the methodology of the social sciences [Studies No. 4]
15. Mouton, J; Van Aarde, AG & Vorster, WS (eds). 1988. Paradigms and progress in theology [Studies No. 5]
16. Frost, M; Vale, P & Weiner, D (eds). 1989. International relations: A debate on methodology
17. Nel, P. 1989. Approaches to Soviet politics
18. Mouton, J & Joubert, D (eds). 1990. Knowledge and method in the human sciences

BASIC CONCEPTS

in the methodology

of the social sciences

Johann Mouton
HC Marais

Assisted by:
KP Prinsloo
NJ Rhoodie

Human Sciences Research Council

First impression 1988
Revised edition, First impression 1990
　　　　　　　　　Second impression 1991
　　　　　　　　　Third impression 1993
　　　　　　　　　Fourth impression 1994
　　　　　　　　　Fifth impression 1996

ISBN 0-7969-0648-3

Translation from **Metodologie van die Geesteswetenskappe: Basiese begrippe** by K F Mauer

Published by:
HSRC Publishers
134 Pretorius Street
0001 Pretoria
South Africa

Printed by Aurora Printers, Pretoria West

CONTENTS

PART 1

PART 2

PART 3

SERIES FOREWORD

One of the major characteristics of science is that a high premium is placed on the validity and credibility of findings. The most important rationale for methodological analysis is therefore to be found in the emphasis which is placed on the scientific nature of research. Stated differently, the aim of research methodology is to develop and articulate strategies and methods by means of which the validity and credibility or research results in the social sciences may be maximized. Broadly speaking, these are also the aims which led to the inception of the HSRC Investigation into Research Methodology.

One of the more specific aims of the research programme on the methodology of the social sciences is to publish a series of reports, monographs, and collections of papers which contribute to the literature in the area. Research reports are published in the Research report series of the investigation, while monographs and collections of papers are to be published in the series in which this monograph appears, i.e. the HSRC Studies in Research Methodology. It is intended that the material published in both series should be representative of the many themes encountered in the field of methodology, and the eventual content will therefore range from philosophical to practical-technical material, and from quantitative-statistical to the other pole of qualitative-interpretative approaches.

As indicated by the authors, the motivation for this particular volume is to be found in the clear need for a greater degree of conscious and systematic thinking about general methodological principles. The aim was to write a book in which considerations of validity that are central to all disciplines in the social sciences would be discussed in an introductory fashion. The manner in which highly complex issues have been simplified and systematized in this volume makes it an excellent introductory text for those who need a clearer understanding of the methodology of the social sciences.

KF MAUER

Preface

Background

Studies on the structure and process of research in the social sciences may be divided into two broad categories. On the one hand, there are those in which the primary emphasis, as far as both style and content are concerned, is on matters of a philosophical nature. On the other hand, there are those works in which the emphasis is on conducting research, and where the bulk of the text is devoted to providing guidelines for the most effective ways of doing research.

Philosophical studies of the social sciences generally focus on the more abstract dimensions of scientific praxis and would typically include studies of the nature of social science, the underlying assumptions and presuppositions, and also the overall aims of social sciences research. The approach is more often than not holistic: social science is analyzed in its relationship to other fields of human endeavour, and in such a manner that issues relating to ethics, human nature and society are also addressed. The primary aim in studies of this nature is to construct consistent conceptions of science or, more specifically, coherent conceptions of the nature and structure of social science, the problems of rationality, objectivity, and truth, different interpretations of social theorizing, and questions relating to the theoretical and practical aims of the social sciences.

Studies belonging to the second group tend to approach the problems of research in the social sciences from a more instrumentalistic or research-technical perspective. These studies typically deal with the following question: "Which specific techniques or methods ought to be used in order to produce valid research findings?" The aim of studies of this nature is to provide the researcher with manuals or practical guides in which the most important methods of operationalizing a research problem, collecting data, and the analysis of the data are explained in detail. Typically, as far as the collection of data is concerned, guidelines are presented on interviewing, the construction of questionnaires, the use of projective techniques, scale construction, and participant and systematically controlled observation. In the case of the analysis of the data, clear and systematic guidelines on quantitative techniques such as descriptive and inferential statistics are discussed. Similarly, relating to qualitative studies, the reader will be presented with material on analytical induction, the grounded theory approach, and the construction of typologies.

Aims

This book, however, does not fall neatly into either of these categories, but is aimed at bridging the gap between them. The problems of research in the social sciences are neither discussed from a philosophical point of view nor, for that matter, from a point of view which represents an emphasis on research methods or techniques. Our primary aim has been to present a systematic analysis of those concepts which are an essential part of the researcher's "intellectual equipment". Emphasis is placed on fundamental methodological concepts which underlie decisions made in the research process, rather than on the methods and techniques themselves. In this way, we hope to encourage a more critical attitude on the part of the researcher.

However, no work on the methodology of the social sciences can be divorced entirely from philosophical considerations. The analysis of concepts such as theory, model, validity, objectivity, and so on, depends to a large extent upon more recent analyses and insights in the philosophy of the social sciences. A related, and important, secondary aim of the book has been to "translate" philosophical terminology and to make it more readily accessible to the reader. At the same time, there are, of course, inevitably direct ties between this work and manuals in which explicit guidelines for conducting research are provided.

By means of an analysis of basic concepts, we have attempted to provide the researcher with a general frame of reference which may be employed to systematize and organize the variety of methods and concepts which are used in research. In order to link the more philosophical and the more technical issues extensive references to both philosophical and technical literature are provided at the end of each chapter.

The senior author has been working in the field of the philosophy of the social sciences for the past ten years: first as a lecturer in the philosophy of social science and subsequently as head of the centre for research methodology at the Human Sciences Research Council. His experience has been that both students and inexperienced researchers, as a rule, have great difficulty in (1) coming to grips with abstract philosophical arguments on the nature of the social sciences, and (2) relating these arguments to their everyday research in disciplines such as sociology, psychology, and so on. On the other hand, regular discussions with social researchers have convinced him that what is needed in the field of research methodology, is not another recipe book of research techniques. Rather, social scientists are in need of a book that provides them with a frame of reference, with a meta-methodological perspective, from which a systematic overview of the available research methods and techniques as well as the underlying principles may be obtained. It is, therefore, hoped that the researcher will use this work together with the many excellent manuals of a more research-technical nature.

Layout

This book consists of three major sections. In the first, which includes chapters 1 to 7, the basic concepts of the methodology of the social sciences are discussed. In the second, chapters 8 and 9, the most important concepts of part one are integrated in discussions on the writing of research proposals and research reports. The third section (appendices) consists of three "case studies" in which the most important methodological principles which were discussed in the preceding sections are illustrated.

The approach that has been followed in the book emphasizes the logical and conceptual relationships between the fundamental concepts of research methodology. It is for this reason that the first part starts out with a chapter in which a model of the research process is developed and which serves as a frame of reference for the rest of the book. This model is used to illustrate how concepts are related, and it also indicates the order in which they will be dealt with in subsequent sections. In Chapters 2 to 5 the most important decisions in the research process are discussed, i.e. formulating the research problem, conceptualization, operationalization, data collection, analysis, and interpretation. The emphasis throughout is on research design considerations: not the decisions and techniques, but rather the underlying considerations of validity. Chapter 6 is devoted to a discussion of the central constructs which not only guide research, but which are also inevitably a product of research, for example, concepts, statements (hypotheses and definitions), conceptual frameworks (typologies, models, and theories), and paradigms. In Chapter 7 the most important similarities and differences between the quantitative and qualitative approaches are explicated by means of the distinctions and basic concepts which were developed and discussed in the preceding chapters. At a more concrete level, information is provided in Chapters 8 and 9 (part two) on how the methodological principles of the social sciences are utilized in the preparation of a research proposal and in writing a research report.

The inclusion of the three case studies in Part III has a threefold aim: First, these studies were selected because we are of the opinion that they provide useful illustrations of "research in action". A number of the basic concepts and methodological principles discussed in Part I are employed in these studies and reference is therefore made throughout Part I to relevant parts in the case studies. The case studies were, however, also selected because they represent three fairly divergent approaches to research in the social sciences: Ferreira's study of an outpatient care centre is typical of qualitative research in the social sciences, Joubert's construction of a typology of value orientations is a good example of conceptual analysis, while Mauer and Lawrence's article provides the reader with a good introduction to quantitative (experimental) research. Finally, we have included a list of questions at the end of each case study in the hope that this will encourage students and researchers to read research articles more critically and systematically.

As far as the different contributions are concerned, the following information is relevant: Chapters 1 to 6 were written by J. Mouton, who was also responsible for the final editing of the manuscript; Chapter 7 was written by H.C. Marais and Chapter 9 by the latter in collaboration with Mouton. Chapter 8 was written by K.P. Prinsloo and the illustrative examples which appear in Chapters 5 and 6 were compiled by N.J. Rhoodie.

Acknowledgements

Originally a much briefer version of this book was used for purposes of internal training at the HSRC. The material was presented in various sessions in the training programmes presented since 1983. In addition, the material also formed the basis of courses in methodology presented at the Rand Afrikaans University (also since 1983) and a number of courses at the Windhoek Academy, Potchefstroom University for Christian Higher Education and Winter Schools in Research Methodology by the senior author. The authors' sincere gratitude is therefore expressed to those individuals who, during these presentations, contributed in some way to the final product by asking questions, passing remarks, and making suggestions which have inevitably led to an improved final document.

The authors also wish to extend their gratitude to various individuals who, at various stages during the preparation of the manuscript, were prepared to offer comments: Dian Joubert, Ricky Mauer, Alet Norval, Gustav Puth, and Willem Schurink. We would particularly like to thank Alet Norval who made considerable contributions as far as the technical editing of the book was concerned, and also Susan Smith who typed the manuscript most professionally under conditions of extreme pressure. Appendices 2 and 3 are reprinted, with the permission of the authors from *Mens en maatschappij*, volume 48(3), 1973 and *The Journal of the South African Institute of Mining and Metallurgy*, volume 74, 1974. We are also indebted to the typing pool for further assistance, to Lynette Hearne for the design of the cover, to Susan le Roux for bibliographic searches, to members of staff of the IRD who assisted with the proofreading of the manuscript, and to the staff of the HSRC's Section for Technical Services for their care with the publication.

Preface to Revised Edition

Since its appearance in 1985 in Afrikaans and in English 1988, *Basic concepts in the methodology of the soial sciences,* has been used as prescribed textbook at most South African universities and in a wide variety of disciplines in the social sciences and humanities. It has also been the major text in more than ten schools in research methodology organized by the Group Information Dynamics (Centre for Research Methodology) since 1986. One can safely state that it has become one of the leading methodology textbooks in South African tertiary education today.

Based upon feedback from lecturers using the book, as well as the response of delegates to the schools in methodology, it is clear that the book is fulfilling its main function, i.e. that of providing an introduction to the fundamental concepts of social sciences research. It is not a substitute, as it was never intended to be, to books on specific research methods and techniques. Rather, by using it in a complementary role to such books, one provides the student with the "best of both worlds". On the one hand, the student is provided with a general frame of reference in which the basic concepts of research in his or her discipline is discussed. On the other hand, he or she is also exposed to a wide range of specific methods and techniques and their applications.

In bringing out a revised edition we decided not to change the contents in any fundamental way. We believe that the book is still as relevant and useful as the first time that it appeared. However, certain smaller editorial revisions are always inevitable. Also, it was decided to make the first chapter — usually found to be the most "philosophical" — a bit more "user friendly" through the introduction of some more detail as well as summaries in strategic places.

We trust that the book will continue to meet the demands of those who embark on research for the first time as well as the "old hands" who refer to it from time to time.

Johann Mouton
September 1990

PART 1

Introduction: The scientific language game

Dimension of social sciences research

The sociological dimension
The ontological dimension
The teleological dimension
The epistemological dimension
The methodological dimension

An integrated model of social sciences research

Intellectual climate
Market of intellectual resources
The research process

Summary

Suggestions for further reading

CHAPTER 1

WHAT IS SOCIAL SCIENCES RESEARCH?

THE SCIENTIFIC LANGUAGE GAME

Our true lover of knowledge naturally strives for reality, and will not rest content with each set of particulars which opinion takes from reality, but soars with undimmed and unwearied passion till he grasps the nature of each thing as it is ... (Plato, *Republic*, 490b)

It is an essential part of being human to strive continually to know oneself and one's environment better. In an important sense, everybody is a philosopher — a lover of wisdom. This "passion to grasp the nature of each thing as it is" (Plato), is manifested primarily in the statements we make about reality. Making pronouncements about that which exists — or believed to exist — again, is an intrinsic component of all meaningful human experience. Although it is true that people may hold many beliefs that are never articulated in words, it is also true that, to the extent that language is essential for meaningful human interaction, making of statements about reality is an essential dimension of human existence. It is, therefore, only natural that a book on the methodology of the social sciences, on the principles which underlie the production and utilization of knowledge, should begin with a closer look at the nature of such statements.

An important characteristic of statements is that they are invariably bound to specific contexts. Different types of statements in different situations or contexts perform different functions, and therefore comply with different

3

criteria. For example, religious communication (in a church or during prayer) differs quite extensively from communication in a social, informal small-group situation such as at a party or barbecue. It has become customary among philosophers to regard each context as analogous to a *language game* (Wittgenstein's term) and to view the different criteria which apply in each context as analogous to the rules of the language game. In the same manner that the rules of chess and draughts differ, so that certain moves (behaviours) are either acceptable or unacceptable depending upon which game is being played, the contextual rules of a party would determine that different behaviours are appropriate from the behaviours which would apply during a religious service.

The language game of this book is the language game of statements made within the context of social sciences research. And the central concern of the book is to analyze the distinctive rules of the language game of the social sciences and to attempt to answer the question: What are the rules of the game which can be employed to distinguish between scientific pronouncements or statements, and those which are regarded as unscientific?

One way of answering this question would be to look at the techniques which we employ in everyday language in attempts to make our statements credible, the ways in which we try to convince others of the reliability or accuracy of what we say, and then to compare these procedures with that employed in the scientific context. Let us consider some common assertions:

S_1: Ice cream is delicious.
S_2: Western Province has the best rugby team in South Africa.
S_3: The divorce rate in South Africa is extraordinarily high.
S_4: Violence depicted on TV is likely to increase the level of aggressive behaviour amongst children.
S_5: The long-term effect of excessive smoking is lung cancer.

Opinions and beliefs about phenomena are usually expressed as statements about reality. We may therefore define a statement as any sentence in which a knowledge claim relating to reality is made. Consequently, statements are sentences in which an identifiable epistemic claim is made (*episteme* is the Greek word for true knowledge). It is for this reason that the study of human knowledge is known as epistemology. Sentences in which demonstrable epistemic claims are made regarding aspects of reality can therefore be distinguished from other types of sentences (e.g. commands or questions) in which epistemic claims are not made.

If we were to give reasons why any of these views are held (Why do you claim that ice cream is delicious?), we might be inclined to follow one of three strategies. We could invoke our personal tastes or subjective feelings, we could refer to some authority figure, or we could simply invoke a casual observation which we have made.

4

(1) Invoking personal preference or subjective feelings

The answer to a question such as that suggested in the previous paragraph would typically be something like the following: I think that ... or, I am convinced that ... or, I feel that ..., and so on. My personal preference has become so ingrained in my total experience that it is hardly likely that another person would be able to convince me that I may be wrong. Strictly speaking, there can be neither right nor wrong as far as personal preference is concerned. If it is my feeling that ice cream is delicious or that the Western Province rugby team is indeed the best in South Africa then logical reasoning is unlikely to convince me to the contrary! In everyday interpersonal communication the basis upon which an argument rests is frequently no more than the invocation of personal preferences. *After having listened to all your arguments to the contrary, I still feel that excessive smoking, though perhaps not in the short term, will inevitably lead to the development of lung cancer.* Logical or empirical evidence will probably not convince me to change my personal judgments in what I regard as matters of taste or preference. By logical evidence we mean that which is based upon the logic of a particular argument, and by empirical evidence we mean arguments based upon specific experiences or observations. It is therefore exactly for this reason that invoking personal taste rules out any logical or empirical test from the start, and that personal taste is unacceptable as a criterion for testing the credibility or reliability of any statement.

(2) Invoking authority

Another way in which people attempt to justify a statement is by invoking the authority of either an individual or an organization. Following this line of thought, statement 5 may have read: The Medical Research Council claims that heavy smoking eventually leads to lung cancer. Statement 2 may, in the same manner, be amended to read: Dr Danie Craven claims that the Western Province rugby team is the best in South Africa. In all such cases the person or institution is invoked because of the associated reputation or authoritativeness. Once again we find that arguments of this nature frequently end in an impasse. *Well, Dr Christian Barnard believes that smoking is directly related to the incidence of cardiac disease, and if that is his opinion, who am I to argue with him?* The important point to bear in mind here is that the person or organization is invoked merely on the basis of the reputation which he, she, or it is supposed to have. This type of arbitrary appeal to authority must be clearly distinguished from references in a scientific study to the published research findings of authoritative scientists. In the latter cases, the appeal is to the "authority" of the research, not of a person or institution.

If in a study of values, I were to cite the work of Rokeach, I would in actual fact be invoking the authoritativeness of his research. It is quite possible to distinguish this acceptable type of invocation from those in the earlier examples. If I were to be asked why I am citing Rokeach, it would be a simple matter to elaborate and to refer to several published studies (which I accept as being both reliable and valid) and his findings on the nature and structure of values. In the same way that invoking personal preference is unacceptable, invoking personal authority is far too arbitrary, subjective and emotional to be of any use as a yardstick for epistemic statements.

(3) Invoking casual observation

A third, and somewhat more sophisticated strategy which is frequently encountered in arguments, is to invoke a number of casual observations which may have been made as support for the argument. To statement 1 I could, for example, have replied: *Well, I have never met anyone who does not think that ice cream is delicious.* Even in the case of statement 3 a more extensive grounding may have been:

> *I travelled quite extensively abroad last year and because I am rather interested in the question of divorce rates, I made a point of reading the newspapers in those countries, and of taking particular note of the number of divorces reported. As a matter of fact I listened to some of the court hearings of divorce cases. If I were to compare what I saw there with my impressions and experience here, I am quite convinced that our country has a particularly high incidence of divorce.*

Although the supporting evidence which the person has cited in this case refers to specific empirical observations, and while it may be regarded as a rough comparative study, the evidence simply cannot conform to the requirements of reliability and validity — demands which are usually regarded as integral criteria for scientific knowledge. The observations were not systematic and they may well have been biassed; consequently the result could be a distorted image of the actual situation. There is also no way in which the observations could be verified by a different observer. The so-called "observations", therefore, remain mere accidental observations which were made under casual and non-systematic circumstances.

The different strategies discussed (and others, for example, appealing to another person's feelings, claiming that the issue is self-evident, and so on) are usually quite adequate for the language games of everyday life. When the primary aim is no more than communicating, understanding, or persuading, we would, as a rule, require very little more than these strategies. When, however, it is our aim to gain valid knowledge of reality (phenomena/events/behaviour) in order to explain it, and also to predict future tendencies and events, when it is the aim to unravel the causes of human interaction or to develop a logical reconstruction of an historical event, a far greater premium is placed upon such values as reliability, credibility, accuracy, validity, and objectivity.

6

FIGURE 1.1

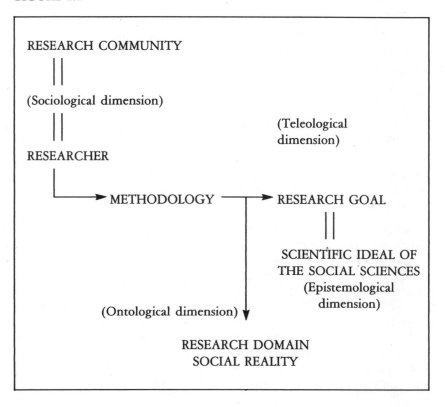

DIMENSIONS OF SOCIAL SCIENCES RESEARCH

In the remaining part of this chapter a model will be presented which embodies a particular approach to the interpretation of the process of research in the social sciences. Although it is not claimed that the model is either exhaustive or universally valid, an attempt has been made to develop a model that include the most important insights which have been gained from recent developments in the philosophy and methodology of science. Following a discussion of the model, we will indicate how the model can be used in distinguishing between good and poor research in the social science.

In terms of this model research in the social sciences would be defined as follows:

Social sciences research is a collaborative human activity in which social reality is studied objectively with the aim of gaining a valid understanding of it.

The following dimensions of research in the social sciences are emphasized in this definition:

7

- the sociological dimension: scientific research is a joint or **collaborative** activity;
- the ontological dimension: research in the social sciences is always directed at an aspect or aspects of **social reality**;
- the teleological dimension: as a human activity, research in the social sciences is intentional and goal-directed, its main aim being the **understanding** of phenomena;
- the epistemological dimension: the aim is not merely to understand phenomena, but rather to provide a **valid and reliable** understanding of reality; and
- the methodological dimension: research in the social sciences may be regarded as **objective** by virtue of its being critical, balanced, unbiased, systematic, and controllable.

It must be emphasized that these five dimensions of research are just that: five aspects of one and the same process. This should be kept in mind when each dimension is discussed separately in the pages that follow. Research can be discussed from various perspectives. From the sociological perspective, one is interested in highlighting the social nature of research as a typical human activity — as praxis. The ontologial dimension emphasizes that research always has an object — be it empirical or non-empirical. When one looks at research within the teleological perspective, one wants to stress that research is goal-driven and purposive. Research is not a mechanical or merely automatic process, but is directed towards specifically human goals of understanding and gaining insight and explanation. The epistemological dimension focuses on the fact that this goal of understanding or gaining insight should always be further clarified in terms of what would be regarded as ''proper'' or ''good'' understanding. Traditionally ideals of truth and wisdom have been pursued by scientists. More recently other ideals — problem solving, verisimilitude, validity, and so on — have been put forward. Finally, the methodological dimension of research refers to the ways in which these various ideals may be attained. It also refers to such features as the systematic and methodical nature of research and why such a high premium is placed on being critical and balanced in the process of research.

The five dimensions are subsequently discussed in more detail.

The sociological dimension

Who would know secret things, let him know also how to guard secrets with secrecy, reveal what is fit to be revealed and set his seal on that which should be sealed up; let him not give to dogs what is sacred, not cast pearls before swine. Observe this law and the eyes of your mind are opened to the understanding of sacred things, and you shall hear all your heart's desire revealed

8

to you through divine power (Quoted in Rossi, P.; Francis Bacon — *From magic to science,* 1957: 29).

This statement, which dates back to 1575, is characteristic of the Renaissance view of the nature of scientific research, according to which knowledge was regarded as esoteric and secret and as something which ought, therefore, to remain solely in the possession of initiates. For this reason it comes as no surprise that the scientist was perceived as some type of *Magus* figure — someone who, by means of exceptional abilities, is able to penetrate the deepest secrets of nature. Some of the best-known scientists of the time, for example Paracelsus, Agrippa and Cardanus, all subscribed to this view. At that stage, for example, the latter wrote *Work has no need at all for partnership.*

Francis Bacon was one of the first people who objected to this *isolationist ideal* in the sciences. In all his published works (which appeared in the early part of the seventeenth century) there is evidence of a clear call for co-operation among scientists for participation in the reform of the scientific edifice (a metaphor which already presupposes the idea of co-operation), and for the exchange of knowledge. It is common cause amongst historians of science that the seventeenth century represents an important turning-point in views on the nature of scientific research. It is therefore not incidental that the development of modern physical science is associated with a greater degree of collaboration and organization. Edgar Zilsel adds a further reason for the seventeenth century having been the golden age of the physical sciences:

> *In the workshops of the late medieval artisans co-operation resulted quite naturally from the working conditions. In contrast to a monk's cell or a humanist's writing chamber a workshop or dockyard is a place where several people work together* (1945: 247).

It has long been known that the scientific revolution of the seventeenth century owes much to the artisan tradition of the fifteenth and sixteenth centuries. These artisans worked in teams in order to solve problems of ballistics, sailing, navigation, warfare, astronomy, and so on. Zilsel's plausible argument is that these working conditions, when compared with those that existed in monasteries, led to co-operation among scientists and eventually to the development of modern science.

Nowadays it is commonly accepted that the sociological dimension of science is a central component in any analysis of what science ought to be. Because these problems are the natural domain of the sociology of science, and in view of the fact that these issues are discussed in great detail in a large number of books on the subject, we shall confine ourselves to some of the more important topics that are dealt with in those discussions.

- Sociologists of science emphasize the fact that scientists operate within a clearly defined scientific community, in invisible colleges (Diane Crane), that they belong to identifiable disciplinary paradigms (Thomas Kuhn),

9

or that they are linked in research networks. As a consequence, one of the central problems is to identify research communities by, for example, using information concerning bibliographic references in journal articles, examining membership lists of scientific associations, and so on.

- A typical theme also concerns the analysis of the social mechanisms which operate within these research communities. In *The scientific community*, for example, Hagstrom develops a model according to which a research community is characterized by the exchange of information for the sake of community-specific rewards. A researcher who produces acceptable scientific information is rewarded by means of publications, by being elected to the editorial boards of learned journals, and so on. Storer (*The social system of science*, 1966) advocates a similar model, except that he interprets scientific information as creative products which are exchanged for academic recognition. A characteristic of both these models is the degree of social control which is attributed to scientific communities — because of the fact that scientists seek recognition they tend to accept the goals and values of the research community. This system of social control is institutionalized in review systems (for example blind peer review) rules for funding, criteria for promotion, and the mechanisms of research management. One of the most important consequences of a mechanism of this nature is that scientists would tend to place a considerable premium on the priority of their discoveries. Although the intensity of this may not be so excessive in the social sciences, it cannot be denied that a great deal of stress is placed on the determination of priorities in the origin of theories and data.

- It is inevitable that considerations which concern mechanisms of social control would also involve moral implications. The growing interest in research ethics during the past decade is indicative of this development. In situations where research becomes highly organized and institutionalized, it is unavoidable that greater emphasis will be placed on issues such as moral values and norms relating to plagiarism, professional conduct, and status, and the right of research participants.

- Another central theme in studies of the sociology of science is the role of ideological (and other non-epistemic) interests in the process of scientific research. As in the preceding case, it is obvious that a conflict of interests is always latent in situations where research has become highly organized, and where external sources of finance, contractors, government departments, and other interest groups become involved. It is also clear that once a specific research community has adopted a point of view with regard to a given interest group or an ideological school, the study of the relationship between ideological assumptions and research within that research community (or even of groups within the community) becomes a most interesting field of study.

10

- Related to the theme of *ideology and research* is the whole issue of the role of meta-scientific and methodological preferences in the social mechanisms of the research community. A question that may arise, relates, for example, to the role of preferences for particular quantitative methods in the selection of articles, the publication of books, and the election of members of editorial boards. Following from this, one may well ask whether the functioning of the social mechanisms is always effective and whether non-scientific considerations do not, at times, cloud the issue. A well-known example which is quoted by Kuhn, illustrates this point: *Lord Rayleigh, at a time when his reputation was established submitted to the British Association a paper on some paradoxes of electrodynamics. His name was inadvertently omitted when the paper was first sent, and the paper itself was at first rejected as the work of some paradoxer. Shortly afterwards, with the author's name in place, the paper was accepted with profuse apologies* (1970: 153).

- Finally, it would be appropriate to refer to a theme which is not strictly sociological, and ought rather to be regarded as belonging to the domain of social psychology. We refer here to the role of motivation, idiosyncracy, personality, and interests in research. In his book, *The subjective side of science,* Mitroff, for example, devised a typology of scientists. He distinguished between the experimentalists (analytical and exact), the middle-of-the-road (a highly flexible thinker), and the speculative theoretician (creative and quite brilliant). In a subsequent publication Mitroff and Kilmann suggested a new classification: the analytic scientist, the conceptual theorist, the particular humanist, and the conceptual humanist. From these few examples it is evident that the personality structure of researchers, their idiosyncratic interest and motivation, thinking strategies, and cognitive preferences are important factors in the practice of social science, and that more research on the part of sociologists and psychologists of science is necessary.

In conclusion, it is clear that the sociological dimension of research cannot be ignored in any analysis of the process of research. In this book we shall refer to sociological factors where we consider that they ought to be taken into account because of their effect on methodological considerations.

The ontological dimension

The term "ontology" refers to the study of *being* or *reality*. Therefore, when we refer to the ontological dimension of research in the social sciences, we have in mind the reality which is investigated in research in the social sciences. This reality is referred to as the research domain of the social sciences.

In general terms, the research domain of the social sciences may be regarded as humankind in all its diversity, which would include human activities, characteristics, institutions, behaviour, products, and so on. It is clear that this diversity permits different perspectives on the nature of the research domain. Phenomena may, for example, be distinguished in terms of observable and unobservable, verbal and non-verbal, or individual and collective dimensions. If a chronological classification were to be adopted, phenomena would vary from historical events through current ones to anticipated events or trends. Further, it would be possible to distinguish between human actions (individual or collective), and the products resulting from human acts such as literature, art, music, and so on. Yet a further distinction could be drawn between human behaviour, on the one hand, and attitudes, opinions, values, and knowledge, on the other. It ought also to be possible to indicate that the distinction between human behaviour and the products of human activities, which is reflected in the distinction between behavioural and human sciences (*Geisteswissenschaften*) is related to the boundaries between observable and non-observable (inferred) behaviour. Exactly how these distinctions are drawn and argued for by different philosophers, however, are not of central importance to this book.

What is important, however, is to realize that individual social scientists or groups of social scientists frequently hold explicit beliefs about what is real and what is not: beliefs which profoundly affect the definition of research problems. Beliefs of this nature will be referred to as *domain assumptions* and will be taken to refer to beliefs about the nature, structure, and status of social phenomena.

In this manner behaviourists differ from psychoanalists about the reality of cognitive phenomena, atomists from holists about the unit of study, positivists from realists about the interpretation of causal relationships in human behaviour, and so on. These topics are discussed in depth in the philosophy of the social sciences. The importance of this issue for methodology is the following: because each researcher, either implicitly or explicitly, makes certain domain assumptions, there must necessarily be differences relating to what is regarded as the research domain of the social sciences. Differences between individual researchers are, however, not the main issue. Rather, the differences between different schools of thought, and between different theoretical approaches is often so radical that the research domains of the various schools show little overlap when they are compared with one another. This is not to say that these differences are unbridgeable. Contrary to the point of view adopted by Thomas Kuhn in his book, *The structure of scientific revolutions,* in which he maintains that different paradigms are incommensurable, our standpoint is that, more often than not, there exists a substantive degree of overlap between different theoretical orientations, models, and methodologies. This problem will receive more attention in chapter 6, when Kuhn's paradigm concept is discussed in greater detail.

In conclusion, it is clear that the variety of perspectives of man and society, associated with divergent domain assumptions, leads to a situation where one

12

cannot talk about **the** research domain of the social sciences. The content of the ontological dimension of research in the social sciences must, as is the case in the other dimensions, be regarded as variable.

The teleological dimension

Aristotle remarked that man is naturally inclined to desire the acquisition of knowledge. According to him this desire stems from a fascination with both the obvious and the more obscure. This early fascination gradually led to an increasing awareness of man's ignorance, and the concomitant necessity for systematic investigation. Two thousand years later, Francis Bacon stated that *knowledge is power*. Through knowledge reality can and must be changed. According to him, this reality had been plagued by sickness, deterioration, and depravity ever since the fall of man. While the Greek ideal of sciences was primarily one of knowledge for the sake of knowledge, the modern ideal, which dates from approximately 1600, is far more pragmatic. Nevertheless, these two ideals of science cannot be regarded as mutually exclusive. If one were to regard the former (knowledge for the sake of knowledge) as the theoretical ideal, and the latter (knowledge for the sake of power) as the practical ideal, then it would be acceptable to postulate that the attainment of the theoretical, and the attainment of the practical are merely two poles of the same dimension. A juxtaposition of, or dichotomy between, the theoretical and practical aims of the practice of science would therefore be unacceptable. The distinction ought rather to be regarded as representing a broad indication of interests than as indicative of the existence of fundamental differences.

When the distinction is understood in this manner, it becomes interesting to pay attention to the existence of various interpretations of the theoretical and practical ideals of science. Depending upon one's philosophical allegiance, it may be possible to regard the theoretical aim of the social sciences as being a description of the rule-governed aspects of human behaviour, the explanation of behaviour in terms of causal laws, the prediction of future behaviour, and so on. Similarly, it would be possible to regard a number of practical aims as important. Such a list might include controlling human behaviour, reforming society by solving social problems, psychotherapy, emancipation of the oppressed, supplying reliable information for public policy, and so on.

Irrespective of which ideal of the social sciences one may support, or which of the major distinctions one chooses to emphasize, the practice of science is invariably goal-directed. This characteristic of the practice of science is referred to as the teleological (*telos* is the Greek word for goal or aim) dimension. Thus far we have merely touched upon the different types of ideals of science which may be encountered in the social sciences. Strictly speaking, however, these problems form part of the domain of the philosophy of the social sciences. In research methodology the problem which must be addressed is somewhat more limited, and relates mainly to the question of research goals.

A variety of classification of research goals are to be found. On the one hand, research is frequently categorized as exploratory, descriptive, explanatory, or predictive. On the other hand, a distinction is drawn between hypothesis-generating and hypothesis-testing research. Irrespective of which type of classification is used, it is clear that the research goal always refers to the immediate goal of a given research project. The methodological implications of the different types of goals, as well as the relationship between research goals and the ideals of social science, will be discussed in chapter 2.

The epistemological dimension

The epistemological dimension of social sciences research may be regarded as the key dimension of social science praxis. As has been indicated a high premium is placed upon the epistemic status of scientific statements. Stated differently, the requirement that statements must approximate social reality as closely as possible is more highly emphasized in the language game of science than in any other language game.

In an important sense, the epistemic dimension may be regarded as the embodiment of the ideal of science, namely the quest for truth. As one may well expect, a study of the history of epistemology reveals a variety of interpretations of the exact nature of this epistemological ideal. Following the leads of Greek philosophy, it was customary to regard certainty and demonstrable proof as the epistemological ideal during the seventeenth century, and even subsequently. In Francis Bacon's book *Novum organum,* published in 1620, he maintained that the goal of all scientific research is to discover not pretty probable conjectures, but certain and demonstrable knowledge, while Rene Descartes's point of view in his 1641 book, *Meditations* on a first philosophy was similarly that the goal of science is to erect the edifice of human knowledge upon a certain and indisputable basis. The assumption that genuine knowledge must necessarily be certain and incorrigible knowledge is also the basis of the more recent logical positivist ideal of verification. In the later history of this movement (after the 1930's), however, a clear shift in the direction of the ideal of probability became evident. The goal, therefore, became to produce statements which were, at least, highly probable, and for which the highest degree of inductive support or confirmation could be demonstrated. In Karl Popper's earlier publication, *The logic of scientific discovery,* he based his methodology of theory assessment upon the logic of modus tollens: although the positivists were correct in rejecting the idea of conclusive verification, he maintained that this did not imply that conclusive falsification could not be retained. Nonetheless, the two approaches are still not unrelated as they share the underlying ideal of total certainty.

14

In chapters 2 and 5 we shall indicate that there are a number of methodological and logical considerations which render the ideal of complete certainty in the social sciences unattainable. This does not, however, imply that social scientists need abandon the ideal of truth. The alternative to rigid objectivism or fundamentalism is neither complete relativism nor scepticism. This is the fundamental epistemological postulate of the book. Because of the complexity of the research domain of the social sciences, and the inherent inaccuracy and fallibility of research, it is necessary to accept that complete certainty is unattainable. The likelihood that research findings may have limited or contextual validity is accepted, while bearing in mind that subsequent research may reveal that it is invalid. It is, therefore, accepted that the epistemic ideal ought rather to be the generation of research findings which approximate, as closely as possible, the true state of affairs. Bearing in mind that it is impossible to know when the truth has been attained, it necessarily becomes essential to strive constantly for the elimination of falsity, inaccuracy, and error in research.

From the preceding it may be concluded that the primary aim of research in the social sciences is to generate valid findings, i.e. that the findings should approximate reality as closely as possible. Following Popper's thinking, it is accepted that one should seek the greatest degree of verisimilitude in statements about reality. Alternatively, one could maintain that scientific statements ought to be approximations of truth in Putnam's terminology. The term validity is probably the most useful to convey the meaning of verisimilitude. In this we follow Cook and Campbell (1979: 37) who say: *We shall use the concepts of validity and invalidity to refer to the best possible approximation to the truth or falsity of propositions ...*

In chapters 2 and 5 a detailed analysis is presented of the factors which present obstacles to the attainment of valid findings, as well as ways in which these factors may be controlled.

The methodological dimension

While the epistemological dimension refers to the status of scientific statements, the methodological dimension concerns what may be called the "how" of social sciences research. In other words, How should research be planned, structured, and executed to comply with the criteria of science? In actual fact, the etymological meaning of the word methodology could be interpreted as the logic of implementing scientific methods in the study of reality. This definition becomes clearer when one bears in mind that the process of scientific research is largely a type of decision-making process. The researcher is required to make a series of decisions of the following nature: Which theory or model is likely to be most appropriate for investigating a given subject? Which research hypotheses concerning the object of study may be formulated on the basis of the selected theory or model? Which measuring instruments and data-collection methods can be used? How should the collected data be analyzed? What does the findings mean and how do they relate to the original formulation of the problem? Methodology, then, is defined as the logic of the application of scientific methods to the investigation of phenomena. According to this definition methodology refers to the logic of the decision-making process in scientific research. We would therefore agree with Kaufman's statement that *research methodology is the theory of correct scientific decisions* (1944: 230).

Because the decision-making process is so complex, and as there are many traps for the unwary, the field of research methodology is defined as a study of the research process in all its broadness and complexity, the various methods and techniques that are employed, the rationale that underlies the use of such methods, the limitations of each technique, the role of assumptions and presuppositions in selecting methods and techniques, the influence of methodological preferences on the types of data analyses employed and the subsequent interpretation of findings, and so on. As indicated in the previous paragraph, one of the fundamental epistemological assumptions in this book is that, because it is a human decision-making process, social sciences research is intrinsically fallible. Seen against this background, the major aim of methodological analysis is to develop a more critical orientation on the part of researchers by eliminating obviously incorrect decisions and, in so doing, to maximize the validity of research findings. Consequently, the basic approach adopted in this book is embodied in the question: How can scientific research be planned and executed to ensure that the findings would be most valid? A tentative answer to this question was suggested in the working definition of social sciences research presented earlier, in which we stated that scientific research is characterized by attempts to ensure that it is objective. It is for this reason that the main thesis of this book is that it is only possible to generate valid findings in the social sciences if the research is objective. We would, however, hasten to add that our interpretation of objectivity is neither positivistic nor objectivistic. "Objective" ought not to be identified with "neutral" or "universally valid". During the course of our discussion, we shall, for example, indicate that there are times when objective research inevitably requires a considerable degree of empathy on the part of the researcher. In the same manner that the criteria of rationality, reliability, and validity are always context dependent, it is impossible to conceive of objectivity in a decontextualized manner. In other words, objectivity is dependent upon the type of research design employed.

In the preceding pages we have attempted to explain the key concepts of our working definition of social sciences research. The five dimensions of social sciences research which we have distinguished are the following:

- social sciences research is a *collaborative* human activity;
- social sciences research is a study of *social reality*;

- social sciences research aims at *understanding* social reality;
- social sciences research is a study aimed at a *valid* understanding of social reality; and
- social sciences research is *objective* research.

In the following section we look at these five dimensions, very briefly, from two very different contexts: the more abstract context of scientific disciplines as against the more concrete context of a specific research project.

The disciplinary and project contexts of research

As we have already indicated, the main focus in this book is on the research process as it is executed by individual researchers. However, it is of course true, that even individual research projects are conducted within the broader contexts of particular paradigms and disciplines. Individual researchers are trained as researchers within a given research tradition or paradigm and this

FIGURE 1.2

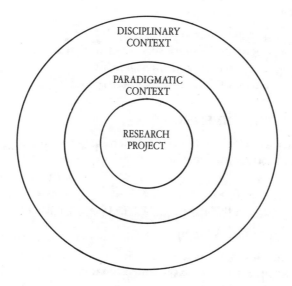

training usually has a lasting effect on the theoretical and methodological preferences of the researcher. It also implies that particular assumptions about the nature, domain, and structure of research are shared with other researchers. If this is viewed within an even broader context, it becomes evident that each discipline in the social sciences consists of a variety of paradigms. This obviously implies that different research models, theories and ontologies will inevitably be found in the discipline within which any researcher conducts his or her research. Individual research projects are, therefore, necessarily embedded in wider disciplinary contexts.

It is useful to apply the distinction between the disciplinary and project perspective to our model of the five dimensions as it sheds more light on the way in which these five dimensions are manifested in research. Because we are looking at these five dimensions again, although from a different perspective, a certain degree of duplication is inevitable.

THE SOCIOLOGICAL DIMENSION

At the level of research in a discipline, the following aspects of the sociological dimension are important:

- The existence of networks or research communities
- Mechanisms of social control
- Issues of research ethics
- The influence of ideologies and interests

At the project level, the sociological dimension is manifested in decisions relating to:

- Individual versus team projects
- The differences between contract versus self-initiated research
- Issues of project supervision and management
- Planning and control of time and resources (people/apparatus/finance)

THE ONTOLOGICAL DIMENSION

At the disciplinary level, the ontological dimension refers to discussions and disputes as to the various ways in which research domains can be defined and classified, e.g.

- Behaviourist *versus* cognitive approaches
- Realist *versus* instrumentalist or nominalist approaches
- Individualist *versus* holist approaches

A similar, but much more concrete and specific discussion is found at the level of projects where the ontological dimension refers to a proper classification of the unit of analysis. Are we, for example, studying -

- Individuals
- Groups or collectivities
- Interactions, or
- Objects?

A more detailed discussion of these issues is provided in Chapter 2.

THE TELEOLOGICAL DIMENSION

This dimension refers to the fact that social science, as a typical human activity, is goal-driven. It is, therefore, not surprising that a whole range of definitions of the possible goals of a discipline are found in the literature. The traditional distinction between theoretical and practical goals is still useful in classifying these goals.

- Theoretical goals such as theory construction or theory building, understanding human behaviour better, explanation and prediction of human behaviour and gaining insight into social reality.

- Practical goals such as the therapy or healing of the human being, improving the quality of life and emancipating the oppressed.

Within the project perspective, it is usual to refer to specific project objectives such as:

- Theoretical: Exploratory, descriptive and explanatory (which includes evaluation and prediction studies) research.
- Practical: To provide information, diagnose and solve problems and planning and monitoring social programmes.

THE EPISTEMOLOGICAL DIMENSION

Various definitions of the epistemic ideal of science and scientific disciplines have been put forward in the history of science, e.g.

- The search for truth (e.g. Plato and Aristotle)
- Certain and indubitable knowledge (e.g. Descartes)
- Empirical adequacy (e.g. Van Fraassen)
- Problem solving (e.g. Kuhn)
- Wisdom/insight (e.g. Maxwell)

It seems inappropriate to claim that a specific project or study will result in truth or even more far-fetched — certain and indubitable knowledge. At this level, we are more inclined to talk of the validity, demonstrability, reliability or replicability of our research findings.

THE METHODOLOGICAL DIMENSION

Within the context of a discipline, the methodological dimension is taken to refer to more or less high-level methodological paradigms or schools, such as:

- Positivism and logical positivism
- Phenomenology or the interpretivist approach
- Critical theory (neo-Marxism)
- Karl Popper's critical rationalism, and
- Scientific realism

At the project level, three general methodological approaches are usually distinguished in the social sciences:

- The quantitative approach
- The qualitative approach
- The participatory action approach

A decision to follow one or a combination of these methodologies, does of course, entail further more specific choices regarding the various methods of:

— data collection (questionnaires/ interviews/ documents);
— data analysis (statistical/ mathematical/ interpretative); and
— inference (inductive/ deductive/ retroductive).

This concludes our discussion of the five dimensions as viewed from the disciplinary and project perspectives. In the final section, these various perspectives are integrated into a model of social sciences research.

AN INTEGRATED MODEL OF SOCIAL SCIENCES RESEARCH

It is the aim of this model to summarize our discussion up to this point and to systematize the five dimensions of social research within the framework of the research process. In doing so, we are following recent models of scientific research as articulated by Gerard Radnitzky (*Contemporary schools of metascience*) and Thomas Kuhn (*The structure of scientific revolutions*). Both of them have articulated models of scientific research in which the social nature of science is taken as point of departure. Both Kuhn and Radnitzky, for instance, emphasize that scientists always do their research within larger networks or communities of scientists which affect the nature of research in various ways. Kuhn's views are discussed in detail in Chapter 6, while many of the central notions of Radnitzky's model are incorporated in the model which is outlined in this section. However, because both Kuhn and Radnitzky developed their models primarily for the natural sciences, it will be necessary to modify them somewhat to make them applicable to the social sciences.

Following Radnitzky, the model can be described as a systems theoretical model. In this model we distinguish between three subsystems which interact with each other and with the research domain as defined in a specific discipline. These are:

— The intellectual climate of a specific discipline
— The market of intellectual resources within each discipline
— The research process itself.

INTELLECTUAL CLIMATE

The term "intellectual climate" is used to refer to the variety of meta-theoretical values or beliefs which are held by those practising within a discipline at any given stage. We are referring to sets of beliefs, values and assumptions which, because their origin can usually be traced to non-scientific contexts, are not directly related to the theoretical goals of the practice of scientific research. By the very nature of social science disciplines, this would include beliefs about the nature of social reality as well as more discipline-specific beliefs relating to society, labour, education, history, and so on. For these reasons, we find that in a discipline like sociology the intellectual climate consists of a variety of beliefs about human beings (behaviourism, humanism, existentialism) as well as definite beliefs about the nature of society (mechanistic, organistic, cybernetic, systems-theoretical). The origin of many of these values may be traced back to traditions in philosophy. Because it has, however, become part and parcel of the intellectual climate of a particular discipline in the social sciences, it has acquired, even if only indirectly, specific theoretical relevance and content.

A further distinguishing characteristic of the intellectual climate of a discipline is the fact that these beliefs tend to display the qualities of postulates or assumptions. Sociological beliefs (which we encounter in positivist thought) to the effect that human beings are passive bearers of meaning and that, for this reason, they are more reactive than active within their environments, or that the research domain of sociology consists of concrete social facts (Durkheim) rather than meaningful interactions (Blumer), obviously display the characteristics of assumptions rather than those of hypotheses. The clear implication is that beliefs of this nature are frequently neither testable, nor were they ever meant to be tested. They constitute postulates or commitments which underlie testable statements.

MARKET OF INTELLECTUAL RESOURCES

The market of intellectual resources refers to the collection of beliefs which has a direct bearing upon the epistemic status of scientific statements, i.e. to their status as knowledge-claims. The two major types are: theoretical beliefs about the nature and structure of phenomena on the one hand, and methodological beliefs concerning the nature and structure of the research process.

Theoretical beliefs are those beliefs of which testable statements about social phenonomena are made. Theoretical beliefs may, therefore, be regarded as assertions about the what (descriptive) and why (interpretative) aspects of human behaviour. It would, therefore, include all statements which form part of hypotheses, typologies, models or theories. Turning once again to sociology, theoretical beliefs would, for example, include all testable statements derived from macro-sociological theories (for example, structural functionalism, conflict theories, symbolic interactionism) and from micro-theories (for example, Simon and Gagnon's theory of homosexual behaviour or Smelser's theory of collective behaviour).

21

FIGURE 1.3

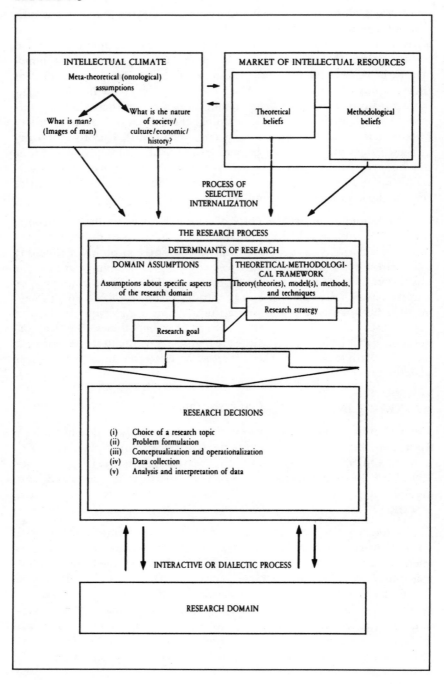

INTELLECTUAL CLIMATE

Meta-theoretical (ontological) assumptions

What is man? (Images of man)

What is the nature of society/ culture/economic/ history?

MARKET OF INTELLECTUAL RESOURCES

Theoretical beliefs

Methodological beliefs

PROCESS OF SELECTIVE INTERNALIZATION

THE RESEARCH PROCESS

DETERMINANTS OF RESEARCH

DOMAIN ASSUMPTIONS

Assumptions about specific aspects of the research domain

THEORETICAL-METHODOLOGI-CAL FRAMEWORK

Theory(theories), model(s), methods, and techniques

Research strategy

Research goal

RESEARCH DECISIONS

(i)   Choice of a research topic
(ii)   Problem formulation
(iii) Conceptualization and operationalization
(iv)   Data collection
(v)   Analysis and interpretation of data

INTERACTIVE OR DIALECTIC PROCESS

RESEARCH DOMAIN

Methodological beliefs are beliefs concerning the nature of social science and scientific research. These beliefs are emphasized in this book. Examples would include different types of traditions in the philosophy of the social sciences — such as positivism, realism, phenomenology, Neo-Marxism, and hermeneutics — and the most important methodological models such as quantitative and qualitative models. In an important sense methodological beliefs are more aligned to those beliefs which form part of the intellectual climate because they frequently entail a postulative aspect. More often than not, methodological beliefs are no more than methodological preferences, assumptions, and presuppositions about what ought to constitute good research. Because there is a direct link, however, between methodological beliefs and the epistemic status of research findings, and because these beliefs can invariably be traced to the context of scientific praxis, they are included as a component of the market of intellectual resources.

THE RESEARCH PROCESS

We now turn our attention to a typical research project. In this context, the main thesis of our model is the following: In the research project the researchers internalize specific inputs from the paradigm(s) to which they subscribe in a selective manner, so as to enable them to interact with the research domain in a fruitful manner and to produce scientifically valid research.

The term *selective* is used in this context merely to convey the notion that the individual researcher tends to incorporate only certain paradigmatic beliefs in his or her own approach. The term *internalize* is used to indicate that the researcher incorporates only those beliefs (for example postulates, theories, models, research models) which are seen as relevant to the specific goal, research problem, and so on. The principle of selective internalizing may explain why researchers do not necessarily adhere to an identifiable paradigm in their research. The constraints which the phenomena place upon the researcher are frequently the determining factor which lead the researcher to adopt either a qualitative or a quantitative approach. The fact that it is possible to demonstrate that many researchers employ a single research model throughout their careers need, therefore, not necessarily be interpreted as a consequence of the "coercive" function of a given paradigm. Frequently it is merely force of habit, sheer convenience, or the power of the socialization process which exists in the lecture halls of universities.

When we focus on the execution of the research project, we make a distinction between the determinants of research decisions on the one hand, and the decision-making process on the other.

Determinants of research decisions

The determinants of the decisions which the researcher is likely to make in research process, may be defined as those task- or problem-oriented beliefs that derive from a given paradigm which have been internalized. It would, therefore, include certain assumptions about the research domain and the specific phenomena, a specific theoretical framework or model, a specific research model and the resultant methodological preferences.

The choice regarding the specific inputs which are selected from a given paradigm tends to be made, as indicated above, as a consequence of the theoretical and methodological demands posed by the research problem. A specific research strategy and research goal that are to be implemented in a project develop as a result of an interaction between the proposed research project and selected beliefs about the phenomena. For this reason, it is essential that we emphasize at an early stage that the content of task- or problem-oriented beliefs (in other words the determinants of research decisions) is the result of the interaction between the researcher (with his or her conceptual framework) and the research domain (more correctly, the researcher's perceptions and definition of the research domain). This process is not chronological, but ought rather to be viewed as a dialectical one. The researcher's perceptions of the domain phenomenon are both antecedent to, and the result of, his or her conceptual frame of reference.

A researcher's framework of problem-oriented beliefs is a determinant of his or her research decisions for the exact reason that these beliefs are involved, to a lesser or greater extent, in every facet of the decision-making process. We shall pay further attention to this matter at a later stage.

Decision-making steps in the research process

An attempt has been made to include the major common denominators of most types of research in this model of the research process. We are convinced that, given the necessary translation, the steps that we have included would be applicable to different types of research. In this context, we would include empirical research, theory building (theoretical research), historical research, conceptual analysis, and so on. Bearing in mind that the model is not meant to imply that the stages of decision making which are discussed necessarily follow a rigid temporal sequence, we also believe that it may be employed to capture the differences which, for example, exist between quantitative and qualitative research. Five typical stages may be distinguished:

(1) The choice of a research topic or theme.
(2) Formulating the research problem.
(3) Conceptualization and operationalization.
(4) Data collection.
(5) Analysis and interpretation of data.

Because the logic of the decision-making stages that are incorporated in the research design is discussed in detail in the next four chapters, we shall present only brief notes at this stage.

First, we regard it as necessary to emphasize the intrinsic interwovenness of (i) the determinants of research decisions, and (ii) the steps of the decision-making process in a research project, a topic to which we alluded in the previous section. The researcher's specific beliefs regarding the domain phenomena and the best interpretation(s) of a particular phenomenon, and assumptions about what constitutes good research, will all play a determining role in the manner in which the research problem will be formulated, the choice of techniques by means of which the central concepts of the theory are to be operationalized, and the manner in which data about phenomena or events are to be collected.

Secondly, we wish to emphasize that the model allows for different types of research. In this model the formulation of problems could refer either to typical empirical problems (for example, What is the relationship between intelligence and scholastic performance?) or to typical conceptual problems (for example, What is the meaning of *structural violence*?). In the same manner, conceptualization and operationalization could refer to the situation where clearly articulated theories and models are employed as the framework for research. Similarly, the concepts could be employed to refer to a situation where the conceptualization is done in a qualitative manner during the course of the research, with the primary aim of determining the concepts of the actors within their social context. It is also possible to demonstrate that data collection need not necessarily only refer to the processes involved in collating data in a quantitative manner, but could as readily refer to information derived from historical documents, biographies, in-depth interviews, and so on. One could go even further and demonstrate that this view would hold for that type of evidence which is generated in the process of conceptual analysis. We shall, however, discuss this problem in more detail in subsequent chapters.

SUMMARY

The first aim in this chapter was to clarify the concept *social sciences research*. In terms of the definition of social sciences research which is used in this book, five dimensions are distinguished. These are the sociological, ontological, teleological, epistemological and methodological dimensions. The fact that we allude to five dimensions of social sciences research is already an indication that these five aspects are conceptually linked. For this reason, we have stressed that these dimensions are mutually determined. When we, therefore, turn our attention to the context of the research process as, for example, in the model of the practice of social sciences research in the previous section, the interdependence of the various dimensions is implied throughout.

The primary goal in the formulation of the model was to draw attention to the fact that a variety of perspectives on research exist. On the one hand, one may emphasize the fact that research is always conducted within the context of a particular research tradition and discipline. Seen from this point of view, it is clearly the sociological dimension that is highlighted. What one would emphasize is, therefore, the existing diversity of meta-theoretical values, methodological models, theoretical frames of reference, and so on. On the other hand, however, one may focus on the individual researcher within the context of a specific research project. Here it is primarily the research process as a rational decision-making process, the determinants of research decisions, and the typical steps which occur within the decision-making process that are emphasized. One of the main objectives of this text is to analyze and reconstruct the logic which underlies this decision-making process.

Suggestions for further reading

1. In the preface we emphasized that the material contained in this book deals with the general methodology of the social sciences, and that issues related to the philosophy of science, research methods, and research techniques are not analyzed. For a discussion of the most important differences between the philosophy of science, research methodology, and research technology, Mouton (1983b) may be consulted. A somewhat dated but still useful book in this general field is that by Kaplan (1964). More recent books which deal with similar issues include Agnew and Pike (1982), Babbie (1979), Denzin (1978), Nowak (1976), and Philliber, Schwab, and Sloss (1980). Although the majority tend to present discussions which merely spell out guidelines, there are sections in each in which the authors deal with general methodological principles.

2. As indicated in the preface, an important goal of this book is to assist readers who intend using it as a first, relatively simple, reference source by guiding them to more advanced publications in the fields of research methodology and the philosophy of science by providing appropriate references. Chalmers (1982) is probably the best introductory text on the philosophy of science currently available. Somewhat more advanced is the text by Koningsveld (1980), while Newton-Smith (1981) is regarded as the most balanced introductory text on the contemporary state of the art of the philosophy of science, although it is probably more suitable for the advanced student. For the real connoisseur, one can hardly do better than to read Asquith and Kyburg (1979) which is generally regarded as the standard reference source.

3. A number of excellent publications on the philosophy of the social sciences has appeared during the past decade. One of the best general introductions is to be found in Bernstein (1976), while his more recent text (Bernstein, 1983) contains a more advanced overview. Further introductory texts in this general area are Benton (1977), Giddens (1976), Keat and Urry

(1975), and Trigg (1985). For the novice in this field, the concise book by Hughes (1980) can be highly recommended, in spite of the fact that he adopts a thematic approach, rather than dealing with different trends like hermeneutics, phenomenology, Neo-Marxism, and realism.

4. In our discussion of the sociology of science we have paid particular attention to the more recent developments in this area. Thomas Kuhn's point of view appears in his 1970 publication. Competent discussions of Kuhn's point of view are to be found in Lakatos and Musgrave (1970), and Suppe (1974). A recent trend is that progressively more attention is being paid to the implications of Kuhn's point of view for the social sciecnes (Barnes, 1982; Gutting, 1980). This issue is addressed in greater detail in chapter 6 of this book.

Radnitzky's systems theory model of scientific research is elaborated in Radnitzky (1970, 1974 and 1980). For an incisive treatment of Radnitzky's point of view, the best source is probably Anderson (1984). For the sociology of science in general, the following texts may all be regarded as good introductions: Barnes (1974), Collins (1982), Hagstrom (1965), Merton (1973), and Storer (1966). Collins (1983) also presents a recent overview of the field which may be regarded as a useful introduction. The most recent developments in this area are, however, to be found in the *Sociology of the science yearbook* which has appeared since 1977.

5. As far as journal articles are concerned, the most important publications in the field of the philosophy of science appear in: *Philosophy of science, British journal of the philosophy of science, Synthese, Kennis en methode*, and *Zeitschrift für allgemeine Wissenschaftstheorie*. Concerning the philosophy of the social sciences, *Philosophy of social science*, and *Human studies* may be consulted.
Encyclopedias on the philosophy of science are rare. At the time of writing we are aware of the existence of only two, both in German.
These are *Wissenschaftstheoretischen Lexicon* (Braun and Radermacher, 1978) and *Enzyklopädie der Philosophie und Wissenschaftstheorie* volume 1) (Mittelstrass, 1980).

Introduction: Social sciences research as a rational activity

What is the meaning of research design?

Viewing research design as maximizing validity

Choice of a research topic

    Self-initiated research
        Wonder
        Theory testing
        Generation of hypotheses

    Contract research

Problem formulation

    Unit of analysis
        Individuals
        Groups
        Organizations
        Social artefacts
        Threats to validity

    Research goals
        Exploratory studies
        Descriptive studies
        Explanatory studies
        Some philosophical remarks on causality

    Research strategy

Resumé

Suggestions for further reading

CHAPTER 2

RESEARCH DESIGN: TOWARDS PROBLEM FORMULATION

INTRODUCTION: SOCIAL SCIENCES RESEARCH AS A RATIONAL ACTIVITY

Chapters 2 to 5 are devoted to a discussion of the dynamics of the process of social sciences research. In the previous chapter we emphasized the fact that the research process is essentially a decision-making process in which the researcher is continuously involved, among other things, in making decisions about what ought to be investigated and how this ought to be done. As we indicated, in the language game of the social sciences high demands are placed upon the validity of scientific statements. This clearly implies that research must be objective and critical. In terms of the topic of this, and the next three chapters, this would require that the researcher make rational research decisions. Although *rational* has become to be seen as a loaded concept in recent philosophy of science, it is still true that in most circles it is accepted that scientific activities must comply with the criteria of rationality. Where differences do occur, they relate to the exact interpretation of what is meant by *rationality*. Because this is not a philosophical treatise in which we can enter into the detail of this problem, we shall confine ourselves to two remarks. The first will deal with what rationality is not, and the second with the meaning which we wish to give to the concept rationality in this book.

A well-known interpretation of rationality is that found in logical positivism and the earlier philosophy of Karl Popper in which rationality is equated with logicality. According to this view, science is rational to the extent that it complies with the rules of logic. On the one hand, the issue has been formalized in the ideals of inductive logic (compare Carnap, Carnap & Jeffrey, and other works), while, on the other hand, in the ideal of deductivism (Popper). In the case of both these approaches, it is assumed that the implementation of logical rules (inductive and deductive inferences) is a necessary and sufficient criterion to ensure the incorrigibility of scientific statements. Harold Brown, in a searching analysis of the logicist interpretation of rationality, states that:

> *Again the project (of inductive logic) is to find an algorithm on the basis of which we can evaluate scientific theories, the assumption being that even if we cannot prove the final truth of an hypothesis, we can produce a set of rules which will allow us to determine the degree to which it has been confirmed by the available evidence. The same ideal controls the falsificationist view of scientific procedure. Popper, realizing that no finite procedure can prove a scientific theory, noted that the logical principle modus tollens provides an algorithm which, given appropriate basic statements, could prove a theory false* (1977: 146-147).

It would be reasonable to claim that rational decision making is understood in both these schools of thought as an algorithmic process in which one decision follows another according to a preprogrammed scheme. However, research projects are neither rigid nor inflexible. The ideal of the positivists in particular, was to ensure that the research process was rational (according to their definition of the concept) and logical so as to eliminate all elements of subjectivity and idiosyncrasy from the outset. It is evident that this interpretation of rationality forms the basis of many handbooks on research methodology in which the research process is often presented as a highly structured and prescriptive series of phases or steps.

One of the most important gains resulting from the "revolution" which Kuhn brought about in modern philosophy of science, concerns the meaning of the concept *rationality*. In his critique of positivism, Kuhn argues that decisions concerning the acceptance or rejection of theories *can never be settled by logic and experiment alone* and that *the competition between paradigms is not the sort of battle that can be resolved by proofs* (1970:). The position elaborated in the next three chapters is that rationality is a characteristic of people and can, therefore, never be intrinsic to either rules or guidelines. In terms of the research model developed in chapter one, rationality must be regarded as the communal property of a social sciences research community. This leads to a situation where research in such a community is invariably judged on the basis of the criteria of rationality. The content of *rationality* is, however, not exhausted because of the fact that it has a sociological character. Certain more generally accepted criteria co-determine what a given research community will regard as *rational decisions* such as, for example, considerations concerning logical consistency, the rule of sufficient evidence, theoretical scope, inter-subjective validity, explanatory success, and so on.

There are, therefore, two sides to our concept of rationality: on the one hand, it is acknowledged that what is regarded as rational (scientifically respectable) is inevitably bound to the values and beliefs of a specific research community. On the other hand, it is similarly acknowledged that criteria exist which have greater scope and validity than for one or two research communities only. One example will suffice to illustrate this point. There may be considerable differences between the adherents of two research traditions or paradigms concerning what ought to be regarded as rational research decisions when the one group accepts a quantitative research model, while the other follows a qualitative model. Those in the first group would regard considerations of external validity (generalizability) as one of the most important requirements, while those in the second group would tend to regard them as being of less importance, if they were to be taken into account at all. Nonetheless, it is likely that the adherents of both these approaches would regard considerations of internal validity, such as making valid inferences and consistent conclusions, as essential conditions for the rational practice of science.

Therefore, in accepting the social nature of rationality, we do not necessarily opt for a standpoint of relativism (cf. Brown, 1985). The assumption that certain criteria of rationality apply across paradigms, ensures that the relativistic alternative is not regarded as the logical alternative to the traditional logicist interpretation. (This argument is discussed in more detail in Mouton, 1986).

Our primary aim in the chapters in which we discuss issues of research design, is to indicate what is meant by rational decision making in the research process. In accordance with the epistemological position adopted in this book (see Chapter 1), this aim is to indicate how the researcher, by employing procedures of rational decision making, may increase the likelihood of generating valid research findings. One of our central presuppositions is that, because scientific research is a human endeavour, it is necessarily fallible. In terms of this assumption (Popper's *fallibilist thesis*), the primary aim of methodological reflection is to increase the ultimate validity of research findings by ensuring that errors and inaccuracies are eliminated by means of rational research decisions.

The existence of a variety of research methods, paradigmatic preferences, and differences in phenomena, suggests that it is erroneous to assume that a single correct research methodology, appropriate for all situations, may be found. More often than not, the researcher will only be able to control for some of the threats to validity and nuisance variables. Rational decision making, therefore, means that the researcher will frequently have to make concessions. For practical and other reasons it is usually impossible for researchers to control

31

for all the factors which may pose a threat to the validity of their findings. It is, nonetheless, possible, by paying attention to nuisance variables in a critical and systematic manner, to ensure that the ultimate research findings are likely to be more valid. This is the primary aim of research design.

WHAT IS THE MEANING OF *RESEARCH DESIGN?*

Selltiz *et al.*, in their classical book on research methodology, define research design in the following manner: *A research design is the arrangement of conditions for collection and analysis of data in a manner that aims to combine relevance to the research purpose with economy in procedure* (1965: 50).

From this definition it is evident that the aim in research design is to align the pursuit of a research goal with the practical considerations and limitations of the project. Clearly, research design implies that research is planned. In our discussion of this topic we adhere fairly closely to the literal (and conventional) meanings of the words *design* and *plan*. The most general use of the words plan and design are probably to be found in the construction industry, where the drawing of building plans or an architectural design invariably precedes the actual construction of a building. In this sense there is a concurrence with the term research design as an exposition or blue print of the research project.

Because *design* in this sense of the word usually implies decisions which are taken beforehand (to ensure that potential mistakes are eliminated, thereby maintaining the lowest possible cost), it has become customary in the practice of research to refer to research design mainly in the context of highly structured and controlled research such as experimental studies. Because experimental research involves the stringent control of all relevant variables to ensure the elimination of possible effects of unknown variables, studies of this nature lend themselves to pre-planning and design. The study of different types of experimental procedures is, for this reason, the most highly developed area of research design.

During recent decades, it has, also, become customary to refer to design within survey research. This is largely attributable to the degree of refinement of sample design techniques. Developments in the field of survey design can also be explained in terms of the highly structured nature of present-day survey research. Compared with this, there is very little published in the literature that addresses the problems encountered in field research, or in research in which the natural environment of the subject is an important feature of the design and where control or accurate planning are ruled out from the outset. The same applies to single case studies, unstructured interviewing, or historical analyses.

32

The meaning of the term research design as we use it in this book is, however, a broadening of the accepted usage. Too much emphasis is placed upon the fact that design and planning are directly related to the degree of structure and control in a research project. Clearly, such a relationship does exist, and it is for this reason that research design will always be more important, and also more effective, in studies in which systematic control and manipulation are possible.

Nonetheless, a further important dimension of the meaning of *research design* is disregarded in the process. The need for design and planning is most evident when errors and inaccuracies have to be eliminated. Even when it is impossible to structure a project fully and to consider each step in detail, it is frequently possible to eliminate certain typical threats to validity at the beginning and also during the course of the project. This is the meaning which we wish to convey by the terms *design* and *research design* in this book. It is now possible to link up to the previous section, and the aim of research design may be formulated in the following manner.

The aim of a research design is to plan and structure a given research project in such a manner that the eventual validity of the research findings is maximized.

Research design is, therefore, synonymous with rational decision making during the research process. Irrespective of how structured or unstructured a research project is likely to be, it is the duty of the researcher to ascertain which general nuisance variables may render the results invalid, and to take every possible step to ensure that these factors are either minimized or eliminated.

Using the accepted decision-making steps in the research process as a frame of reference, we present, in chapters 2 to 5 an explanation of the factors which may threaten the overall validity of a project. We must, however, emphasize that we shall deal with a broad range of nuisance variables which may occur across a broad spectrum of research in the social sciences. It should be clear that it is highly unlikely that all the factors which we shall discuss will ever occur in a single research project. For this reason, it is the task of the reader to decide which of the factors discussed are likely to affect the validity of the research findings.

VIEWING RESEARCH DESIGN AS MAXIMIZING VALIDITY

As indicated in the previous section, the model of research decisions constitutes the frame of reference of this chapter and the subsequent ones. In this model we distinguish between the following five typical research decisions:

(1) Choice of a research topic.
(2) Problem formulation.

(3) Conceptualization and operationalization.
(4) Data collection.
(5) Analysis and interpretation of data.

In this chapter we shall deal with the first two steps, while the last three are dealt with in chapters 3, 4 and 5.

In our discussion of each of these five steps, we shall present:

(i)   a brief explanation of what is involved in the particular decision-making step;
(ii)   a discussion of the most important threats to validity which typically occur in this context; and
(iii)   an indication of which steps may be taken to counteract or eliminate the effect of those threats to validity.

CHOICE OF A RESEARCH TOPIC

In this section we discuss the choice which the researcher exercises concerning which phenomenon or phenomena are to be studied. Particular attention will be paid to the reasons which underlie the choice of research designs.

Self-initiated research

WONDER

Research may be conducted for a variety of reasons. Quite often, the motivation is mere inquisitiveness about an interesting phenomenon or about something which presents a puzzle. An interesting example of this is to be found in the well-known research of Stanley Milgram. He wanted to find an explanation for the extreme cases of mass aggression which had been recorded in recent history, such as the mass extermination of millions of Jews in Nazi concentration camps or the killing of civilians at My Lai during the Vietnamese War. His hypothesis was that the phenomena could not be adequately explained by notions of the so-called sadistic personality. An alternative explanation was that, given the circumstances surrounding the events, the main reasons were to be found in obedience to authority. To investigate this hypothesis, he designed a series of experiments.

The basic design included an experimenter and two subjects. The subjects were informed that the study dealt with the manner in which people learn. By spinning a coin, one of the subjects was designated as the teacher and the other as the pupil. Following this, the pupil was strapped into an electric chair, and the learning task was begun. A panel with 30 switches was placed in front of the teacher. The switches were marked in increments of 15 volts, with the first marked 15 volts and the last 450 volts. At increments of 60 volts, descriptive phrases appeared on the control panel: *light shock, moderate shock, intense shock, extremely intense shock, danger: tremendous shock*

34

and finally three X's. The *teacher* was instructed by the experimenter to apply shock to the pupil every time he gave an incorrect answer, beginning with 15 volts and incrementing the voltage by 15 volts with each successive error. In actual fact, the spinning of the coin had been manipulated, and the pupil was an accomplice of the experimenter.

Although the pupil was not shocked at all, he simulated increasingly painful reactions until the intensity reached 300 volts, after which he displayed no reaction whatsoever. The suggestion, therefore, was that he had become unconscious at that stage. What the experimenter was, in fact, investigating, was the amount of shock that the subject (the *teacher*) would be prepared to apply before refusing to continue. Despite the fact that the subjects believed that the pupils were being shocked in an extremely painful manner, more than 60 % were prepared to continue with the experiment right up to the end. Milgram's conclusion was that people could be induced to display aggressive behaviour when it occurred under the instruction of an authority figure. Although this study gave rise to a lengthy debate on the subject of research ethics, it remains nonetheless, an excellent example of how a researcher, stimulated by a puzzling situation, conducted original research.

Inquisitiveness about behaviour and phenomena which appear to be somewhat atypical has frequently been the major reason for embarking on a study. In the same manner, research has been conducted on behaviour in nudist colonies, on homosexual behaviour in public toilets, on behaviour in cinemas where pornographic films are shown, and on the behaviour of people in psychiatric hospitals.

THEORY TESTING

An important category of research is motivated by the testing of existing models and theories. An interesting example of research of this nature is Kingsley Davis's (1961) evaluation of structural functionalism. His argument was that prostitution plays a demonstrably utilitarian function in society, by virtue of the fact that it operates as a safety valve. He argued that prostitution provides an opportunity to indulge in types of sexual behaviour which would be regarded as deviant within the context of the normal family structure, and that prostitution, in fact, contributes to the maintenance of the family system. In a similar manner, people have attempted to indicate that structural functionalism does not provide an adequate explanatory model for some types of behaviour. Research in which another theoretical model, symbolic interactionism, has been employed has been conducted on the same phenomenon in an attempt to demonstrate the inadequacy of functionalist interpretations. A useful example is to be found in the work of Howard Becker (1963). According to his argument, an important factor which influences a person's involvement in a deviant career is to be found in the extent to which the public labels such a person as deviant. According to him labelling has a negative influence on the person's self-concept, but a more important consequence is that the person concerned (for example, a prostitute, a homosexual, a criminal) will tend to become even more closely associated with the deviant behaviour.

GENERATION OF HYPOTHESES

Compared with the preceding examples, researchers frequently have to investigate phenomena about which few established models or theories exist. In this type of situation, researchers have to attempt to generate new models or hypotheses by using exploratory studies. Such models or hypotheses can then be used as point of departure in subsequent research. A category which is important here is the type of phenomenon which has been the subject of intense investigation in one culture, but which has not yet been investigated in another. From Schurink's (1979) study it is clear that prostitution has been the subject of intensive research reaching over a period of several decades in the USA, but that very few studies of this phenomenon had been conducted in South Africa. The importance of this type of consideration becomes even clearer when research amongst the different cultural groups is considered.

Contract research

An important characteristic of contract research is that it is nearly always directed at solving social problems. The person or organization contracting the research has a clear practical interest in the research, and tends to require specific information about the research topic at fairly short notice. In this regard an important difference exists between applied research and self-initiated research which, more often than not, originates primarily from the interests of an individual researcher and therefore tends to display the characteristics of theory-related research or so-called basic research.

The importance of the distinction between self-initiated and contract research is to be found in the different ways in which the ultimate validity of the research findings may be affected. In self-initiated research the choice of a research design is primarily the responsibility of the individual researcher. In the case of contract research, on the other hand, the problems to be researched are usually reasonably clearly defined. There are two issues which are of importance here.

In the first instance, it should be clear that, even in the case of self-initiated research, the choice of a research design is only partially at the discretion of individual researchers. As a result of the context within which master's or doctoral studies are conducted, students select a research theme in consultation with the supervisor concerned often as a result of research initially conducted by the supervisor. One of the most important conclusions that Kuhn reached in his study of normal science, was that a large degree of agreement was to be found amongst the adherents of a specific research paradigm on what ought to be investigated and even on how this ought to be done. There can be few places where this is more clearly illustrated than in the choice of research topics by postgraduate students which frequently bears the mark of their mentors.

The mere fact that the choice of a research topic is co-determined by the interests of the supervisor or the research team within which the researcher works, need not necessarily pose any threat to the eventual validity of the findings. That a practice of this nature may not be to the ultimate benefit of the department or discipline is, however, also clear when the same tradition is continued year in and year out without any constructive innovation. A risky situation does, however, develop when the choice of a research topic or the eventual formulation of the research problem is of such a biased nature that important research and literature are excluded on a *priori* grounds or, even worse, that certain types of interpretations or explanations are likely to receive priority over competing interpretations from the outset. This leads us to the second difference between contract and self-initiated research.

Because the choice of a research topic is, by definition, not in the hands of the researchers in the case of contract research, they have a greater responsibility to ensure that the formulation of the problem is as objective and critical as possible. It is entirely unacceptable that contract research should be regarded as implying that the organization requesting the research determines the direction thereof, and the manner in which data are collected and analyzed at the stage of entering into the contract.

Thus, although threats to the validity of research exist in both self-initiated and applied research they need not present insuperable obstacles to the researcher. The sanction associated with an established tradition of self-initiated research is, in itself, one of the most important safeguards against unscientific research in the face of the necessity for conducting contract research. In this context the existing mechanisms of social control — criticism and debate in research communities — fulfil an important role in ensuring the validity of findings.

PROBLEM FORMULATION

The choice of a specific research design is the first step in the identification of what is to be investigated. The next step involves getting an exact indication of the nature of the "object" of the investigation (individual, group, organization, social interaction or social object) and of which aspects, characteristics or dimensions of the "object" need to be researched. For this reason it is customary to formulate the research problem in the form of a series of questions. For example:

- What is the nature of the social interaction in a gay club?
- What is the relationship between intelligence and creativity respectively and the ability to solve abstract problems?
- What were the primary causes that led to the Soweto riots?
- Why is alienation such a common characteristic of urbanized people of our time?
- What are the essential characteristics of structural violence compared with physical violence?
- In what way do the political attitudes of present-day youth differ from those of ten years ago?

It is clear that research problems are usually worded in a form beginning with: What is or was...? What happened...? Why did x ...? What are the causes of...? How much...? How many...? To what extent...?

The exact formulation of a research problem is related to a number of factors. From the previous section it is evident that the research motivation (self-initiated or contract) exerts an important limitation on the problem formulation. In this section, we shall pay attention to three factors which co-determine the manner in which research problems are formulated: the unit of analysis, research goal and research strategy.

Unit of analysis

Once a decision has been reached on the broad area of the investigation, the researcher has to decide what is to be investigated, i.e. the nature of the unit of analysis. If one were to pose the question: ''What area are you investigating?'', a researcher would readily reply' ''Social disintegration, political attitudes relating to change, the population explosion, juvenile delinquency, alcoholism, or whatever.'' It is, however, clear that each of these replies is merely a broad indication of the general area which is to be investigated. For a more exact indication of the research problem, it is necessary that the specific unit of analysis be identified. Following Babbie (*The practice of social science*) four main categories of units of analysis may be distinguished:

INDIVIDUALS

Individual human beings are probably the most common typical *object* of research in the social sciences. Even when groups, communities, or populations are studied, it is customary to study individuals, and then to aggregate the data collected in this manner for the group concerned. Clearly, the researcher is often interested in specific categories of individuals such as students, constituents, politicians, academics, factory workers, and so on. In cases of this nature a certain number of individuals are studied as representative of the particular population which was initially identified.

GROUPS

Collectivities of individuals are also frequently studied as groups as, for example, in the case of families, gangs, census blocks, couples, and so on. The reason for studying groups rather than individuals is to be found in the fact that groups possess characteristics which are not necessarily applicable to the behaviour of individuals. Families (but not individuals) share values of *loyalty* and *cohesiveness*; while gangs display norms which include *solidarity* and *collective responsibility* — their own code of behaviour. For the exact reason that groups possess their own characteristics, it is necessary to try to understand and explain the functioning of either families or gangs in terms of those characteristics. It would, quite simply, be wrong to attempt, for example, to consistently try to understand the behaviour of groups in terms of the characteristics of the individual.

ORGANIZATIONS

Formal social organizations such as companies, churches, universities, academic departments, factories, and supermarkets are frequently used as the unit of analysis. Here, as in the previous case, attention is once again focussed on the unique qualities of these social organizations such as organizational structure, lines of authority, promotional policy, the representativeness of minority groups on the pay roll, labour relations, and productivity.

SOCIAL ARTEFACTS

In a general sense, the term "social artefacts" is used to refer to all *products* of human behaviour. Babbie distinguishes between social objects such as books, paintings, cars, buildings, and songs, on the one hand, and social interactions such as marriage ceremonies, court hearings, traffic offences, divorces, race riots, prostitution, and juvenile delinquency, on the other.

The classification of individuals, groups, organizations and social artefacts is taken a stage further by Babbie. Thus far we have referred to the *characteristics* of these four units of measurement in general terms. More specifically, it is possible to distinguish between the conditions, orientations, and actions of individuals, groups, organizations, and social artefacts. Although such a refinement facilitates understanding in the majority of cases, it does not invariably do so. Bearing in mind that social groups and organizations usually differ only in terms of intensity and degree, they have been included under the same category in the table that follows. The table, therefore, includes only the most significant refinements. Empty cells indicate that a particular refinement would not have been enlightening.

	CONDITIONS	ORIENTATIONS	ACTIONS
INDIVI-DUALS	sex/age/educational level/ marital status/ occupation	opinions/attitudes/values/ preferences/dislikes/biases	voting behaviour/ strikes/church attendance/aggression/television viewing/educational attainment.
SOCIAL GROUPS AND ORGANI-ZATIONS	size/structure/ locality/cohesiveness/group spirit/management composition	organizational policy/functions/ regulations and procedures/company strategy	gang crime/ company mergers/ club activities.
SOCIAL OBJECTS	length/size/ quality/genre/ style/composition/ frequency of themes.		
SOCIAL INTER-ACTIONS	appearance/ locality/ duration/ kinds of people involved/intensity	motivation/ goals/motives/ strategies	

The table of units of analysis and of what Babbie refers to as research themes can clearly be expanded by cross tabulating the units of analysis against each other. Both these approaches illustrate how research problems can be generated, and also how extensive the research domain of the social sciences really is.

Another important dimension that determines the unit of analysis is the dimension of time. It is possible to distinguish between diachronic or longitudinal studies, on the one hand, and synchronic or cross-sectional studies, on the other.

* **Diachronic/longitudinal** studies involve the investigation of units of analysis over an extended period of time. This category could, for example, include the study of changes in political attitudes over a period of time, or research into the origin and development of a particular socio-political move-

ment such as Inkatha or the Nazi movement in Germany during the period between the end of World War I and that of World War II.

Different types of longitudinal studies like cohort studies or panel studies are usually included in this category. Cohort studies refer to research in which a particular sub-population (for example, people born between 1940 and 1949) is studied with a view to assessing the changes which occur over time. Although the sample in each study may differ, it will consistently include subjects drawn from the sub-population which was originally defined. Panel studies are similar to cohort studies with the exception that each follow-up study would include the same individuals in the sample. An example of this type of study would be if the political attitudes of a group of constituents were to be investigated month by month for the duration of an election campaign.

* **Synchronic/cross-sectional** studies are those in which a given phenomenon is studied at a specific point in time. For example, studies of the attitudes of people or the value systems of a particular sample at a certain time.

This distinction between synchronic and diachroniç research would apply to most of the cells in the preceding table. It merely serves to illustrate how complex the research domain of the social sciences is, and to show the variety of potential research topics.

THREATS TO VALIDITY

The two most important threats to the validity of a study regarding the unit of analysis are to be found in (i) the so-called ecological fallacy and in (ii) reductionistic tendencies.

(i) **The ecological fallacy** involves, for example, arriving at conclusions about groups when the subjects of the study are individuals. The inverse would also apply where conclusions are reached about individuals when the participants in the study are groups. The following is an example of the latter fallacy: Assume that we are conducting a post hoc analysis of election results. Further assume that our interest is in the amount of support received by the only female candidate in the local city council elections. We have data at our disposal on the voting patterns in the different wards and also census data on the demographic composition of the wards. According to our analysis we find that there is a greater degree of support for the female candidate in wards with a larger proportion of younger voters. One would be inclined to conclude that younger people are more likely to vote for a female candidate. In doing this we would be in danger of committing the ecological fallacy. It might just as well have been the older voters in the wards with greater proportions of younger voters who voted for the female candidate. The problem which arose is related to the fact that we used wards as our unit of analysis to arrive at conclusions about the behaviour of individual voters.

(ii) The term **reductionistic** tendencies is used here to refer to the situation where researchers tend to consider and present only those explanations and interpretations which are embedded in discipline-specific variables. For practical and theoretical reasons a sociologist would only consider common sociological variables (values, norms, roles) when investigating a particular phenomenon; economists only economic variables (supply and demand, marginal values); and a psychologist only psychological variables (personality types, motivation). If a person working in a particular discipline were, however, to go so far as to postulate that the view that he or she holds is the only correct approach to the phenomenon, or if he or she were to maintain that his or her interpretation is the only viable one, there is clear evidence of reductionism. The tendency to explain all phenomena in terms of economic variables is known as economic reductionism, in psychology it is called psychologism, and in sociology it is labelled sociologism. If an event like the 1976 Soweto riots were to be studied, one may, within this framework, expect political scientists to pay attention only to the political frustrations of the group; economists only to the economic problems associated with income and expenditure; sociologists to the discrepancy between role expectations and role perceptions, relative deprivation, and the influence of living conditions on quality of life. The problem arises when one of these approaches is absolutized at the expense of the others.

The obvious solutions for these two types of research errors are (i) a critical awareness of the unit of analysis when conclusions are reached about the data, and (ii) a critical awareness of the limitations of the scope of a given discipline. An ecological fallacy involves a threat to inferential validity. Claims made in the conclusions reached, must be supported by the data or information collected. The issue of inferential validity is dealt with in detail in Chapter 5. As far as (ii) is concerned, the limitations of any single discipline make it desirable that interdisciplinary strategies be used. By involving consultants and colleagues from other disciplines, the probability of reductionism is, to some extent, reduced.

Research goals

The research goal provides a broad indication of what researchers wish to attain in their research. Is the aim of the project to describe, to explain, or to predict, or is the aim exploratory? Is it to evaluate some practice or programme? It is possible to distinguish between three basic types of studies: exploratory, descriptive, and explanatory studies. Both classificatory and correlational studies are grouped under the category of descriptive studies, while predictive and evaluative studies are regarded as sub-categories of explanatory studies.

EXPLORATORY STUDIES

As clearly indicated in the term, the goal which is pursued in exploratory studies is the exploration of a relatively unknown research area. The aims of such studies may vary quite considerably. They may be:

- to gain new insights into the phenomenon;
- to undertake a preliminary investigation before a more structured study of the phenomenon;
- to explicate the central concepts and constructs;
- to determine priorities for future research;
- to develop new hypotheses about an existing phenomenon.

In their book on research methodology, Selltiz *et al.* emphasize three methods by means of which exploratory research may be conducted:

(i)   a review of the related social science and other pertinent literature,
(ii) a survey of people who have had practical experience of the problem to be studied,
(iii) an analysis of "insight-stimulating" examples.

Because exploratory studies usually lead to insight and comprehension rather than the collection of accurate and replicable data, these studies frequently involve the use of in-depth interviews, the analysis of case studies, and the use of informants. Hypotheses tend to be developed as a result of such research, rather than the research being guided by hypotheses. The most important research design considerations which apply here are, the need:

(i)   to follow an open and flexible research strategy, and
(ii) to use methods such as literature reviews, interviews, case studies, and informants, which may lead to insight and comprehension.

The best guarantee for the completion of an exploratory study is to be found in the researcher's willingness to examine new ideas and suggestions and to be open to new stimuli. The major pitfall to avoid is allowing preconceived ideas or hypotheses to exercise a determining influence on the direction or nature of the research.

DESCRIPTIVE STUDIES

The spectrum of descriptive studies includes a large variety of types of research. On the one hand, it is possible to emphasize the in-depth description of a specific individual, situation, group, organization, tribe, sub-culture, inter-action, or social object. On the other hand, one may emphasize the frequency with which a specific characteristic or variable occurs in a sample. A distinction may also be drawn between descriptive studies with a contextual interest (see the next section on *research strategy*) and descriptive studies with a more general interest. This distinction is also closely related to the distinction which may be drawn between qualitative and quantitative research.

The description of phenomena may also range from a narrative type of description (as in historical analysis) to a highly structured statistical analysis. The latter type of description is characterized by the use of a systematic classification of variables by means of frequency tables, arithmetic means, medians, cross tabulations, and so on. Nonetheless, classification which need not necessarily be quantitative in nature may also be the basis of other types of descriptive research. A good example of this is to be found in Joubert's (1973) typology of value orientations on the basis of specified general principles. The construction of a typology or taxonomy may therefore be regarded as typically classificatory in nature.

The majority of examples to which we have referred thus far involve the description of domain phenomena in terms of separate variables or characteristics. The exception has been historical description where a specific (chronological) relationship between events is postulated. When descriptions are constructed by means of the relationships between variables, it is usually referred to as a correlational study. The researcher does not conclude with a list of frequencies or arithmetic means (univariate statistics) but goes further by postulating relationships between, for example, intelligence and scholastic achievement, or age and political attitudes. In statistical terms, these relationships may be estimated in a variety of ways which include correlations, other measures of association, regression analyses, analyses of variance, factor analyses, and so on (bivariate and multivariate statistics).

From the discussion thus far it is evident that the term *description* has developed into an umbrella term used in many different types of research. The single common element in all of these types of research is the researcher's goal, which is to describe that which exists as accurately as possible. Depending upon the researcher's preference for qualitative or quantitative research methodologies, and his or her choice of either ideographic or nomothetic strategies, the meaning of the phrase *to describe accurately* would vary with the context.

The range of contexts include conceptual analysis (the construction of typologies and taxonomies), historical analysis (narrative description), the reconstruction of single cases (individuals to groups), and the use of univariate and multivariate descriptive statistics (frequency tables, correlations, analyses of variance).

One of the most important considerations in descriptive studies is to collect accurate information or data on the domain phenomena which are under investigation. As indicated in the preceding paragraph, the meaning of the term *accurate* will vary from one study to the next depending upon a variety of factors. We shall return to this issue in chapter 4 where the question of data collection is addressed in greater detail.

44

EXPLANATORY STUDIES

The major aim of explanatory studies is to indicate causality between variables or events. The researcher may, for example, not be satisfied merely to show that a relationship exists between intelligence and scholastic achievement but wishes to indicate the direction of the relationship (high intelligence results in better scholastic achievement). The major aim is, therefore, to attempt to explain a given phenomenon (such as good scholastic achievement) in terms of specific causes (such as high intelligence). Even in this simple example it is clear that a valid explanation cannot be achieved unless it is possible to show that intelligence is the sole cause of good scholastic achievement. In this example there are obviously a large number of possible explanations for high scholastic achievement: the motivation of the pupil, the family background and socio-economic status of the family, the nature of the curriculum, and so on.

A valid causal explanation must, therefore, meet three central requirements:

(i)   that a demonstrable relationship exists between the phenomena or, stated differently, that the causal (or independent) variable covaries with the dependent variable, and
(ii)   that there is a specific sequence of cause and effect (temporal sequence),
(iii)   that a specific phenomenon is the real cause of y.

The example which we employed in the previous paragraph is, of course, rather artificial as in modern approaches to the study of causality it is accepted that an event may be the result of a number of causes. The assumption of unilinear causality has, therefore, been replaced by a more sophisticated approach to the study of causality in the social sciences. (Cf. the references to causal inference/models at the end of the chapter).

There is a direct relationship between explanatory research and predictive and evaluative research. If it were possible to construct a causal model of scholastic attainment showing the influence of intelligence, motivation, and family background on scholastic attainment, in other words, how scholastic attainment is proportionally influenced by the presence of these variables, it ought, in principle, to be possible to make generally valid predictions of future scholastic attainment.

In evaluation research we are primarily concerned with the assessment or evaluation of the effectiveness of a given practice, intervention, or social programme. The following is an example of this type of research: In an attempt to improve the scholastic attainment of children in Namibia, a school readiness programme was introduced for all first grade children in the country. After a period of three years a researcher was instructed to establish the effectiveness of the programme. The task of the researcher was to determine whether the introduction of the programme had led to a noticeable increase in the scholastic attainment of the children: it was expected of the researcher to indicate a causal relationship between the programme and attainment. It is therefore clear that the fundamental principle of explanatory research is also to be found in evaluative research.

The two major types of research design by means of which causality may be indicated are experimental and quasi-experimental designs (see the discussion of research designs at the end of chapter 5).

SOME PHILOSOPHICAL REMARKS ON CAUSALITY

Thus far we have discussed causality only within the limits imposed by highly structured and controlled research contexts. The meaning of *causality* in social sciences research is, however, a very complex issue. There are few social scientists who would regard *causality* as a synonym for *physical* or *natural causality*. A characteristic of the approach adopted in the natural sciences is that it is accepted that causality may only be defined in terms of an underlying natural law. Philosophers of science who adhered to the logical positivistic tradition were inclined to believe that whatever it was that caused events to occur in conjunction with each other as if they were causally related, should be explained in terms of the existence of laws of nature. This point of view led to the well-known deductive-nomological model of scientific explanation as explicated by Carl Hempel.

Critics of the positivistic tradition argued that similar laws had yet to be discovered in the social sciences. They concluded that the existence of causal relationships in the social sciences could not be inferred. The debate in the philosophy of science on this topic is far too complicated to discuss it in detail in this book. Basically it amounts to adopting a point of view in favour of the existence of causality in the explanation of human behaviour, as opposed to a point of view which denies the existence of causality and which has its roots in a form of voluntarism. Those who adhere to the latter point of view assume that because human activity is free it cannot be explained by postulating causal relationships. Nonetheless, a third point of view has developed in recent philosophy of the social sciences (see the work of Bhaskar and Simon in the reference list). The fundamental postulate of this point of view is that causality forms part of human activities but without necessarily accepting the existence of an underlying law of nature.

A powerful justification for this point of view is presented by Michael Simon:

> *The fact that one particular occurrence is what made the difference in one particular case does not imply that it would have made a difference in other, similar cases. Causality does not have to entail determinism... We do not have to accept determinism to the extent that we believe that causes and effects are identifiable as repeatable types. But the fact that causal uniformities must be presupposed in order*

for particular causal claims to be validated does not mean that these claims must be universal in character (1982: 115).

Simon's point of view is that causality underlies the physical laws that we would, for example, encounter in nature (for example, the law of gravity) but not that physical laws form the basis of causality. For this reason, it is possible to refer to causal relationships without having to accept the existence of an underlying physical law. If we bear in mind that the debate about determinism is dependent upon the acceptance of the principle of universal causality, in which causality is linked to the existence of physical laws, the question of the tension between causality and free will becomes irrelevant. According to Simon, it is possible to accept the existence of free will, of free human choice and decision making, of human beings as reasonable creatures, while also accepting causality in human activities. In this he joins the lengthy and prominent tradition in action theory in which it is accepted that the reasons for human activities may simultaneously be the causes of human activities. Briefly, he employs the following argument: When we say that a person's activity has been caused by another activity or event, we are, in fact, not saying anything more than that he or she had a reason for behaving in a particular manner. The fact that I may have ascribed my behaviour to a preceding intention or motive or another event, therefore implies that my acceptance of the intention, motive, or other event was, in fact, the cause of my behaviour.

> *What we mean when we say that a person has been caused to act in a certain way is that he has been given a reason for acting in that way and that he has acted for that reason. When the same reasons produce similar actions in different people, we do not have to believe that these elements are linked by causal laws. Similar conditions give rise to similar actions because people appraise their common situations similarly and because the desires they have or have produced in them incline them toward making similar choices* (Simon, 1982: 124-125).

An important implication of this point of view is that causal explanations need not necessarily only be limited to experimental or quasi-experimental situations. Schurink, in a number of qualitative studies (1970, 1976), investigated the causes of prostitution: why prostitutes embark upon this type of activity and why the behaviour is maintained. When specific reasons are found by means of interviewing techniques (financial reasons or peer group pressure), the researcher is justified in claiming that these considerations constitute some of the most important causes of prostitution. The fact that a prostitute maintains that social pressure on the part of her friends is the most important reason which gave rise to her decision to prostitue herself, implies that peer group pressure or differential association may be regarded as an important cause of prostitution. This type of causal explanation is not in conflict with a point of view in which it is maintained that people have free will to exercise choices, for the simple reason that it is not accepted that all prostitution is caused by peer group pressure.

Explanatory research therefore also includes research of an unstructured and qualitative nature. Explanations of human behaviour in terms of motives, intentions, reasons, or goals are also valid causal explanations. In a similar manner, causal explanations are employed in historical analysis. The reasons for the Voortrekkers having wished to leave the Eastern Cape that are contained in Piet Retief's Manifesto may justifiably be regarded as one of the considerations which led to this historical event. The fact that an explanation of this nature may not be universally valid, does not lead to its being a less acceptable explanation.

In conclusion, attention should be paid to the fact that combinations of different research goals are, naturally, possible. A given project may be both descriptive and explanatory, or it could begin as an exploratory study and eventually develop into a descriptive study.

In this discussion of the different types of research goals, the whole question of the associated research strategy has also begun to emerge. Because there is a close link between the choice of a research goal and the choice of a research strategy, we now turn our attention to the latter. Following this, we shall pay attention to considerations that bear upon the issue of validity.

Research strategy

Since 1894 when Wilhelm Windelband proposed the distinction between nomothetic and ideographic research strategies or methodologies, it has become customary to classify social sciences research into one these categories. It may be useful to take a look at exactly what Windelband said. The most lucid description of this distinction is to be found in the following statement:

> *In their quest for knowledge of reality, the empirical sciences either seek the general in the form of the law of nature or the particular in the form of the historically defined structure. On the one hand, they are concerned with the form which invariably remains constant. On the other hand, they are concerned with the unique, immanently defined content of the real event. The former disciplines are nomological sciences. The latter disciplines are sciences of process or sciences of the event... If I may be permitted to introduce some new technical terms, scientific thought is nomothetic in the former case and ideographic in the latter case* (1980: 175).

Throughout his discussion, Windelband emphasizes that the classification which he proposes is a methodological classification, and that it does not relate to a classification of the scientific content as such. As he notes, the same

48

subject could be studied in both a nomothetic and an ideographic manner. It is important to note that both these strategies are equally valid — there is no suggestion whatsoever that one may be more scientific than the other. As a matter of fact, Windelband goes so far as to suggest that one ought to conceive of the two approaches as being mutually dependent.

Thus, ideally, it is possible to distinguish between two types of research strategies. On the one hand, one would find those broad strategies by means of which it would be possible to search for generally valid laws of science which form the basis of actions or behaviours. On the other hand, attention is paid to the single unique event or phenomenon and its structural coherence. The fact that Windelband emphasized the interdependence between the nomothetic (literally: law stating) and the ideographic (literally: uniquely descriptive), should serve as sufficient reason to be cautious about trying to impose a rigid dichotomy here. If one were to probe more deeply into the basis of this distinction, it becomes clear that it can be reduced to a one-sided emphasis on the similarities between phenomena (nomothetic) or to a one-sided emphasis of the differences between phenomena (ideographic). When using the nomothetic approach, it is customary to emphasize the commonalities or similarities between phenomena, while an ideographic approach would, in turn, be used to emphasize that which is unique or distinctive in a situation or an event. For this reason it ought to be regarded as more appropriate to regard nomothetic and ideographic as the extremes of a single continuum. All research involves the description of both similarities and differences. Depending upon whether the similarities in differences are emphasized or whether the differences in similarities are emphasized, one would be able to refer to nomothetic or ideographic strategies.

In our discussion of causality in the previous section, we indicated that, strictly speaking, it is incorrect to identify causality with the laws of nature. It is possible to explain human behaviour without claiming to postulate universal laws of human nature. For this reason, we propose a different distinction from that between nomothetic and ideographic research (the term *nomothetic* inevitably implies an identification of causality with the laws of nature); namely, a distinction between research which is of greater contextual interest, on the one hand, and research that is more representative or of greater general interest, on the other.

On the one hand, phenomena or events are studied because of their intrinsic interest. On the other hand, events or phenomena are studied for the interest which they may have as representative examples of a larger population of similar events or phenomena. In the first case, the phenomenon is studied in terms of its immediate context. In the second case, the phenomenon is studied because it is regarded as representative of a larger population or universe of similar phenomena. In subsequent sections we shall refer to the former as studies involving a **contextual** research strategy, while the latter are referred to as studies involving a **general** research strategy.

Typical examples of studies which are of contextual interest are those in the historical sciences (where a specific historical event is subjected to a searching analysis), the "hermeneutic" sciences like languages, arts, jurisprudence, and theology (where a specific text or work of art is the object of analysis), and the social sciences where the aim may be to subject a single case, a group, or a sub-culture to a searching investigation.

Well-known examples of the last category include Bogdan's study of a single transsexual (Jane Fry), Whyte's study of a specific sub-culture (Street Corner Society), and, obviously, the multitude of ethnographic studies in which the object of investigation is a single tribe. In all the examples cited, the primary aim of the investigators is to produce an extensive description of the phenomenon, event, or group within the context of the unique setting of the domain phenomenon. As a rule, the phenomenon is studied because of the intrinsic interest which the researcher has in the topic.

In contrast with the above, the aim of a researcher is often to study a representative number of events or people with a view to generalizing the results of the study to a defined universe. It is important to note that a strategy with *a general interest* clearly implies that it is possible to generalize to a defined universe or population. Typical examples of research that is of generalizable interest are experimental studies, comparative research, and various types of surveys. While studies which have contextual interest are bound to the unique context of the domain phenomenon, studies which are of generalizable interest ought, strictly speaking, not to be limited by time, place, space, or the variability or uniqueness of the particular group which has been studied. It is for this reason that the sample is selected to be as representative of the total population as possible: the group which is investigated is thus merely a sample, but it is important to note that it is a sample which is representative of the universe.

Notwithstanding the close logical relationship between contextual and general interest (ideographic and nomothetic strategies), it is essential that the researchers be clear about the strategy which they intend following before embarking upon the project. The implications for the eventual validity of the research are far reaching. At this stage we should draw a further distinction between internal and external validity which is directly related to the earlier distinction made between contextual and general interest. In the remainder of the text, the term *internal validity* will be used to refer to the fact that a study has generated accurate and valid findings of the specific phenomena which have been studied. We may therefore refer to a project as having produced internally valid results if the constructs were measured in a valid manner, the collected data are accurate and reliable, the analyses are relevant for the type of data, and the final conclusions are adequately supported by the data. The term *external validity* refers to a further stage in the research process, and that is that the findings of a given project are generalizable to all similar cases. Stated differently, the findings have greater validity than merely for the project in which they were generated. It would therefore be correct to regard *external validity* and *generalizability* as synonymous. These distinctions are summarized in the following diagram:

STEPS IN THE RESEARCH PROCESS AND CONSIDERATIONS OF VALIDITY

INTERNAL VALIDITY

Conceptualization .... Theoretical validity
Operationalization .... Measurement validity
Data-collection .... Reliability
Analysis and interpretation .... Inferential validity

EXTERNAL VALIDITY

Are the findings generalizable to the defined population?

It should be clear that internal validity logically precedes external validity. In other words, it would not be possible to claim that research findings are externally valid unless they can be shown to be internally valid. Research in which the contextual interest is emphasized would, therefore, place the highest premium on internal validity, while research with a generalizable interest would also have to comply with the requirements of external validity.

Bringing the discussion of research strategies and research goals together, it it possible to represent it in the following manner:

RESEARCH STRATEGY		
RESEARCH GOAL	**Contextual interest (internal validity)**	**General interest (internal and external validity)**
Exploratory research	Overview of phenomena by means of case studies and in-depth interviews.	Overview of phenomena by means of exploratory surveys.
Descriptive research	Case studies, in-depth interviews, participant observation.	Sample surveys.
Explanatory research	Contextual explanations by means of case studies, historical analysis.	Experimental and quasi-experimental studies.

51

Our discussion of problem formulation culminates in the question of what the criteria of internal and external validity are. The most important threats to internal and external validity, namely invalid constructs, inaccurate measurements, unreliable data, invalid conclusions (internal validity), and non-representative samples (external validity) are discussed in chapters 3 to 5. The most important point made in this chapter, has been that the conscious and critical choice of a specific unit of analysis, research strategy, and research goal hold obvious implications for the relative importance of the internal and external validity of a research project. Concerning the choice of the unit of analysis, we demonstrated the dangers inherent in the ecological fallacy and in reductionism. Neither of these threats to the eventual validity of a research project are, however, insuperable, and may be dealt with fairly readily by a critical and systematic researcher. A far bigger threat to the general validity of the research would be if the researchers, at this stage of the project, had not yet determined whether or not they would wish to generalize to a defined universe. The answer to this question is directly related to their choice of a specific research goal.

Methodological requirements for validity are obviously a good deal more strict for explanatory research than they would be in the case of exploratory research. This problem will, however, be discussed again towards the end of chapter 5 where a summary of the most important characteristics of the most typical research designs is presented.

RESUMÉ

Our primary aim in this chapter has been to introduce an important theme in the area of research design. In this chapter, as well in the three that follow, we focus on design considerations in social sciences research. Bearing in mind our original definition of research design, that it ought to be employed to maximize the ultimate validity of research findings, the following chapters are devoted to a discussion of considerations of validity in the research process. Our aim is not to discuss specific methods and techniques in the research process, but rather to review such methods and techniques from the vantage point of considerations of validity. In the present chapter our primary focus has been on the most important decisions which have to be taken to enable a researcher to arrive at a valid problem formulation.

In our discussion of considerations that influence the choice of a research design, we emphasized that, especially in the case of contract research, the choice of a research design is frequently beyond the control of the researcher. This situation does not necessarily pose an insuperable threat to the validity of the project. In our discussion of the difficulties surrounding problem formulation, we paid attention to the choice of the unit of analysis, research goal, and research strategy. The most important issue which emerged from this discussion is the distinction which may be drawn between internal and external validity. This distinction is clearly a function of the researcher's choice between either a contextual or a generalizable study. The specific considerations that influence validity will, however, be discussed in more detail in the following chapters.

As we indicated in the first two sections of this chapter, the term *research design* is used in a much broader sense in this book than one would normally encounter in books on research methodology. For this reason, some of the topics discussed in this chapter would, as a rule, not be regarded as problems relating to the question of research design. Viewed against the background of our definition of the aim of research design, it is, however, evident that the researcher needs to consider such issues as the unit of analysis, research goals, and research strategy, at an early stage in the research process so as to ensure that bias and threats to validity are not built into the research design. The issues discussed so far may mostly (if not entirely) be eliminated by the researcher being sensitive to these issues and by adopting a critical stance. The nature and extent of the validity considerations which are to be discussed in the following chapters are, however, likely to pose a much greater challenge to the ingenuity and critical abilities of the researcher!

Suggestions for further reading

1. Trigg (1973) offers an elementary discussion of the issue of rationality and of the far-reaching implications of a consistent relativism. Two books of readings which contain representative discussions by those in favour of rationality, as well as those opposed to this point of view, are those of Wilson (1969) and of Hollis and Lukes (1983). A more advanced text in which the argument in favour of rationality in science is discussed in detail, is that by Newton-Smith (1981). Kekes (1976) deals with the same issues from a Popperian frame of reference.

2. Detailed treatments of general research methodology are to be found in the texts by Doby (1954), Selltiz et al. (1965), Krausz and Miller (1974), Golden (1976), Babbie (1979), Agnew and Pike (1982), and Abrahamson (1983).

3. To facilitate the choice of a research topic, any of the many research indices in the social sciences may be consulted. A list of some of these is provided below:

   Abstracts in anthropology; Behavioral abstracts; Bibliographie linguistique/linguistic bibliography; Bibliography of philosophy; Book review index; British education index; British reports, translations and theses; Bulletin of information on current research on human sciences concern-

ing Africa; Canadian education index; Child development abstracts and bibliography; Children's book review index; Children's literature abstracts; Cognitive development abstracts; Communication abstracts; Criminal justice abstracts; Criminology and penology abstracts; Criminology index; Current bibliographical information; A current bibliography on African affairs; Current geographical publications; Current index to journals in education; Current index to statistics; Current research in library and information science; Documentation in public administration; Dissertation abstracts international; Education index; Educational documentation and information; Family studies abstracts; Geo abstracts social and historical geography; Historical abstracts; Human resources abstracts; Humanities index; Index to international public opinion; Index to periodical articles by and about blacks; Index to scientific reviews; Index to social sciences and humanities proceedings; Index to South African periodicals; Informationsdienst Bibliothekswesen; International African bibliography; International bibliography; International bibliography of economics; International bibliography of historical sciences; International bibliography of social and cultural anthropology; International political science abstracts; Inventory of marriage and family literature; Key to economic science and managerial sciences; Language and language behavior abstracts; Language teaching and linguistics abstracts; Library and information science abstracts; Library literature; London bibliography of the social sciences; Management abstracts, Digests and reviews; Marketing and distribution abstracts; Multicultural education abstracts; Numismatic literature; Peace research abstracts journal; Pedagogische bibliographie; Personnel and training abstracts; Personnel literature; Philosopher's index; Police science abstracts; Population index; Psychological abstracts; Public affairs information service bulletin; Reader's guide to periodical literature; Religious and theological abstracts; Religious and theological resources; Research into higher education abstracts; Resources in education; Resources in vocational education; Sage race relations abstracts; Scimp European index of management periodicals; Social science citation index; Social sciences index; Social work research and abstracts; Sociological abstracts; South African national bibliography; Statistical theory and method abstracts; Studies of women abstracts; Subject guide to books in print; Technical education abstracts; Television news index and abstracts; Tijdschrift voor filosofie bibliografisch repertorium; TMA: Top management abstracts; United Nations documents; United States political science documents; Urban studies abstracts; Work related abstracts; Work study and 0 and M abstracts, and World agricultural economics and Rural sociology abstracts.

4. More detailed attention is paid to the issue of the formulation of the research problem in Babbie (1979), Williamson *et al.* (1977), and Smith (1975). A comprehensive discussion of the most important research goals may be found in Selltiz *et al.* (1965).

5. Ryan (1970) may be consulted for an overview of the philosophical debate surrounding the issue of causality, although Simon's (1982) treatment of the topic probably represents a more modern point of view. An approach which approximates that of Simon, is to be found in the work of Bhaskar (1979) and of Giddens (1979).

CHAPTER 3

RESEARCH DESIGN: CONCEPTUALIZATION AND OPERATIONALIZATION

INTRODUCTION

In our discussion in the previous chapter of the factors influencing the formulation of the research problem, it was evident that different types of research impose different demands regarding the necessity for an initial explicit statement of the problem, and for the formulation of hypotheses. In research of an exploratory nature, the aim is to arrive at the formulation of explicit research hypotheses by initially adopting a flexible approach. In more quantitative research, in which the aim is to test hypotheses, the researcher begins with a reasonably clear statement of the problem and the hypotheses. In this chapter we shall assume that we are dealing with research in which a clear statement of the problem and a set of hypotheses is the point of departure. Obviously, this could well be the case in both quantitative and qualitative research; in both descriptive and explanatory research. It is also important to note that this would apply equally to more theoretical research (for example, conceptual analysis and theory building) and empirical research (which involves the collection of new empirical data).

Karl Popper, in particular, was responsible for placing a new emphasis on the role of problem formulation in science. One of the most common myths about scientific research, is that it could be conducted in the absence of a clearly formulated problem. This myth, which Alan Chalmers calls *naive in-*

ductivism, refers to the belief that objective research obtains when a researcher approaches the research domain in an open-minded and receptive manner, thereby eliminating all bias. According to this approach, data collection is regarded as a process in which data are registered in a passive or receptive manner. For the naive inductivist, then, the major threat to the validity of data is to be found where the researcher approaches the phenomena with either preconceived ideas or hypotheses. Popper, in clear contradistinction, indicates that the research process originates in the identification of either an empirical or conceptual problem. Problems of this nature develop ... *especially when we are disappointed in our expectations, or when our theories involve us in difficulties, in contradictions; and these may arise either within a theory, or between two different theories or as a result of a clash between our theories and our observations* (Popper, 1963: 222).

In Chapter 2, we discussed, in some detail, various ways in which research problems are generated. In this chapter we devote our attention to the considerations which should be taken into account during the further articulation of the formulation of the problem in order, eventually, to collect reliable data about a certain phenomenon. As indicated in the title of this chapter, at least two distinct stages can be identified in the transition from formulating the problem to collecting data, namely conceptualization (or conceptual explication) and operationalization. The easiest way in which the relationship between conceptualization and operationalization can be explained, is to look more closely at the notion of a *concept*.

CONCEPT AND MEANING

We can begin by defining concepts as the most basic linguistic constructions by means of which people order and categorize reality. They are no less than the "pigeonholes" into which we sort the chaotic and unsystematised content of our experiences. Concepts may therefore be regarded as the primary instruments which we employ in coming to grips with our experiences. Concepts are symbols of meaning. They are symbolic constructs which we employ when we refer (or try to refer) to phenomena. But the concept of "meaning" needs to be explicated. A well-known approach is to define *meaning* more clearly by referring to the two basic elements or dimensions of a concept, namely its connotation (*sense*) and its denotation (*reference*).

The connotation or sense of a concept like *culture* would refer to what we mean or intend when we use the concept. Although it would certainly be correct to claim that the connotations that people attach to concepts are influenced by their experiences in life (so-called subjective connotations), it is also the case that there is a sufficiently large degree of concurrence in our use of everyday concepts to make interpersonal communication possible (so-called conventional connotation). In spite of the fact that the use of a concept such as culture may be subjectively determined, it would, nonetheless, be possible to postulate that, by mutual agreement, we have included connotations such as *finesse, refinement*, and *appreciation of literature and art* as part of the conventional connotation of the concept.

The denotation or reference of a concept would refer to the set of phenomena, entities, events, characteristics, behaviours, or processes which exist in reality, and which are included when we use that concept. The denotative dimension of a concept would, therefore, refer to a specific and clearly defined (hopefully) set of entities or phenomena in reality. Consequently, the denotation of the concept *culture* would include such phenomena or events as literary traditions, folk songs, national flags, religious practices, rites, and works of art.

For the purposes of this discussion, our brief introduction to the meaning of *concept* has to suffice. Bearing in mind the earlier distinction between internal and external validity, we are now in a position to formulate the following two general guidelines as a primary requirement for internal validity:

(1) the connotations of the central concepts have to be clear, unambiguous, and articulated; and
(2) the denotations of the central concepts in the formulation of the problem have to be accurate indicators of the connotations.

Clearly, it would be logical to refer to (1) and (2) respectively as the connotative and denotative validity of concepts or constructs. In the remainder of the book these terms will, however, be used as synonyms for theoretical validity (connotative validity) and measurement validity (denotative validity) as these terms are currently used in the literature. In the next section we shall discuss conceptualization as a process aimed at gaining internal theoretical or connotative validity, while operationalizing will be discussed as a process by means of which internal measurement validity (denotative validity) is pursued.

CONCEPTUALIZATION

The term *conceptualization* is used in this text as a synonym for *conceptual analysis* or *conceptual explication*. Assume that a researcher has decided to conduct a study to establish the relationship between political conservatism and racial prejudice. Even for a person not trained in sociology, and particularly in South Africa, it would be quite evident that the concepts conservatism and racial prejudice have many connotations. In pre-scientific everyday life these concepts form part of individuals' commonly held attitudes and value orientations. In the language game of the social sciences, the concepts have become embedded in a variety of models and theories in sociology and political science. It is clear that a familiarity with the most important theories relating to the research problem is an essential precondition for an adequate conceptualization.

59

One of the most striking characteristics of theories in the social sciences is the occurrence of highly abstract and multidimensional concepts. In the social sciences it is unavoidable that we have to employ concepts such as values, culture, solidarity, maturity, meaning, power, peace, revolution, alienation, anomie, structure, function, rite, religion, depression, social distance, anxiety, aggression, motivation, intelligence, success, and many more.

Many of these concepts have their origins in the language game of the social sciences and are, therefore, usually linked exclusively to certain theories or models. However, even concepts such as power, freedom, and revolution, which are part and parcel of everyday life and language, are given new meaning when they become integrated in a theory in the social sciences such as, for example, that of Karl Marx. The fact that concepts acquire meaning, or even new meaning, within a conceptual framework such as a theory, a model, or a typology, has led philosophers of science to refer to such concepts as *theoretical concepts* or *constructs*. As we shall indicate in the following section, the aim in empirical research is to operationalize such constructs in a meaningful manner by making them either measurable or observable. The basic technique by means of which the connotations of theoretical concepts or constructs are explicated, is by means of theoretical or constitutive definition, whereas the denotations of such concepts are explicated by means of operational definition or operationalization. In the following section, we pay a good deal of attention to the manner in which a highly theoretical sociological concept such as *alienation* may be explicated by means of theoretical definition. Following this, the concept *theoretical validity* will be defined more clearly.

An example: Alienation

Although Hegel was the first author to have used the term *alienation* in a theoretically interesting manner, it is generally accepted that it was Karl Marx who first developed a consistent and systematic theory concerning the concept. Marx agreed with Hegel's contention that alienation was a reality which arises when the individual feels that he or she has lost control. Marx, however, differed from Hegel, Feuerbach and others in his view of the origin of alienation, viewing it as resulting from economic factors, and more specifically as a consequence of capitalism:

> *In what does alienation consist? First that the work is external to the worker, that it is not a part of his nature, that consequently he does not fulfil himself in his work but denies himself... His work is not voluntary but imposed, forced labour. It is not the satisfaction of a need, but only a means of satisfying other needs. The object produced by labor, its product, now stands opposed to it as an alien being, as a power independent of the producer... The performance of work is at the same time its objectification. This performance appears, in the sphere of political economy, as a vitiation of the*

worker, objectification as a loss and as servitude to the object, and
appropriation as alienation (quoted in Nisbet, 1974: 291).

One can only really understand this paragraph when it is borne in mind that
Marx afforded central importance to the concept of man as labourer or mak-
er (*homo faber*). Man attains self-realization by means of his labour or productivity. According to Marx, the capitalist system as it existed at the time of
his writing, resulted in man being alienated from the product of his labour
by a system of inequality and injustice. This system consists of two clearly
identifiable classes: the owners (bourgeoisie) and the workers (proletariat).
The fundamental inequity of the system is situated in the nature of production relations: in relative terms the worker contributes more to the production process, while the owner derives a far greater benefit. The worker's
productive ability is reduced to an object (reified), i.e. regarded as merely
another commodity on the market. Alienation, therefore, inevitably results
when that which is intrinsic to the existence of man is reduced to a mere
object or commodity.

It is within this economic theory of alienation that we encounter the first clear
definition of the connotation of the concept. Despite the fact that it is a highly
theoretical and abstract concept, we now have a clearer grasp of what is meant.
The reason for this better grasp of the meaning of the concept is because
the relationship between alienation and better-known concepts such as *labour,
production relations*, and *inequality* have been established within the framework of a theory. It is evident that these concepts are still highly abstract terms.
Nonetheless, the fact that the term *alienation* has been embedded in an in-
tersystemic relationship with these other concepts, has undoubtedly led to
a more exact definition of its meaning.

In 1959 Melvin Seeman published an article (*On the meaning of alienation*)
in which he further advanced the conceptual explication of *alienation*. His
point of departure was that it was possible to define modern mass society
more clearly by emphasizing five essential structural elements:

(1) the development of impersonality and a reduction of relationships as a
    result of position;
(2) the development of a bureaucracy that leads to secularisation;
(3) an increase in social differentiation and specialisation of tasks;
(4) increasing social mobility, and
(5) an increase in scale or bigness.

According to him these five elements are fundamental to three alienation
relevant factors: (1) a loss of control of work and product, (2) a lack of integration within large organizational structures, and (3) a low level of accessibility to reward values. Seeman maintained that the objective alienation
in mass society eventually leads to five social-psychological phenomena:

61

(1) powerlessness,
(2) normlessness,
(4) isolation,
(3) self-estrangement, and
(5) meaninglessness.

Each of these five phenomena are then defined in greater detail. Powerlessness refers to the expectation on the part of an individual that he does not have complete control of his behaviour. Normlessness refers to the expectation that socially unacceptable behaviour is required in order to attain specific goals. Meaninglessness may be defined as a low expectation that it is possible to make meaningful predictions about the future consequences of behaviour. Isolation is a tendency to attribute little value to convictions or ideals which are typically highly valued. Self-estrangement indicates a degree of dependence upon specific forms of behaviour for expected future consequences of behaviour.

Once again it is evident that we are dealing with a coherent theory. An elucidation of the reasons which lead to alienation is provided (expanding bureaucracy, increased social mobility, increased impersonality, and so on), as well as a further explication of the meaning of *alienation*. As in the case of Marx, it is clear that conceptual analysis by means of theoretical definition consists of the explication of the concept by the use of other concepts which are frequently better known. In the present case the concepts powerlessness, normlessness, meaninglessness, isolation, and self-alienation were used.

In other definitions of alienation different dimensions of the concept are emphasized. Keniston pays attention to the distinction between alienation from society and self-alienation:

> *In societies in which the transition from childhood to adulthood is unusually painful, young people often form their own youth culture with a special set of anti-adult values and institutions, in which they can at least temporarily negate the feared life of the adult... (Self-alienation refers to) alienation of man from his own creative potentialities, imbedded in his fantasy life* (1960: 163-164).

In his typology of the dimensions of alienation, Stroup (1961) included the following: indifference, isolation, self-estrangement, powerlessness, loneliness, meaninglessness, disenchantment, and anonymity. In the same manner it would be possible to demonstrate how various scientists have attempted to define the term *alienation* more exactly in different theories and typologies. We shall, however, conclude with these examples.

Theoretical validity

If one were to analyze what happens during the process of theoretical definition, the following emerges: Concepts, or rather constructs, such as, for example, *alienation* typically consist of many shades of meaning — a variety of connotative elements. Theoretical concepts are rich in connotation. One could also use the analogy of a field of meaning to illustrate this idea. Wittgenstein uses the term "family of resemblances".

Within a given field of meaning, certain shades of meaning are more closely associated than others. Together, these shades of meaning within a field of meaning, constitute the meaning of the concept. The association between specific shades of meaning, that is, the central dimensions of meaning, is clearly not a coincidental matter — it is not simply given. It is only within the framework of a theory, a model, or a typology that the dimensions of meaning — the associations — may be systematised through the process of definition. And this is the function of theoretical definition: to arrange or systematize the most important dimensions of meaning of theoretical concepts logically.

To arrange logically would, in this context, imply that the logical rules of correct classification, the rule of mutual exclusion and exhaustiveness, must be adhered to. This may be explained in the following manner: Assume that we wished to develop a classification of types of societies on the basis of their level of development. The classification which we develop is the following: industrialized societies, agrarian societies, and high-technology societies. This simple typology would, clearly, not be acceptable because there is a large degree of overlap between the first and third categories; they do not exclude one another completely. This principle will be addressed in more detail at a later stage (chapter 6).

Using the example of alienation, we have been able to demonstrate that a good theoretical definition implies that (1) the essential dimensions of meaning of a concept have been identified, and (2) that these dimensions are, as far as possible, mutually exclusive. Judged on face value, it would appear that Stroup's typology does not entirely comply with the second of these requirements: the dimensions isolation and loneliness, as well as those which he called indifference and disenchantment, could be regarded as overlapping categories. Seeman's five dimensions, on the other hand, appear even upon cursory inspection, to be valid (exhaustive and mutually exclusive) categories.

Rose, following the lead of Phillips (1966), introduced the term *internal theoretical validity* and listed three characteristics of acceptable theoretical explication. These are *clarity*, *scope*, and *systematic import*. Rose described each of these terms briefly as follows:

> *Clarity is the concept's potential for leading to indicators, which depends on the degree to which it implies a chain of lower-level concepts; scope is the breadth (or narrowness) of the class of phenome-*

na to which the concept applies; and systematic import is the extent to which the concept is used in propositions and theories (1982: 40).

In our preceding discussion of conceptualization we emphasized the same aspects. In summary it would be possible to repeat the most important considerations:

(1) The purpose of conceptualization or conceptual explication is to specify the central shades of meaning of a concept in a logically systematic manner. The best way of doing this is by conducting a thorough study of the literature on those theories of which the concept forms an integral part. In addition to this, it is clear that competent conceptual analysis is also a function of the extent to which the researcher is capable of imaginative speculation and creative insight.

(2) The researcher ought to be able to derive a clear idea of the field of meaning of the concept on the basis of his overview of theories (Rose's scope). The next step would then be to explicate the dimensions that underlie the various shades of meaning in a logically correct manner. As we have indicated, it is particularly important that attention be paid to the requirement of mutually exclusive classification.

Once the considerations mentioned under (1) and (2) have been complied with, there is a high probability that a theoretically valid conceptualization has been attained.

Because the connotative and denotative dimensions of concepts are so closely related, the ultimate test of a theory, model or typology, is the extent to which it leads to valid information of the phenomena that it is supposed to describe or explain. At this point in the research process, the emphasis, therefore, shifts to the problem of measurement and the ways in which valid measures can be attained.

OPERATIONALIZATION

Operationalization or operational definition consists of the development of a measuring instrument by means of which it is possible to obtain accurate data about specific phenomena. If we were to use the example of alienation, operationalization would imply that the researchers have to develop a measuring instrument by means of which they will be able to collect reliable data about the phenomenon called *alienation*. The researcher's aim could, for example, be to attempt to determine the extent to which alienation may be regarded as a characteristic of people, groups, or organizations. A further aim may be to determine whether an existing theory or theories provide a correct interpretation of alienation. Irrespective of what the specific research aims may be, and irrespective of what unit of analysis is to be chosen, and even whether the approach will be qualitative or quantitative, it is essential that the concept *alienation* should be rendered measurable.

It would obviously be quite absurd, for example, to approach individuals and to ask them whether they are alienated. Similarly, taking up a position on a street corner or in a factory, and trying to observe whether people are alienated would be equally ridiculous. The obvious, and most common, approach would be to collect data on the theoretical concepts by means of indirect measurement. This would, for example, mean that a list of questions or items which are assumed to be elements of the phenomenon called *alienation* is compiled, and that these are presented to a group of people in an interview situation. If one were, for example, to administer say twenty items which deal with aspects of alienation (without at any stage mentioning the concept *alienation*), it ought to be possible to gain an overall impression of the person's position with regard to the phenomenon. As we indicated at an earlier stage, the denotative dimension of a concept relates to the particular phenomenon, or characteristics of a phenomenon, that is associated with the use of the concept. The process of operationalization therefore involves compiling a list of real characteristics denoted by the concept for the purpose of measurement. With the construction of a measuring instrument (scale, questionnaire) the items or questions are regarded as indicators of the list of denoted characteristics.

The most commonly used technique of indirect measurement in the quantitative tradition is to be found in scale construction. Further to our example of alienation, we shall now pay attention to Dean's (1961) construction of a scale of social alienation that is directly based upon Seeman's typology.

An example: Dean's social alienation scale

Dean regarded three of Seeman's dimensions as most typical of the construct *alienation*. These were powerlessness, normlessness, and, what he referred to as social isolation. He subsequently formulated a number of questions relating to each of these dimensions which he believed would, in total, define the dimension more clearly. The item format required that each item be rated on a five-point scale: Strongly agree, Agree, Uncertain, Disagree, and Strongly disagree.

Item scores ranged between 4 (Strongly agree) and 0 (strongly disagree). Five of the items were negatively worded, necessitating a reversal of the scoring pattern. Sub-scale scores were used to determine an individual's level of powerlessness, normlessness, and social isolation, as well as a total scale score to determine his or her overall level of alienation. According to the scheme used, a score of 96 (24 x 4) would indicate a maximum level of alienation, with a score of 48 representing a neutral score. For illustrative purposes, a few items from each sub-scale are reproduced here:

Social isolation

1. *Sometimes I feel all alone in the world.*
2. *Real friends are as easy to find as ever.*
3. *There are few dependable ties between people any more.*
4. *People are just naturally friendly and helpful.*

Powerlessness

5. *I worry about the future facing today's children.*
6. *There are so many decisions that have to be made today that sometimes I could just blow up.*
7. *There is little chance for promotion on the job unless a man gets a break.*
8. *We are just so many cogs in the machinery of life.*

Normlessness

9. *People's ideas change so much that I wonder if we'll ever have anything to depend on.*
10. *Everything is relative, and there just aren't any definite rules to live by.*
11. *With so many religions abroad, one doesn't really know which one to believe.*

The nature of the measuring instrument is determined by a variety of factors: the problem formulation, the methodological preferences of the researcher, the nature of the phenomenon, and so on. If the phenomenon of alienation were to be studied amongst a smaller group of people, it is likely that the researcher would employ qualitative methods such as in-depth interviews and participant observation. The manifestations of alienation as they occur in literature or the media such as newspapers or letters in newspapers, could be investigated by means of one of the forms of content analysis that are available. More quantitative studies of alienation will probably be conducted by means of some form of interview schedule or questionnaire.

It is essential that the central concepts in an investigation be operationalized, irrespective of the type of data collection technique that is envisaged. In the preceding example we have indicated the nature of such operationalization in a quantitative study. However, even in a qualitative study where, for example, we are interested in investigating the degree of alienation evinced by a group of people displaying pathological behaviour (for example, rapists), the investigators would have to have a clear grasp of the denotative dimensions of alienation. If this were not the case, the investigators would be unable to identify the manifestations of alienation correctly in the unstructured interviews, with the consequence that they would be unable to collect reliable data on the phenomenon. Similarly, in the case of content analysis it is necessary for the researcher to develop a category system in which the central denotative components of the concept alienation have been accounted for, before it is possible to analyze newspaper reports or letters to newspapers.

Measurement validity

It is clear that an important question at this stage is: When are the operationalizations of concepts or constructs valid? When does an operationalization comply with the requirement of measurement validity. In the field of measurement theory it has become customary to distinguish amongst a number of types of measurement validity which are presented schematically:

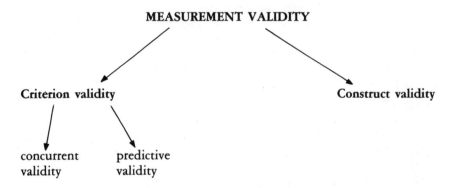

Given the fact that there are numerous introductory texts in the field of measurement theory (see list at the end of this chapter), brief descriptions of each concept will have to suffice.

CRITERION VALIDITY

According to Nunnally we refer to criterion validity *when the purpose is to use an instrument to estimate some important form of behavior that is external to the measuring instrument itself, the latter being referred to as the criterion* (1978: 87). An example from everyday life is when we use the number of distinctions attained by matriculants as a predictor of academic achievement at university. If a high positive correlation were to be found between number of distinctions and academic achievement, the former may justifiably be regarded as a good predictor of the latter.

This is an example of predictive validity — the criterion which is employed to determine whether the measurement is valid is situated in the future. If, in the example of alienation, it were possible to develop criteria of the manifestations of alienation, it ought to be possible to predict future manifestations by means of an alienation scale.

When, on the other hand, the criterion and other measures are taken simultaneously, we refer to this as concurrent validity. The following is an example of concurrent validity: If scores on an intelligence test and examination marks were to be obtained at the same time, and if the scores were found to be highly correlated, the test could justifiably be regarded as a valid indicator of the examination marks.

CONSTRUCT VALIDITY

How to obtain construct validity is probably one of the most difficult problems in social sciences research. Earlier in this section we referred to the fact that the social sciences are characterized by the existence of highly theoretical concepts or constructs: concepts that are derived from scientific theories and which cannot be inferred inductively from the observation of human behaviour. The methodological problem that arises is the following: How does the researcher really know that the items which are included in the scale or questionnaire actually measure the construct which the items are supposed to represent?

How, for example, can Dean be certain that the 24 items actually measure *social isolation, normlessness*, and *powerlessness*? A few examples will serve to illustrate the complexity of the issue. Item 10 (*Everything is relative and there just aren't any definite rules to live by*) and item 11 (*With so many religions abroad, one doesn't really know which to believe*) could, for example, also measure something akin to *relativism*. Item 7 (*There is little chance for promotion on the job unless a man gets a break*) could, for the sake of the argument, be regarded as a measurement of *fatalism*. From the above it follows that construct validity refers to the extent that a scale, index, or a list of items measures the relevant construct and not something else.

Three of the threats to construct validity that Cook and Campbell include in their discussion of the subject are:

Inadequate preoperational explication of constructs, mono-operation bias and mono-method bias (1979: 64-66). Under the first heading Cook and Campbell refer to the effect of poor conceptualization on construct validity: *A precise explication of constructs is vital for high construct validity since it permits tailoring the manipulations and measures to whichever definitions emerge from the explication* (1979: 65). This issue was addressed in the previous section in which conceptualization was discussed. The second and third threats to construct validity are related: mono-operation bias refers to the situation which arises when single indicators or measurements of a construct are employed, while mono-method bias refers to the situation resulting from using the same type of measurement technique for collecting data on the construct which is being investigated. In view of the fact that the latter issue is discussed in the following section, we shall limit ourselves to some remarks on the question of mono- operation bias here. Cook and Campbell define this concept in the following manner: *Since single operations both underrepresent constructs and contain irrelevancies, construct validity will be lower in single exemplar research than in research where each construct is multiply operationalized in order to triangulate on the referent* (1979: 68).

Referring back to our example of alienation, it ought to be clear that mono-operation bias would have occurred if Dean had used one item only to obtain a scale score. Although it has become customary to employ scales which contain multiple items for each construct, it cannot be denied that it still happens that far too many measurements of attitude still rely on single items to measure the respondent's attitudes to a variety of subjects. When, however, multiple indicators (so-called multiple operationism) are used there are a number of techniques which may be employed to assist in determining the construct validity of theoretical concepts. One such technique is factor analysis. The following example has been slightly adapted from the work of Krausz and Miller (1974: 24-25). The example is a simple illustration of the principle underlying the use of factor analysis in the determination of construct validity.

Assume that the theory that we are employing contains the constructs *status* and *intelligence*. Further assume that six indicators are used to measure these constructs: income, length of training, value of fixed assets, problem solving ability, figure recognition and reading comprehension. This could be represented in the following manner:

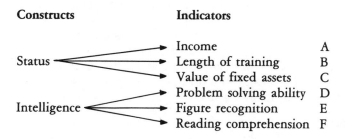

Constructs	Indicators	
	Income	A
Status	Length of training	B
	Value of fixed assets	C
	Problem solving ability	D
Intelligence	Figure recognition	E
	Reading comprehension	F

Basically, factor analysis involves an analysis of the intercorrelations between indicators. In the present example, one would expect high intercorrelations between A, B, and C, and also between D, E, and F. We would also expect that very low or zero correlations would be found between the indicators of status (ABC) and intelligence (DEF). If this pattern of correlations were found, it would suggest the existence of a common factor underlying A, B, and C, and a second factor underlying D, E, and F. It should be emphasized that the technique of factor analysis is limited to the identification of factors on the basis of the intercorrelations between indicators. It remains the responsibility of the researcher to demonstrate the relationship between factor I (ABC) and factor II (DEF), and the theory that is being used. It should be clear that *demonstrating the relationship* is a matter of interpretation, and that alternative interpretations could exist. Referring once again to the example of alienation, one would expect that Dean would have found high intercorrelations between items 1 to 9 (social isolation), 10 to 18 (powerlessness), and 19 to 24 (normlessness). He would, however, have expected low correlations between the items that measure social isolation, normlessness, and powerlessness respectively.

So far we have limited our discussion to the problems surrounding operationalization in quantitative studies. Strictly speaking, it is obvious that one cannot refer to operationalization (in the more technical sense as we have used it so far) in the case of qualitative studies. Nonetheless, the same methodological problems concerning the relationship between theory (constructs) and measurement or observation exists. The specific problems are, however, somewhat different.

One of the major distinguishing characteristics of qualitative research is the fact that the researcher attempts to understand people in terms of their own definition of their world. In terms of Becker's distinction, the focus is on an *insider-perspective* rather than on an *outsider-perspective*. In qualitative research the natural and subjective components of the sample are emphasized. It is for this reason that qualitative research is also referred to as naturalistic research. From a naturalistic perspective, one of the major assignments in research of this nature is correctly to identify the *native* or *indigenous* concepts or conceptualizations of the subjects being investigated. It is only after the researcher has correctly identified the indigenous concepts, or use of concepts, that the researcher will attempt to integrate them within the framework of an existing social scientific theory or model. The approach would, therefore, more accurately be classified as *inductive*, rather than *deductive* when it is compared with quantitative research (cf. chapter 5). A leading qualitative researcher, Norman Denzin, defines *operationalization* in qualitative research in the following manner:

> *Naturalists link their theoretical components to the empirical world through the collection of behavior specimens. They operationalize those concepts through a careful analysis of their specimens. Starting with loose sensitizing definitions of their concepts, they empirically operationalize the concepts only after having entered the worlds of interaction that they wish to understand... They include as many behaviors as possible as indications of the concept in question, through the use of naturalistic indicators which represent any segment of the subjects: behavior that reflects one, or describes, a sociological concept. An indicator is naturalistic if it derives (prefera-*

bly spontaneously) from the subjects: world of meaning, action, and discourse — it is not imposed on that world by the observer (1978: 103).

Typically, the concepts which are generated in qualitative research are, therefore, concrete concepts — concepts which accurately reflect the world of the sample. An illustration of this may be found in Schurink's study on prostitution (1983). An explanation of the subjective connotations that the actors attribute to concepts like *steamers, swaaiers, spinster*, and *lani* therefore, constitute an integral part of the eventual interpretation of the behaviour in question. Qualitative researchers, quite correctly, claim that concepts of this nature possess a large degree of construct validity because of the fact that they are rooted in the world of the subjects. An obvious limiting factor with concepts of this nature is their limited interpretative scope. For the exact reason that these concepts are part of the world of meaning of a given group, they will usually also display highly limited generalizability.

RESUMÉ

This concludes our discussion on the considerations of validity that are relevant to conceptualization and operationalization. We have distinguished between theoretical validity (connotative validity) and measurement validity (denotative validity) on the basis of the distinction that may be drawn between the connotative and denotative dimensions of concepts. In spite of the distinctions, we have emphasized the close correspondence between these two types of validity throughout our discussion. On the one hand, theoretically sound concepts are of little value if they do not pave the way to good empirical research. On the other hand, valid measurement presupposes adequate conceptual explication. If one were to assume at this point that the researchers have dealt with the most important threats to theoretical and measurement validity by means of systematic research design and competent planning, it is evident that they still have to contend with the unusual demands related to data collection in the social sciences. This is the topic of the next chapter.

Suggestions for further reading

1. Popper has presented a further elaboration of his point of view on the nature of scientific problems in Popper (1973). A recent publication in which a detailed discussion is presented on the differences that are to be

found between theoretical and conceptual problems in the physical sciences is that by Laudan (1977). A special category of problem is that which current theories in a discipline cannot solve — the so-called anomalies. Kuhn (1970) was the first to have addressed this theme, while it became a central construct in Lakatos's (1970) philosophy of science.

2. The debate which has raged in the philosophy of science for the past two decades on the question of meaning, or more specifically reference, is competently summarised in Papineau (1979). Newton-Smith (1981), Scheffler (1967), and Suppe (1974) also present discussions of the topic.

3. The term *internal theoretical validity* is thoroughly discussed by Rose (1982). Further references on the question of operationalization may be found in Kerlinger (1973) and Smith (1975). Feigl (1970) and Hempel (1958) present representative points of view on the problems in the philosophy of science that underlie operationalization. The texts by Blalock (1982) and Zeller and Carmines (1980) represent reasonably advanced discussions on operationalization and measurement validity.

4. As far as we are aware, the concept, *triangulation*, was suggested by Norman Denzin. Denzin (1978), as well as Smith (1975) may be consulted for a detailed discussion of this concept. The term *multiple operationism* was originally formulated by Campbell and Fiske in their classical article in 1957. The problem of conceptualization and *operationalization* within the context of qualitative research is discussed by Filmer (1972). Further references are also provided at the end of chapter 7 of this text.

Introduction

Sources of data, reactivity and control

The requirement of reliability

Observation effects
Researcher effects
Researcher characteristics
    (i)   Affiliation of the researcher
    (ii)   Image of the researcher
    (iii) Distance between researcher and participant
Researcher orientations

Participant effects
Participant characteristics
    (i)   Memory decay
    (ii)   Omniscience syndrome
    (iii) Interview saturation

Participant orientations
    (i)   Role selection
    (ii)   Level of motivation
    (iii) Response patterns

Measuring instrument effects
Context effects

More reliable observation

Triangulation
Ensuring anonymity
Establishing rapport
Covert research
Control group
Training
Choice of fieldworkers
Reliability of measuring instruments
Constructive replication

Resumé
Suggestions for further reading

CHAPTER 4

RESEARCH DESIGN: DATA COLLECTION

INTRODUCTION

The distinctive nature of the research domain of the social sciences poses the greatest challenges to the methodological ingenuity of the researcher. The fact that human beings are being investigated in the social sciences creates problems not encountered in the physical sciences. We concentrate on three important characteristics of human beings as being relevant to the topic of this chapter, that is, the fact that they are rational, historical, and normative beings.

Rationality refers to the fact that human beings possess the ability to reason about their existence; the ability to make reasoned and free decisions that determine their future. Rationality does not only imply awareness, but, more importantly, also self-awareness. One may, in terms of ethnomethodological theory, state that human beings are capable of defining their situatedness in the world. Human beings do not only react to stimuli — they interpret, define, and behave proactively.

The fact that human beings are rational beings also accounts for their historicity. That human beings are capable of creative and culture-forming acts, is the direct cause of human history. Human beings create their own history but they are, simultaneously, the products of history. The fact of historicity not only means that human beings have a past, present, and future, but also that they have tradition, culture, and hope or, stated differently, that they possess an historical consciousness.

It follows from both the preceding that humans are normative beings. They do not merely behave in a reasoned manner, but reasoned in terms of what they regard as desirable and proper. Human beings behave in accordance with their value orientations, their norms concerning what is perceived as right and wrong. These are dimensions of human existence that also grow and change historically, and which are subject to human development.

The implications of these aspects of human existence are far-reaching when human beings participate in scientific investigation. Human behaviour is neither static nor predetermined, and patterns of behaviour tend to vary over time. In an important sense, individuals are unique beings: each with their own set of value-orientations, own preferences and norms, own wishes and desires, and unique convictions and ideals. In the following discussion on the methodological considerations which apply in the data collection process, the manner in which these aspects of human existence pose some of the most important threats to the validity of research findings, will become clear.

SOURCES OF DATA, REACTIVITY AND CONTROL

Quite different from the situation in the physical and earth sciences, and on a much larger scale than in the biological sciences, the participants in research in the social sciences are, to a greater or lesser extent, aware of the fact that they are being studied. Depending upon the nature of the particular source of data, and the manner in which the data are collected, human beings, when they participate in research, are aware of this situation, and tend to react to it. In the literature on methodology, this phenomenon has been known as *reactivity* since the publication by Campbell (1957). We shall employ this term in a broad sense in this section to indicate the phenomenon that human beings react to the fact that they are participants of research. This reaction appears in a variety of forms, for example, resistance to being interviewed or to completing questionnaires, supplying inaccurate information as a result of apathy, wilfulness, modifying behaviour or information with the aim of creating a better impression, or deliberately misinforming the researcher. We shall discuss the different manifestations of human reactivity in the process of data collection in the following section. It is, however, important to take note of the fact that reactivity is an important variable, depending upon the nature of the source of data.

Following Manheim's (1977) scheme, it is possible to divide sources of data in the social sciences into two main categories with two subcategories in each.

(1) Human behaviour and human characteristics.
(2) Products of human behaviour and of human characteristics.

(1) Human behaviour and human characteristics

Manheim distinguishes between two main categories — on the one hand, verbal behaviour (for example verbal or written responses to questions posed by the researcher) and, on the other, all observable behaviour and characteristics. Included in the first category are those forms of human behaviour which only become accessible by means of indirect observation such as one finds in questionnaires, interviews or projective tests. The second category includes all forms of individual behaviour, social interaction, and observable characteristics such as gender, number of individuals, physical locality, non-verbal behaviour, stature, and so on. In this category, methods of direct observation are generally used to collect data. Examples would include structured or controlled observation in experimental situations, and participant observation in non-structured situations. The distinction which we have drawn between structured and unstructured observation is clearly not equally applicable in all situations (see also Groenewald, 1986). Nonetheless, it provides a *rough* systematisation of data collection techniques which is useful for the rest of the discussion.

(2) Products of human behaviour and of human characteristics

Manheim divides this category into two sub-categories — physical traces and archival sources. Physical traces are defined as any physical evidence that has been left from earlier human behaviour. In accordance with Webb's subsequent refinement of this category, physical traces are further sub-divided into erosion measures and accretion measures. Examples of erosion measures would include the wear of floor tiles at museum exhibits, the erosion of library books, and the patterns of wear of clothing such as shoes which may be employed as indications of human activity. Examples of accretion measures would, for example, include the number of empty liquor bottles per week in refuse cans, pot shards, and the placing of buildings.

Archival (or documentary) sources refer to the extensive collections of records, documents, library collections or mass media material that have been amassed. It would clearly also include well-known material such as census data, life statistics, ecological and demographic data, personal documents like diaries, autobiographies, letters, and case studies. Other types of archival sources include mass media material like newspaper reports, the content of radio and television programmes, and film material. Webb *et al.* (1966) also refer to less well-known material such as inscriptions on tombstones, sales records, suicide notes, the records kept by nurses on patients, and voting records.

It was Webb and Banks who first drew attention to the existence of *differential reactivity*. Data sources where human beings are directly involved (category 1) are regarded as highly reactive sources, whereas those where human beings are only indirectly involved (category 2) are much less likely to be regarded as reactive sources.

Reactivity becomes the largest single threat to the validity of research findings when human behaviour or characteristics are the source of data or information. Excluding covert observation, and irrespective of whether data are collected by means of indirect or direct observation, human beings as respondents or research participants are aware of the researcher and usually react to this situation in one way or another. Obviously, the products of human activities such as documents or texts cannot react to the fact that they are being researched. It should, nevertheless, be borne in mind that the products of human behaviour are the result of decisions and cognitive processes — that the products are the sedimentations or objectifications of the human spirit (in Hegel's terminology). This is, for example, manifested in the fact that the researcher, when studying a text, has to be mindful of the original intention or aim of the author and of the researcher's own historicity. The rationality of human beings is obviously also manifested in the products of human behaviour. Although data sources in the second category are unlikely to display reactivity to any marked extent, it cannot be ignored. In the remainder of this section, we shall, however, pay attention to the threats to the validity of findings which are associated with the first category.

An obvious reaction to the high level of reactivity of some sources of data is to attempt to control for this. The researcher could, for example, attempt to minimize the threats to validity by imposing a greater degree of structure on the observations, or by exerting more control on the research situation.

The best examples of this type of control are to be found in experimental research designs. One such form of control is the practice of assigning participants to experimental and control groups on a random basis to control for the possible effects of individual differences. Quite frequently, the participants of such research are isolated in a laboratory situation removed from their natural environment so as to limit the effects of external nuisance variables. Banks drew attention to the interesting phenomenon that these control measures vary positively with the degree of reactivity of the specific observation technique employed. Stated differently, the greater the number of controls that the researcher builds into the research situation, the more likely the participants are to be reactive. Because of the fact that laboratory conditions such as isolation and random assignment to treatments does not form part of the everyday existence of the subjects, it is likely to result in artificial and atypical patterns of behaviour. As Groenewald (1986) quite correctly states, the researcher is faced with an insoluble dilemma — while, on the one hand, it is desirable to use observation techniques that elicit as little reactivity as possible in order to ensure the highest level of validity, it is, on the other hand, equally desirable to employ observation techniques that make it possible to exercise the greatest possible control.

Therefore, those sources of data collection in which use is made of direct observation (systematic and participant observation), or indirect observation (questionnaires and interviews) lend themselves to the possibility of control by, for example, making use of appropriate statistical techniques. As we have, however, indicated, these sources of data are also highly reactive. The second main category of sources of data, physical and archival sources, is not, however, as readily amenable to control. In a certain sense, the data are already given. While the researcher is able to sample the source of newspaper reports or issues of magazines in content analysis, for example, the basic text which is used as the primary source of data, is determined. The reverse of this situation is, of course, that these categories of data are low on reactivity and, for this reason, do not pose as big a threat to the eventual validity of the findings.

The fact that reactivity and control are positively correlated, illustrates a point which we made earlier in this book, namely that methodology in general, and research design in particular, inevitably involves compromises. It is required of the researcher constantly to weigh the advantages and disadvantages of a number of issues against each other, and eventually to decide upon those measures which, as a whole, are likely to increase the validity of his findings to the greatest extent.

THE REQUIREMENT OF RELIABILITY

The central consideration of validity concerning the process of data collection is that of *reliability*. Essentially, this is the requirement that the application of a valid measuring instrument to different groups under different sets of circumstances should lead to the same observations. Smith defines reliability by posing the following question:

> *Will the same methods used by different researchers and/or at different times produce the same results?* (1975: 58).

From these definitions it is clear that the reliability of observations or data is influenced by four variables: the researcher(s), the individual who participates in the research project (in future referred to as the participant), the measuring instrument, and the research context or the circumstances under which the research is conducted.

In the section in which we deal with the question of the nuisance variables that may influence the reliability of observations, we shall interpret these four variables in the widest possible sense. The researcher refers to the project leader, the interviewer, the experimenter, the participant observer, or the field worker. The participant could refer to the individual who is being observed, who is being questioned (the respondent), or to a group of people who are being observed or questioned. The measuring instrument may refer to a highly structured instrument (questionnaire or interview schedule), or to an unstructured instrument such as a list of unstructured items or a list of observation categories. Finally, the research context refers to both the broad spatio-temporal circumstances under which research is conducted (for example, a particular year in a specific country with a specific socio-political system), and the specific spatio-temporal setting.

A further distinction is drawn between the characteristics and orientations of the researcher and the participant. Researcher or participant characteristics refer to attributes such as gender, nationality, age, socio-economic status, educational level. These characteristics are known as organismic variables. Researcher or subject orientations refer to attitudes, opinions, expectations, preferences, tendencies, and values. These distinctions may be represented in the following manner:

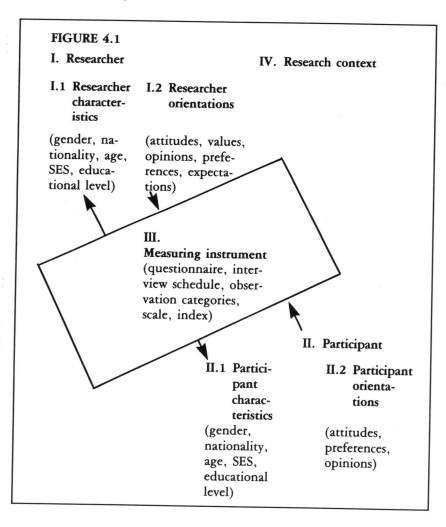

FIGURE 4.1

I. Researcher

IV. Research context

I.1 Researcher characteristics

I.2 Researcher orientations

(gender, nationality, age, SES, educational level)

(attitudes, values, opinions, preferences, expectations)

III.
Measuring instrument
(questionnaire, interview schedule, observation categories, scale, index)

II. Participant

II.1 Participant characteristics
(gender, nationality, age, SES, educational level)

II.2 Participant orientations
(attitudes, preferences, opinions)

In accordance with common usage in the literature on experimental design, we shall refer to the consequences of the nuisance variables associated with each of the four variables as *effects*: researcher effects, participant effects, measuring instrument effects, and context effects. Researcher effects are those negative consequences (relating to validity) that are directly attributable to the researcher. Similarly, measuring instrument effects are those negative consequences, or that lack of validity, that may be directly attributed to some aspect of the measuring instrument, and so on.

Observation effects

We shall employ the term *observation effects* in a broad sense to indicate researcher, participant, measuring instrument, and context effects. Although the examples to which we refer in the following section are mainly derived from the experimental and survey research literature, it ought to be clear to the reader that they have a wider applicability, and also refer to unstructured forms of observation.

RESEARCHER EFFECTS

Our discussion of researcher effects is divided into two sections; in the first, we discuss those effects which are associated with researcher characteristics, and in the second, those associated with researcher orientations.

Researcher characteristics

Some of the most important researcher effects associated with specific researcher characteristics or attributes, relate to the affiliation of the researcher, the image that the researcher has with the research participants, and the distance between the researcher and the participants as a result of differences between the characteristics of the researcher and those of the participants. The latter category is, therefore, not only the consequence of researcher characteristics, but it arises from the interaction between the characteristics of the researcher and those of the participants.

(i) Affiliation of the researcher

The organisation with which the researcher is associated may result in responses being biassed. If the interviewer is employed by a highly influential organisation that is known for the quality of its research, it is likely that respondents will be more highly motivated to answer questions seriously and authentically. Universities and large research organisations usually have reputations of this nature. Should the interviewer, however, be associated with an organisation which causes suspicion or with a completely unknown organisation, it is likely that respondents will react more negatively to the interview situation. Atking and Chaffee (1972), for example, found that the affiliation, or presumed affiliation, of inteviewers played an important role in research related to government control of violence in television programmes. In those cases where the respondents, who were parents, thought that the interviewer represented some government body, they were more inclined to give extreme responses to questions. See also Hyman's (1954: 185 *et seq.*) discussion of the influence of sponsorhip on responses.

(ii) *Image of the researcher*

In an important study Jack Douglas (1976) discusses the problems surrounding conflict in research. According to him a tacit assumption in research has always been that the participants naturally wish to co-operate with the researcher, and that they would obviously provide valid and reliable information. Douglas, however, maintains that the assumptions of the *investigative paradigm* are much more realistic. *The investigative paradigm is based upon the assumption that profound conflicts of interest, values, feelings and actions pervade social life* (1976: 55). On the same page he also states that *conflict is the reality of life; suspicion is the guiding principle*. If this were to be regarded as excessively pessimistic, Douglas reminds us that in everyday life members of the public are regularly confronted with a variety of *suspect strangers* who require information from them. *Spies, counterspies, police, detectives, prosecutors, judges, psychiatrists, tax collectors, probation officers, ... investigative journalists and all others involved in the vast array of investigative occupations in modern society and the most obvious practitioners of the investigative paradigm* (1976: 56).

In a variety of studies conducted by Douglas, including some in massage salons and on nudist beaches, he found that suspicion and mistrust were the rule rather than the exception. One manifestation of mistrust was in avoidance or evasive responses. *Rather than being the exception, I suspect such evasiveness is the common situation in field research: People rarely tell the whole truth as they see it about the most important things, but they are generally being evasive or misleading rather than lying. A field researcher must understand this and the reasons for it: Primarily a fear of exposure, of being caught in a lie, and an unwillingness to appear less than absolutely 'moral' to an academic stranger* (1976: 65-66).

The image of the researcher with participants is frequently that of a stranger, an outsider, or an intruder. In the research conducted by Douglas these issues were probably given greater prominence as a result of the sensitive nature of the research that he was conducting. It appears fairly obvious that girls in massage salons would regard the researcher as a suspect — the possibility cannot be excluded that he is a policeman.

In his inaugural address, Schutte (1983) drew attention to the negative image that researchers may have, particularly when they are involved with cross-cultural research in South Africa. Not only do language and cultural differences contribute to the fact that the (White) researcher is regarded as suspect by the (Black) participant, but the socio-political situation also plays a part.

> On the every-day level of communication he (researcher) is much more readily perceived as the informer attempting to gain access to inside information. He is almost comparable to the 'enemy within the gates', as Mayer defined the witch, as somebody who becomes familiar with the internal matters of a group but who maintains outside affiliations and loyalties. Black communities have become used to the informer, and there are various ways of keeping him happy by feeding him bogus 'information'. Similarly our researcher runs the risk that professional interests he intends to serve may not be recognized in the light of the subjects' past experiences. Rather his activities may be regarded as those of some official serving the interests, not of professional social research, but those of the state apparatus or some bureaucracy (1983: 10)

The examples that we have discussed have all related to fairly general perceptions of the researcher as a suspect or stranger. At a considerably lower level Brislin et al. (1973) use the term *rudeness* as an all-embracing term to refer to the researcher as someone who interrupts the normal activities of the respondents. It is, however, evident that a variety of issues, like the affiliation of the researchers, their interests, cultural background, and the time and place of the research all contribute to the image of the researchers: the positive or negative perception that the participants are likely to have of them.

(iii) *Distance between researcher and participant*

Rather than discuss researcher and participant characteristics separately, we will pay attention to the manner in which differences between the researcher and the participant may result in negative consequences in the context of observation.

A large body of research has been conducted in an attempt to establish which effects result from differences between the researcher and the participant. In some of the most important findings, the existence of racial effects, gender effects, status effects, urban-rural effects, and even styles of dress effects have been indicated. We shall pay some attention to a few of these studies.

In a recent study Campbell (1981) found race-of-interviewer effects similar to those found in earlier studies by Hatchet and Schuman (1974) and also by Hyman (1954). His final assessment of the situation was that racial differences between the interviewer and the participant result in a significant degree of bias. These biasses are, however, limited to those items in which the race of the respondent is explicitly mentioned by the interviewer. The direction of the observed bias is also constant in the sense that respondents consistently provide responses that are favourable to the race to which the interviewer belongs.

In a study on pre-marital sex, Zehner (1970) found that the responses of male participants were not influenced by the sex of the interviewer. In comparison, female participants tended to be far more reticent when they were interviewed by female interviewers. In his study on controversial issues related to sexual intercourse, Rangonetti (1970) did not, however, find any significant differences between the answers provided by those who were interviewed by male and female interviewers respectively. What he did find, however, was that respondents were significantly more open in their responses when they were interviewed by a single interviewer, irrespective of the sex of the interviewer, than they were in a group interview situation.

Mendras (1969) attempted to establish whether differences in rural and urban background between the interviewer and the participant had an influence on response bias. Giles and Chevasse (1975), in turn, attempted to establish whether the style of dress of the interviewer had an influence on participants' responses. Their conclusion was that style of dress could have a greater influence on responses than the perceived status of the interviewer!

In a recent publication, Sudman and Bradburn (1982) found that the distance which is created between participant and interviewer as a result of interviewer and participant characteristics, cannot be seen as a separate issue from the content of the questions posed. It has already been noted that racial differences are only found when the content of the question includes a reference to the race of the respondent, and that sex differences were only found in Zehner's study when the items referred to sexually sensitive themes. According to Sudman and Bradburn, the perceived threat of a question is of greater importance than the other issues. People are simply reluctant to reply to questions which deal with sexual behaviour, alcohol consumption, traffic offences, the possession of firearms, and the use of drugs.

It is, therefore, hardly surprising that when questions are posed that relate to sexual behaviour, which is, in any event, a sensitive topic, and these questions are posed by male or female interviewers, gender effects will be observed. The same would apply if questions on race relations were to be asked by White or Black interviewers.

Researcher orientations

From research which has been conducted over a broad spectrum it is possible to conclude that the eventual observations are clearly influenced by the prejudices, expectations, attitudes, opinions, and beliefs of the researcher,

84

and that this applies equally to an interview, a laboratory, or a field situation.

Hyman attempted to systematize the influence of researcher orientations as follows: He identified three types of orientation effects in interview situations: *bias-producing cognitive factors within the interviewer, attitude structure expectations*, and *role expectations*. In the first category Hyman included those cognitive factors which could result in specific expectations as far as respondents' answers are concerned, and which are unique to the interviewer such as his or her particular beliefs and perceptions. Hyman, as an example, quotes the following passage in which a female interviewer discusses her attitudes towards respondents:

> *When asked whether she could make guesses about the attitudes of the respondents, she replied: 'I often get fooled. On Russian questions I perhaps unconsciously make guesses. But if I do that I'm likely to write down what I think. Therefore I try not to.' But when the issue is pursued by asking her whether there are any characteristic types of respondents, she says: 'Once they start talking, I can predict what they'll say ...* (1954: 58)

As Hyman quite correctly states, expectations of this nature may constitute an important source of bias if the interviewer is led by them in his or her further probing, classification of responses, and so on. Under the second category that Hyman refers to as attitude-structure expectations, he draws attention to the fact that some interviewers tend to believe that the attitudes of respondents are likely to display a uniform structure. This leads to a situation where the interviewer expects the respondent to answer later questions in a schedule in accordance with responses provided earlier on. This situation is clearly reflected in a statement like: *Once they start talking, I can predict what they'll say* (Hyman, 1954: 59).

The third category of orientation effects, perhaps more appropriately referred to as **expectancy effects,** (or role expectations as Hyman calls them), is defined in the following manner: *We might conceive of role expectations to denote the tendencies of interviewers to believe that certain attitudes or behaviors occur in individuals of given group memberships, and therefore to expect answers of a certain sort from particular persons* (1954: 61). Role expectations, which frequently lead to the development of rigid stereotypes, are particularly prevalent in those cases where men have certain views of female roles, where Whites have particular conceptions about Blacks, youth about the aged, or the inverse, and so on. As an illustration of this phenomenon, Hyman refers to the remark by a male interviewer who said: *I just don't think the average woman has as much social consciousness as the average man* (1954: 61)

Rosenthal and his co-workers systematically studied similar expectancy effects in experimental studies. One of the best-known studies on *experimenter ex-*

pectancy effects was conducted by Rosental and Fode (1963) with laboratory rats. The experimenters were undergraduate psychology students who were led to believe that they would acquire practice in established experimental procedures. One half of the experimenters were led to believe that the rats that they would use had been bred from exceptionally intelligent blood stock, while the other half were also inaccurately informed that the rats were less gifted. In actual fact, the rats had been selected at random from a homogeneous rat colony and there was, therefore, no difference as far as their *intelligence* was concerned. The final results confirmed the expectancy effect: the first group of experimenters, who had expected their rats to learn more quickly, reported that this had indeed been the case, whereas the second group with the supposedly dull rats, reported that their rats had not acquired the skills as quickly.

In a recent review of the literature on interviewing techniques, Campbell *et al*. (1981) point out the existence of a similar orientation effect which they refer to as *reinforcement* and *feedback*. They draw attention to the fact that in several studies it has been indicated that when the interviewer provides positive feedback by, for example, saying *um-hum* or *good*, this has a definite influence on subsequent responses. It is evident that systematic approval on the part of the interviewer as far as some of the responses are concerned, could have a clear biassing effect on the information obtained.

PARTICIPANT EFFECTS

The mere fact that human beings are studied, leads to atypical behaviour. It is probably accurate to claim that the first description of participant effects in the literature of the social sciences is to be found in the publication by Roethlisberger and Dickson (1939). Four researchers, Mayo, Roethlisberger, Whitehead, and Dickson, embarked upon a research project at the Hawthorne factory of the Western Electric Company in 1927. The original intention in the research was to study the effects of working conditions such as temperature, lighting, rest periods, working hours, and so on, on worker productivity by observing six female workers. The interesting, and unexpected, finding was that the workers' performance increased irrespective of which one of the variables was manipulated. Irrespective of whether working hours were increased or reduced, and rest periods lengthened or shortened, productivity increased consistently. The researchers interpreted their findings as meaning that the employees felt flattered to have been able to participate in the experiment! It has subsequently become common practice to refer to this type of participant effect as the Hawthorne effect.

Referring to the same effect, Selltiz *et al*. (1959) called it the guinea-pig effect.

If people feel that they are 'guinea-pigs' being experimented with, or if they feel that they are being 'tested' and must make a good impression, or if the method of data collection suggests responses or stimulates an interest the subject did not previously feel, the measuring process may distort the experimental results (1959: 97).

As in the previous section, we shall distinguish between effects which result from characteristics that are inherent in the participants, and those that are the result of participant orientations.

Participant characteristics

In the preceding section we paid attention to the influence of some of the better-known participant characteristics such as gender, racial group, and status in the interaction between researcher and participant. We now turn briefly to three further well-known subject effects: memory decay, the omniscience syndrome, and interview saturation.

(i) *Memory decay*

According to Smith (1975) the researcher has to accept that there is a natural decay in the ability to remember events which is positively correlated with (i) the length of time that has elapsed since the occurence of the event, (ii) the irregular occurence of the event, (iii) the relative unimportance of the event, and (iv) decreased accessibility to relevant data relating to the event.

(ii) *The omniscience syndrome*

Some respondents appear to believe that they are capable of answering any question. It is, therefore, imperative that the researcher be sensitive to this type of effect to avoid the inclusion of responses that are not authentic. Brislin et al. (1973) discuss this phenomenon in more detail.

(iii) *Interview saturation*

Pareek and Rao (1980) quite correctly indicate that some members of society, and particularly those who live in the metropolitan areas, have become so used to market surveys, for example, that they tend to reply to questions in a mechanical and superficial manner. Apart from the fact that a response of this nature can be identified in the interview situation, initial refusal or reluctance on the part of the respondent is usually also a good indication of an *over-saturated* respondent.

Participant orientations

(i) *Role selection*

One of the most far-reaching participant effects is associated with the participant's perception of his or her role in the research setting. Webb et al. quite appropriately indicate that:

> By singling out an individual to be tested (assuming that testing is not a normal condition) the experimenter forces upon the subject a role-defining decision — What kind of person should I be as I answer these questions or do these tasks? (1966: 16).

Webb *et al.* draw attention to the fact that the role selection effect is likely to be manifested in a variance between *don't know* responses and the measurement of imaginary attitudes and opinions. If, for example, the instructions to the interviewee were to read: *You have been selected as part of a scientifically designed sample... It is important that you answer all questions...*, it is clear that the importance and uniqueness of the respondent are emphasized. When instructions of this nature assume an important role in the interview situation, it is not at all difficult to predict that fewer *don't know* responses will be found, and that a greater number of imaginary attitudes and opinions will be measured.

(ii) *Level of motivation of the participant*

One of the most important variables that can influence the validity of the data collection process either positively or negatively, is the level of motivation of the participant. The level of motivation is clearly influenced by a variety of factors such as interviewer characteristics, contextual factors, and the manner in which the questions are phrased. Two issues may be emphasized in this context: the degree of interest that the topic has for the interviewee, and the extent to which he or she is likely to be threatened by the questions that are posed. It has been possible empirically to demonstrate that the more interesting the respondent finds the topic, the more highly motivated he or she will be which, in turn, results in an increase in the response rate. As we indicated earlier, the *level of threat* posed by the questions will have an important bearing upon the willingness of people to respond to them, and also on their level of motivation. Questions that relate to highly private issues are likely to be perceived as threatening by the majority of respondents, and they are likely to respond in a completely unreliable manner. It is for this reason that Cannell and Kahn emphasize that: *it is the interviewer who must make the interviewing experience and task sufficiently meaningful, sufficiently rewarding and sufficiently enjoyable to attain and maintain the necessary respondent motivation* (1968: 574).

(iii) *Response patterns*

One of the most important types of observer effect in interviewing is the occurrence of systematic response patterns which are generally referred to as *response sets*. A number of authors, including Cronbach (1946), Kolson and

Green (1970), and Webb *et al.* (1966), have discussed this matter. Kolson and Green, for example, draw attention to the existence of the tendency to *gamble* among children who are not certain of the meaning of items. Similar response patterns that have been noted, particularly when the meaning of items is obscure, include the tendency to endorse only the extremes on scaled items (*extreme checking style*), or to check the mid-points of the scale (*central tendency*). For the purpose of our discussion, we shall pay more attention to two well-known types of response pattern: **social desirability** and **acquiescence response set.**

The Hawthorne effect is clearly an example of a social desirability tendency. As Selltiz *et al* succinctly state the matter: *Most persons will try to give answers that make themselves appear well-adjusted, unprejudiced, rational, open-minded and democratic* (quoted in Smith, 1975: 136). Rosenberg was also able to confirm that those individuals who attained high scores on Marlow-Crone's Social Desirability Scale were more inclined to supply extremely positive responses than those with low scores on the scale.

The tendency to answer either yes or no to virtually all the items in a questionnaire or scale is referred to as acquiescent response set. As early as 1937 Sletto found that respondents were more likely to agree with a statement than to disagree with the inverse of that statement. In a more recent and detailed study of this issue, Schuman and Presser (1981, chapter 8) were able to confirm earlier findings on this topic. Apart from the fact that they were able to confirm the existence of this type of response pattern (it can produce differences that range between 10 and 15%), they also found indications that this phenomenon is more likely to occur amongst respondents with a low level of education than amongst, for example, university graduates. Schuman and Presser, however, maintain that we have not yet built up a sufficiently large body of research into the phenomenon of acquiescent response set to be able to provide an adequate interpretation of the reasons underlying this type of response pattern.

MEASURING INSTRUMENT EFFECTS

In the literature, observer effects that are directly related to the nature and structure of the measuring instruments are dealt with almost exclusively within the context of questionnaire or scale effects. In view of the fact that these effects are dealt with in detail in two recent publications (Schuman & Presser, 1981; Sudman & Bradburn, 1982), we shall merely list the most important effects.

(*i*)   *Item or question sequence effects*
(*ii*)   *Open and closed question effects*
(*iii*) *Don't know effects*
(*iv*)   *Midposition effects*

(v) *Questionnaire length effects*
(vi) *Item sensitivity effects*
(vii) *Leading question effects*
(viii) *Fictitious attitude effects.*

Not only are these effects discussed in detail in the publications that we have mentioned, but a variety of techniques by means of which they can be controlled for are also discussed (for example random ordering of items, balancing of positive and negative times, and so on).

CONTEXT EFFECTS

In discussing the research context, it is possible to distinguish between the broader spatio-temporal factors that are determined by historical, socio-political, and economic factors, and the narrower research setting within which the experiment, interview, or observation is conducted.

Concerning the former, it is essential that the researcher be sensitive to the following types of factors:

- The time during which the researcher is conducted. In both longitudinal and cross-sectional studies the time during which the research is conducted may, for example, play a determining role in people's attitudes and preferences. Particularly in the case of longitudinal research where changes in behaviour or attitudes are investigated, significant changes could be the result of external events such as elections, civil unrest, or increasing unemployment.

- **Cultural** factors such as habits, traditions, customs, and institutions. There are numerous examples in the anthropological literature in which researchers, to their ultimate detriment, failed to take local conventions and customs into account in the design and execution of their research.

- **Political** factors such as the existence of interest groups, a lack of freedom, and intimidation. We have already referred to Schutte's inaugural address in which he focusses attention on the influence of the socio-political situation in South Africa, indicating the manner in which it influences confidence and participants' perceptions of researchers.

As far as the specific research setting is concerned, Lutynska (1970) distinguishes between four categories of *research setting*:

(1) the private residence of the respondent
(2) the respondent's place of employment
(3) a cafe, restaurant, or similar public area, and
(4) a park, street, garden, and so on.

The importance of this issue is associated with the perceived *neutrality* of each setting. In the first two, the respondent is familiar with the setting, but

90

the researcher is not. The third and fourth categories are, however, neutral territories. In studies in which the influence of the research setting was investigated, it was, for example, found that the researcher's impressions of the participant's home or place of work, frequently led to significant biasses in the data. The respondent's role (see our earlier discussion on role selection) is also directly influenced by the research setting. In the domestic setting a person's role as father may be more noticeable, whereas his role as employer or supervisor may be more noticeable in the work place.

More reliable observation

The wide range of observer effects indicates the extent to which reactivity plays a role in the investigation of human behaviour. It would be quite impossible for any researcher to identify all observation effects, and to account for them. The purpose of research design is, however, to increase the eventual validity of research findings by systematic planning and by structuring a research project in such a manner as to minimize the combined effects of nuisance variables. It is for this reason that we now pay attention to a number of ways in which the researcher is able to control for some of the effects. Our exposition does, however, not address the detail of the issues; this may be found in the publications cited. Our primary concern is with the broad issues.

TRIANGULATION

Researchers ought to accept as a general principle that the inclusion of multiple sources of data collection in a research project is likely to increase the reliability of the observations. Denzin coined the term *triangulation* to refer to the use of multiple methods of data collection. Campbell and Fiske (1959) suggested a similar strategy which they called *multiple operationism*. All these concepts relate to the use of a variety of methods which, as a result of their complementarity, may be employed to correct for their respective shortcomings.

It is important to bear in mind that specific types of data collection are designed for the acquisition of certain types of data. Morris Zelditch (1962) distinguished between three types of information in his seminal article: frequency distributions, incidents or events, and institutionalised norms and status. For each of these types of information there is a prototypical method of data collection: the use of surveys for information concerning incidents, and the use of informants or interviews for information on norms and status. Zelditch's classification merely illustrates that each type of method has specific limitations. By employing different methods of data collection in a single project we are, to some extent, able to compensate for the limitations of each.

We have, in an earlier section, drawn attention to the fact that not all methods are equally reactive. It is, therefore, an important principle that more reactive methods (such as direct observation) ought to be supplemented by less reactive methods (such as the use of documentary sources).

Two examples of triangulation ought to suffice to illustrate the advantages of such an approach. One of the observation effects that has been identified is associated with item sensitivity. We have specifically indicated that items in which issues relating to race and sex are addressed are likely to result in considerable response variability, particularly when the race and gender of the interviewer have not been controlled for. In the event of such variation occurring in response to sensitive questions, it appears likely that more reliable information may be obtained by doing a follow-up study in which in-depth interviews are used. In a similar manner, it ought to be possible where historical events are being investigated, and where memory decay may play an important part, to increase the reliability of the information by making use of documentary sources like diaries and letters.

ENSURING ANONYMITY

As indicated by Schuman and Presser (1981), respondents tend to be reluctant to supply information to interviewers on sensitive matters. A similar problem occurs in studies of sensitive behaviour such as in so-called deviant behaviour. Douglas indicated that subjects tend to be unusually reluctant or unwilling to participate because they regard the investigation as an invasion of their privacy. The fact that his investigations concerned situations of a sensitive nature — massage parlours and nudist beaches — obviously contributed to this kind of response.

One possible strategy would be to emphasize the anonymity of responses and observations whenever possible. Instead of using face-to-face interviews, it may, for example, be possible to use postal surveys or telephone surveys. Nevertheless, respondents are not necessarily convinced that the latter approaches actually ensure their anonymity. As far as the study of so-called deviant behaviour is concerned, the assurance that the investigator will not identify the respondents in any manner (see Schurink's use of *noms de plume* in his study on prostitution (1983)), must be regarded as a minimum requirement for establishing greater validity.

ESTABLISHING RAPPORT

A strategy which differs from the former is to attempt to establish the best possible interpersonal relationship or rapport with the respondent. It ought to be clear that this strategy is necessarily time consuming, and that it is not always possible to employ it. For example, Douglas (1976) reported that a year had elapsed before they discovered that one of their most trustworthy participants had been using a *nom de plume* all along.

The advantage of a solid interpersonal relationship between researcher and participant is that it acts to neutralize initial distrust. It is also clear that it can act as a control for role selection effects. If the respondent trusts the interviewer, the need no longer exists to play a role of some sort. The establishment of good rapport can also serve as a control for context effects.

COVERT RESEARCH

A more drastic strategy is to make use of some form of covert research. Covert observation may assume a variety of guises. Basically, it amounts to the respondent being deceived about the actual purpose of the research, or about the identity of the researcher. In cases of this nature all possible measures are taken to ensure that the participant does not become aware of the fact that he or she is part of a research project. A good example of this type of research is Simon Holdoway's study of police activities. Holdoway (1982) went so far as to join the police, undergo the necessary training, and spend several months serving as a policeman doing patrol duties. With a single exception, nobody knew that his eventual aim was to conduct a sociological study of police activities.

Covert research is particularly applicable in studies in which use is made of participant observation or interviewing. These are studies in which it is essential for the researcher to establish close ties with the group being investigated, but where he or she wishes to prevent them from discovering his or her actual identity. Other types of covert research are encountered where researchers disguise the fact that research is being conducted. An example of this is to be found in the study conducted by Schwartz and Skolnick (1962) in which letters of application for employment were manipulated to investigate the effect of a criminal record on *suitability for employment.*

For a more detailed discussion of experimental designs in the natural context (field experiments) where some form of disguise is used, the reader may refer to Campbell (1969). One of the most common examples of deception in laboratory experiments is to be found in so-called blind and double blind designs. In blind experimental designs the participants do not know whether they are part of the experimental or control groups, whereas in double blind experimental designs there is the additional requirement that the experimenters do not know whether they are dealing with the experimental or control group.

It is obvious that effective covert research is a useful strategy for countering the general guinea-pig effect: if the participants are not aware of the fact that they are being studied it is unlikely that they will be able to react to the investigation. Covert research also controls for expectancy effects. In the example of the double blind experimental design, one of the most important causes of expectancy effects is eliminated.

Although the use of covert strategies (disguise, deception, withholding information) is one of the most effective ways of minimizing, or even eliminating, observation effects, there are fundamental ethical objections to the wholesale use of this approach. Covert research necessarily implies that the subject is deceived, or that his or her right to privacy is broken, or that he or she has to be lied to. The dilemma with which the researcher is confronted, is therefore how to weigh the moral interests of the subject against the interests of science. A number of authors have proposed suggestions about how to neutralize the negative ethical implications of covert research. One approach involves asking the permission of the subject to use the information gathered immediately upon completion of the study while obviously still ensuring the anonymity of the subject. Martin Bulmer's Social *research ethics* (1981) may be consulted for an excellent exposition of the ethical implications of participant observation and covert research.

CONTROL GROUP

It has always been the norm to make use of control groups in experimental studies wherever possible. Apart from the experimental group, to which the specific experimental treatment is applied, or in which given interventions are made, a comparable control group is used which does not undergo the experimental treatment. In an attempt to ensure that the experimental and control groups are comparable, use is made of techniques such as the random assignment of participants to either the experimental or control groups (*randomization*), or to the *matching* of participants in the two groups. If significant differences were to be found in the experimental group which have not occurred in the control group, it would be reasonable to conclude that the experimental interventions (or the implementation of the so-called independent variable) have been the cause of the observed difference. By making use of a control group, it is possible to control for participant effects such as maturation, history, and selection effects. We would, however, recommend that researchers who intend making use of an experimental approach in their research, should carefully study the most important participant effects that are likely to occur in different types of experimental design, and what measures may be taken to eliminate these (Cf., for example, Cook and Campbell's excellent book (1979) on quasi-experimentation).

TRAINING

The adequate training of experimenters, interviewers, research assistants, field workers, and so on, is a necessary precondition for any research. One of the specific aims in training of this nature, is to counteract researcher effects. In our discussion of researcher effects, we drew attention to the negative consequences of researcher orientation effects, and particularly to those associated with researcher expectation effects. The chances of obtaining accurate observations are increased when, for example, interviewers are given clear instructions as to the aims of the project, the importance of accurate interviewing is emphasized, or the need for consistent interviewing is made clear. Thorough pre-training is also likely to eliminate or reduce the occurrence of some of the other researcher effects that we have not mentioned, such as the inaccurate noting of responses, coding errors, classification errors, and many more.

SELECTION OF FIELD WORKERS

The origin of one of the most important researcher effects is to be found in the distance between researchers and participants. Although different factors, such as context or level of motivation, result in greater degrees of distance between researchers and participants, researcher characteristics such as gender, race, age and style of dress, are some of the most important factors that fall under this rubric. An obvious solution to this problem is to exercise due care in the selection of field workers. Those field workers who share as many characteristics of the sample as possible (like gender and race, for example) ought to be given preference.

RELIABILITY OF MEASURING INSTRUMENTS

In the case of structured measuring instruments such as scales and psychological tests, a number of standard techniques are available by means of which reliability may be estimated. Four of the better known techniques are (i) the use of parallel forms, (ii) the test-retest method, (iii) the split-half method, and (iv) the method of internal consistency. Any standard text in the field of measurement theory (for example Carmines & Zeller, 1979) and test theory (see Nunnally, 1964, 1978) would include a discussion of these techniques.

The aim of techniques of this nature is to determine the reliability of measuring instruments, and specifically the extent to which the particular scale or test is likely to yield the same measurements upon repeated application.

In those cases where these methods are not applicable, the researcher could still make use of pilot studies to test the items or the observation categories that are to be employed. Excessive variance or large numbers of non responses could, for example, either be an indication that the items are ambiguous or that they are unusually sensitive. The major importance of pretesting, and the use of methods such as those mentioned earlier, is that they enable the researcher to determine the most important measuring instrument effects, and to eliminate them.

In conclusion, it is hardly possible to over-emphasize the importance of the principle of replication. As Barber (1976: 87) quite correctly notes, a variety of factors make exact replication in the social sciences virtually impossible. Following Lykken's (1968) lead, Barber argues in favour of more constructive replication by stressing that *more investigators should attempt to confirm empirical relationships that were claimed in earlier reports while the replicator formulates his own methods of sampling, measurement, and statistical analysis* (1976: 87).

Constructive replication implies that the researcher wishes to control the findings of an earlier study by investigating the same problem for a different sample and/or by using a different research design.

RESUMÉ

At the beginning of our discussion on data collection we emphasized the distinctive nature of the research domain in the social sciences. Three aspects were emphasized: the rationality, historicity, and normativeness of man. In the preceding discussion we have presented ample evidence of different manifestations of these uniquely human dimensions in the field of social research.

The fact that the term *observer effects* was used as a general term for the different effects that complicate the data-collection process, may have created the impression that human rationality, historicity, and normativeness were used in a singularly negative sense. The aim of the discussion of the various types of researcher effects was, however, rather to sensitize the researcher to the variety of ways in which human nature may influence research findings. In suggesting certain control measures and design considerations to counteract problems related to observer effects, the aim is not to deny the human dimension of the research process. On the contrary, emphasizing the necessity of research design is quite probably the greatest recognition one may give to the unusual nature of the research domain in the social sciences!

Suggestions for further reading

1. For an introduction to the design of survey research and to the construction of questionnaires, the following texts may be consulted: Bateson (1984), Belson (1981), Marsh (1982), Moser and Kalton (1971), and Rosenberg (1968). Any of the general methodology texts in the reference list would also contain an introductory chapter on the design of questionnaires.

2. The two best-known data collection techniques in field research and ethnography, participant observation and unstructured interviewing, are discussed in: Burgess (1982 and 1984), Gordon (1984), Johnson (1975), Lofland (1971), McCall and Simons (1969), Spradley (1979 and 1980).

3. Plummer's (1983) book on the analysis of documents of life (diaries, letters, and so on) is an excellent overview of the field and also contains an extensive list of references. As far as quantitative content analysis is concerned, the publications by Berelson (1952), Holsti (1962), and Krippendorf (1981) may be consulted as introductory texts. In the same manner, Hakim's text on the secondary analysis of existing sources of data (especially census statistics) represents a good introduction to the field.

4. The literature on the field of scale construction, and particularly the construction of attitude scales, is extensive. The following references are, therefore, merely an overview of some of the best-known sources: Baird and Noma (1978), Dawes (1972), Edwards (1957), Fishbein (1967), Henerson (1978), Miller (1970), and Oppenheim (1966).

5. The book by Webb et al. (1981) remains the best introduction to the field of non-reactive measures, while Bales (1950) is the classical text in the field of controlled observation. Compare Smith (1975) for more recent studies on these topics.

Introduction

Research as a logical process: The requirement of inferential validity

A typology of research designs

CHAPTER 5

RESEARCH DESIGN: ANALYSIS AND INTERPRETATION

INTRODUCTION

As background to the concepts *analysis* and *interpretation*, and the relationship between them, we present the following excerpt from a sociological investigation in some detail. A discussion of what is understood by *interpretation* and *analysis* is presented immediately following the relevant section.

An example: The Reiger Park disturbances

> *Reiger Park: 9 May 1981. At approximately 14h00 an altercation developed between a number of Coloureds and some of the taxi drivers who were employed by an Indian businessman. The cause appeared to relate to a refusal on the part of the Coloureds to get into the Indian's taxi-cabs. At this juncture, one of the taxi drivers (an Indian) produced a firearm and wounded one of the Coloureds. Following this the Coloureds who were present left for Reiger Park where they looted and set fire to cars and shops that belonged to Indians. The situation was exacerbated by other looters exploiting the chaos which had arisen by burgling shops. Several shots were fired during the night. Apart from 21 individuals who were admitted to hospitals suffering from gunshot wounds, several others, were wounded. Three rabble rousers were injured as a result of police action. Three*

Coloured youths were fatally wounded. In the ensuing violence three shops, a house, a garage, and several cars were destroyed by fire.

What actually led those involved to behave as they did? In a qualitative study which was conducted immediately after the incident (the data were collected on 11 and 12 May), Schutte and Van Wyk tried to find an explanation for these events.

The research data were collected by means of discussions with members of the City Council of Boksburg, members of the Boksburg station of the South African Police, inhabitants of Reiger Park, and from an analysis of newspaper reports. In the newspaper reports a number of different causes were suggested for the revolt: racial conflict between Coloureds and Indians was suggested by one source whereas another attributed the events to the chronic housing shortage which was also deteriorating in the area concerned. After the data had been collected they were analyzed and interpreted in terms of Smelser's theory of collective behaviour. A brief exposition of this analysis is presented.

Smelser regards uninstitutionalized collective behaviour as the uninstitutionalized mobilization of a community to act towards the reduction of one or more constraints in a social system by changing a component of behaviour. In this definition uninstitutionalized behaviour refers to acts that deviate from what a given society has come to regard as acceptable; constraint to factors in the system which place intolerable restrictions upon the community; and collectivity to a group of people within a community or to the community as a whole.

According to Smelser's theory, six social circumstances or determinants are required before a given type of collective behaviour will be manifested. Apart from this it is necessary that the determinants should be present at a sufficient level of intensity, and that they should combine in a specific pattern. The reason for this is that successive stages will make successive contributions towards reaching the ultimate stage which is the actual incident of collective behaviour.

The six determinants of collective behaviour are:

- *structural conduciveness, a determinant which occurs when the institutional patterns within a given society have greater potential to lead to certain types of collective behaviour (the possibility of race riots are greater in those societies in which racial differences are accentuated);*

- *structural strain which occurs when certain circumstances within a social structure result in strain or the disturbance of the relationship between different components of behaviour;*

- *generalized beliefs occur when a given collectivity believes that the cause of the strain is to be found within the structure;*

- *contributory incident, which is the immediate cause that leads to the incident;*

- *mobilization of participants, where a group of people are mobilized to collective action at a given moment; and*

- *social control or measures which prevent, interrupt, or redirect the development of other determinants at various levels. These measures are, however, only activated once the incident has started.*

In the research, this theory was used as a frame of reference to analyze the events relating to the Reiger Park disturbances.

Structurally conducive events: *It would appear that a structurally conducive milieu had been created as early as 1961 when Zindabad (later Reiger Park) was proclaimed a Coloured residential area and Coloureds from the surrounding residential areas which included Indian residential areas were moved there. According to some of those involved, the movement of the Coloureds was executed with a degree of impatience as they were given a limited amount of time to move to Zindabad. From information which became available, it would appear that the City Council of Benoni ordered some of the Coloured businessmen to move from the Benoni municipal area in the absence of compensatory business premises being available in Boksburg. The resulting feeling of resentment was exacerbated by the fact that 14 Indian families were not, in turn, ordered to move from Reiger Park to a residential area which had been proclaimed for Indians. It is, therefore, clear that the factors in the structure that could facilitate collective behaviour were present at the level of available facilities.*

Structural strain *developed in Reiger Park as a result of the population growth in the town, and the concomitant shortage of land available for expansion, housing facilities, and business premises.*

Generalized beliefs: *From interviews conducted with those who were dissatisfied, it became apparent that a generalized belief had arisen, and had been propagated, to the effect that the Indians who were resident in Reiger Park were the major cause of all problems in the town, including that they were the major obstacle in the way of alleviating the housing pressure with which the rest of the population was confronted. An example of this is to be found in the belief amongst the Coloureds that the land on which the Indian shops were situated had originally been earmarked for dwelling houses. The factual situation was that the land had not been zoned for residential purposes at all, but had been set aside for a community centre.*

Precipitating event: *From the course of events which led to the disturbances, there can be little doubt that the incident which had led to the Coloureds behaving violently towards some of the Indian properties, had been the shot fired by an Indian taxi driver at an East Rand railway station.*

Mobilization of participants: *It would appear that a large number of the inhabitants had been persuaded to behave collectively at a meeting held on the evening preceding the eruption of the disturbances. It can also be accepted that one or more leaders took the initiative in starting the destruction of property.*

Social control *is a determinant that embraces all other determinants and exerts some influence during each stage. With the incident at Reiger Park it is evident that ineffective measures of social control contributed to the fact that strain factors led to a violent eruption. The last houses to have been built in Reiger Park were completed in May 1976 and 402 apartments were built in 1976. Although the inhabitants had made representations to the City Council of Boksburg on a number of occasions, it would appear that the serious nature of the problem had not been accepted. With the development of generalized beliefs concerning the presence of Indians in the area unsuccessful representations were made to the Boksburg City Council from time to time via the local Management Committee.*

Conclusion

From the preceding analysis of the revolt in which Smelser's theory of collective behaviour had been used as a point of departure, it is evident that it would be incorrect to refer to the situation as a race riot as some of the local newspapers had done. Had this been the case, one would have expected the consulting rooms of the Indian medical practitioner as well as the Chinese-owned store to have been dealt with in a similar manner. Both these buildings either adjoined, or were part of, properties that were looted.

From the application of Smelser,s theory of collective behaviour it is evident that the actual cause of the hostilities could be related back to the substantial shortage of housing resulting in poor living conditions, and the ineffective communication system available to the inhabitants to relay their grievances to the City Council. As a result of the ineffective communication system generalized beliefs developed which were often unfounded, and resulted in the Indians in Reiger Park being branded as scapegoats. A single spark was all that was required to ignite the powder keg that had developed.

Discussion of the concepts *analysis* and *interpretation*

This case study offers a striking illustration of what is meant by the concepts *analysis* and *interpretation*. Traditionally, scientists tended to juxtapose analysis against synthesis. Analysis, then, is understood to mean the resolution

102

of a complex whole into its parts, while synthesis may be regarded as the construction of a whole out of parts. By means of analysis the constituent variables or factors that are relevant to the understanding of a phenomenon or an event, are isolated. By means of synthesis the relationships between these variables are reconstructed to provide an insight into the causal factors associated with the events or factors being studied.

In this chapter we shall use the term *interpretation* rather than *synthesis* to emphasize the *interpretative* dimension of explanation in the social sciences.

How does analysis and interpretation occur? It would also be possible to ask the same question as follows: How are data systematized in a meaningful manner by means of analysis and interpretation? Basically, there are two answers that may be offered to these questions which involves a deductive and an inductive strategy respectively.

(i) In the deductive strategy the researcher embarks upon a research project with a clear conceptual framework in mind. This may be a model, a theory, or a typology or a set of explicit hypotheses. A framework of this nature leads to a relatively rigid manner of conceptualization, operationalization, and data collection, and it will ultimately constitute the frame of reference for analysis and interpretation. As we indicated in Chapter 2, this type of strategy is typical especially in hypothesis testing and in explanatory studies.

(ii) In the inductive strategy, the researcher would embark upon the project without an explicit conceptual framework, and merely use general and vague hypotheses or guesses to guide the research. Research of this nature is far less structured. Once the data have been generated, the researcher attempts to discover relationships or patterns by means of close scrutiny of the data. The data are analyzed and interpreted by means of inductive abstraction and generalization. The eventual result is that such a strategy will result in a more systematic explanation or even a conceptual framework such as a typology. It should be clear that the inductive strategy is particularly appropriate to hypothesis-generating studies or to studies of an exploratory and descriptive nature.

One should, nonetheless, not conclude on the basis of the preceding paragraphs that these two strategies are mutually exclusive. There are numerous examples of studies where a combination of these strategies are used. It is, for example, possible that a researcher starts out using the inductive approach and generates new hypotheses in the process. Once such hypotheses have been formulated, the researcher can proceed with a testing of the hypotheses (deductive approach).

If one were to analyze the Reiger Park study, it is clear that the researchers used a more deductive strategy. The explicit point of departure for the study was to use Smelser's theory of collective behaviour as an explanatory framework. It is possible to summarize the logic of the project in the following steps:

I Statement of the problem: What were the contributory factors to the Reiger Park disturbances?

II Conceptualization and operationalization: Smelser's theory of collective behaviour. According to the theory, data have to be collected on six variables: structural conduciveness, structural strain, and so on.

III Data collection: By making use of more qualitative methods (interviews and analysis of newspaper reports), data relating to the relevant variables are collected.

IV Analysis and interpretation: The data are analyzed in terms of the categories of Smelser's theory. The eventual interpretation presents an indication (see Conclusion) of the manner in which the events may be understood if we accept that the theory is approximately true. The conclusions reached by the authors are supported (inductively) by the data which had been collected, i.e. the study provides additional confirmation of Smelser's theory.

It is now possible to indicate more explicitly what analysis and interpretation involve. In the case of this study, the analysis of the data were carried out by employing Smelser's theory. The relevant variables have already been identified in the theory. The task of the researchers was thus to identify the relevant determinants of collective behaviour in the data. They were required to indicate which data fitted the category of *generalized beliefs*, which data could be classified as related to the category of *structural conduciveness*, and so on. Analysis as a process of resolution is, therefore, relatively easily accomplished when an existing theory is used as a frame of reference.

It is evident that the manner in which the data are eventually interpreted is also suggested by the theory. According to Smelser's theory, the six determinants are essential preconditions to uninstitutionalized collective behaviour. When these six determinants are found to be present, it is likely that this type of collective behaviour will follow. The fact that the researchers had gathered sufficient evidence (according to themselves) about the presence of the six determinants in the given situation, led them to conclude that: *The cause of the hostile outburst can be related to the real shortage of accommodation and the ineffective communication channel by means of which residents could direct their grievances to the City Council.*

It is quite evident that the final interpretation is based upon two issues:

(i) Are the data which have been collected reliable?

(ii) If it were to be assumed that the data are reliable, do they provide adequate support for the conclusion?

The first issue is primarily related to the question of reliable data collection, as well as to those steps in the research process which precede it. It is for this reason that we have stressed in the preceding chapters, that the research process ought to be regarded as an integrated whole. The reliability of observations is directly related to the validity of the theory that is used and the manner in which a study has been operationalized. This is clearly illustrated in the example of the Reiger Park incident. The theory that was used played an important part in the data collection as it sensitized the researchers to the relevant data categories. If further research were to have shown that the theory was in fact invalid, it would clearly also have had far-reaching implications for any subsequent set of data collected on the basis of the theory.

The second question is one that is not often posed in methodology texts. Even if one were to accept that the data were sufficiently reliable, the possibility remains that the data may not provide adequate support for the conclusions based on them. There is, for example, a possibility that other interpretations of the same events may be advanced. An outsider may well be inclined to say that an alternative interpretation, to the effect that the incidents were simply race riots, had not been adequately refuted.

It is, however, important to bear in mind that all conclusions that are reached on the basis of collected data, always involve logical inference. The question that has to be posed is whether the inferences that are drawn, and whether the conclusions that are reached, are valid. The methodological criterion that applies in this case, and the subject of this chapter, is **inferential validity**.

A few remarks on analysis

We have deliberately decided not to pay detailed attention to the process of analysis in this chapter. We focus on the inferential validity of the interpretation phase — the final stage in which the researcher presents his or her conclusions or explanations of the phenomenon. One of the reasons for not having treated analysis as a separate issue, is related to the example which has been discussed. When data analysis is conducted in studies that are highly structured — the type of study in which the course of the research is largely directed by a given frame of reference — analysis is less of a problem. In such cases the validity of the analysis depends upon the validity of the framework that is used.

The second reason for not paying detailed attention to the issue of data analysis, follows from the extremely sophisticated statistical techniques that are employed in quantitative research in the social sciences. The developments in the fields of descriptive techniques and quantitative analysis have provided researchers with a wide variety of analytical techniques. Developments in the field of computer technology have also resulted in a situation where not only fairly simple univariate techniques are accessible, but where complicated multivariate techniques are much more readily available than was the case a few decades ago. The major threats to validity in the application of these techniques are clearly systematized in the majority of standard methodology texts. Examples relate to the fact that certain types of techniques are applicable only to certain types of data (compare the requirements relating to the level of measurement — nominal, ordinal, interval, and ratio), or that certain techniques may only be used provided the distribution of the data is normal, or provided the sample has been randomly selected. Statistical considerations of this nature are, however, beyond the scope of this book.

The most important reason for not discussing analysis as a separate theme in this chapter is, however, to be found in the fact that the criterion of inferential validity applies equally to data analysis. Analyzing data involves making inferences. Even the relatively simple process of assigning data to certain categories involves an inferential process. Although this inferential process is not nearly as complicated as that which is involved in the interpretation of results, it would be an error to regard it as merely a mechanical process. Philosophers of science such as Winch (1958) have emphasized that the process of identification (for example, when a researcher decides that a given form of behaviour belongs to category A rather than category B) contains a demonstrable interpretative element. The methodological requirement of inferential validity, therefore, not only applies to the final stages of the interpretation of results, but also to analysis and, as we shall argue in the following sections, to every other form of decision making in the research process.

RESEARCH AS A LOGICAL PROCESS: THE REQUIREMENT OF INFERENTIAL VALIDITY

In this section we shall focus on the research process as a typical example of logical argumentation. Irrespective of the exact nature of a research project, it is possible to regard any research project as an extended logical argument.

Logical argumentation

Larry Wright (1982: 4) defines an argument as *the (usually) dispassionate marshalling of support for some statement (or viewpoint, or conclusion or position)*. In the same manner that an individual would argue a case in everyday communication by citing evidence in its support, the social scientist attempts to muster scientific evidence in support of a specific point of view. More specifically, one may say that it is the aim of the social scientist to demonstrate the validity or invalidity of a given theory or model (or even interpretation, or finding) by mustering sufficient evidence.

Apart from the considerations of validity discussed in the preceding chapters, we now turn to a further criterion of validity that is referred to as inferential validity. The term inferential validity refers to the validity of the logical inferences (both inductive and deductive) that are drawn during the execution of a research project.

If it is so that the research process can correctly be characterized as a logical argument, then it becomes an obvious requirement that any research study has to comply with the rules of logic — the rules of valid argumentation. We shall, therefore, begin with a brief discussion of the term *argument*. The following is the basic scheme of a typical argument:

S_1
S_2 (Statements that are offered as support for or as
S_3 evidence of the conclusion reached -- also known as
S_4 the premisses of the argument)

C (Conclusion)

Let us begin with an example from everyday usage: *There is no doubt that Pretoria drivers are the worst in the country. Just pay attention to the manner in which they ignore red traffic lights and stop signs. And it is hardly necessary to refer to the ill-mannered way in which they cut across traffic lanes without indicating their intention of doing so and how they force their way into lanes without considering other drivers!*

This argument can be represented schematically in the following manner:

S_1: Pretoria drivers ignore red traffic lights
S_2: Pretoria drivers ignore stop signs
S_3: Pretoria drivers force their way into traffic lanes
S_4: Pretoria drivers change lanes without giving the necessary signals

----

C: Pretoria drivers are the worst in the country.

The schematic presentation clearly illustrates that the relationship between the premisses and the conclusion is one of support. The premisses support the conclusion or lead to it. The process whereby the speaker arrives at a conclusion from premisses, is known as the drawing of inferences. One may identify two types of relationship between premisses and conclusion, namely inductive support and deductive support. The former is referred to as inductive inference or induction, while the latter is referred to as deductive inference or deduction. The differences between induction and deduction will be discussed in due course.

It is interesting to note that the example above does not constitute a valid argument: the argument does not comply with the requirement of inferential validity. A closer inspection reveals that the premisses (s_1 to s_4) do not provide sufficient support for the conclusion (C). Stated somewhat differently, on the basis of s_1 to s_4 one would, at best, be able to arrive at the conclusion that Pretoria has poor drivers — but certainly not that they are the worst in the country. While it may be true that they are the worst, this conclusion cannot be substantiated by the supporting evidence. The important point that we wish to make is the following: even if it is accepted that the supporting evidence (the premisses) is true (in this case that s_1 to s_4 are true), the possibility remains that it does not constitute sufficient evidence for the conclusion. The problem in cases of this nature, is usually that the conclusion is broader than implied by the premisses. At the same time, our example also illustrates that inferential validity is not associated with the truth or reliability of the premisses (for the sake of the argument it is accepted that they are true), but rather with the relationship between the premisses and the conclusion.

We may, therefore, attain inferential validity if:

(1) The supporting evidence is relevant to the conclusion, and

(2) the supporting evidence offers adequate support for the conclusion.

It is usually easy to meet the first condition (the requirement of relevance). Assume that we were to add the following to the premisses in the preceding example:

s_5:   Pretoria is the capital of the Transvaal.

Although this statement happens to be true, it is clearly quite irrelevant to the conclusion. If, however, we were to add the following premise to the argument — s_6: *The accident rate in Pretoria is the highest in the country*, we would have more relevant supporting evidence. Not only is the statement in s_6 relevant, but it also increases the likelihood that the conclusion (to the effect that Pretoria drivers are the worst in the country) is true. Adding s_6 would be regarded by some people as adequate evidence for the acceptance of the conclusion (The second condition of adequate support). In the final case, the inclusion of s_6 could mean that the argument as a whole complies with the requirement of inferential validity. The supporting evidence (s_1 to s_4 and s_6) could then be regarded as providing both relevant and sufficient evidence in support of the conclusion. To explicate the notion of sufficient evidence more thoroughly, we shall discuss an example which has been taken from Larry Wright's *Better reasoning*. The example also illustrates the fact that gradations may exist in the relationship between premisses and conclusion. In other words, specific evidence may support a conclusion to a greater or lesser degree.

An example: The assassination of John F. Kennedy

Suppose that one were to consider various arguments in favour of the statement that President Kennedy had been shot by Lee Harvey Oswald (this would be C, the conclusion of each argument). The first argument that could be advanced in favour of C, would be the following:

s_1:   Shortly after the assassination Lee Harvey Oswald was noticed in the book depository from which the shots had been fired.

C: Lee Harvey Oswald assassinated President Kennedy.

Although s_1 does lend some support to C, it is evident that this does not constitute a strong argument in favour of the conclusion. The addition of s_2 could, however, make some difference:

s_1:   Shortly after the assassination Lee Harvey Oswald was noticed in the book depository from which the shots had been fired.

s_2:   Oswald's palm print was found on a rifle left close to the window from which the shots had been fired.

C: Lee Harvey Oswald assassinated President Kennedy.

There can be little doubt that the addition of s_2 increases the evidence in support of the conclusion. Nonetheless, if this evidence were to be presented to a jury, it is unlikely that the members would be satisfied with the adequacy of the evidence. Assume, however, that we were to add two further pieces of evidence:

s_1:   Shortly after the assassination Lee Harvey Oswald was noticed in the book depository from which the shots had been fired.

s_2:   Oswald's palm print was found on a rifle left close to the window from which the shots had been fired.

s_3:   An eye witness identified Oswald as the assassin.

s_4:   According to the ballistic tests that the fatal shots could have been fired from the rifle (in s_2).

C: Lee Harvey Oswald assassinated President Kennedy.

The support for C offered by the arguments s_1 to s_4 appears to be overwhelming. In a court of law it would probably be regarded as sufficient evidence.

As Wright, quite correctly, indicates, the case against Oswald would have been watertight if evidence of the following nature could also have been obtained. Assume that the owner of the book depository from which the shots were fired had been concerned about the security of his store. As a precautionary measure he had had closed-circuit television installed, and the whole episode had been recorded on tape. The quality of the recording was also of such a nature that there could not be the slightest trace of doubt that it had indeed been Oswald who had fired the shots.

With each new piece of evidence more support accumulates for the conclusion, and the argument in favour of the conclusion becomes stronger. With the addition of the final video-taped evidence, it would appear that the case has been conclusively proved. It is no longer possible to arrive at an alternative conclusion on the basis of the evidence presented. One is virtually compelled to accept C. And yet, the possibility still exists that Oswald was not the assassin!

Assume, says Wright, that the evidence just referred to had been fabricated. Assume that an amazingly ingenious plot had been hatched against Oswald with a view to frame him for the murder of President Kennnedy. With this aim in mind, an exact replica of the book depository had been built elsewhere and equipped with similar video cameras; a similar motorcade had been arranged, someone who bore an unusually close resemblance to Oswald did everything that the real Oswald was supposed to have done, everything was recorded, the actual video tapes were replaced with the forged tapes, and so on. Obviously, this is not the type of evidence that anyone, and particularly not a jury, would regard seriously. Nonetheless, it remains a logically tenable explanation of the existing evidence. Stated differently: the conclusion (C) does not necessarily follow logically from the evidence because of the fact that this conclusion, although outrageous, is also conceivable.

Now, it is possible to remove all possible doubt by changing the argument in such a manner that C must necessarily follow from the premisses. We could try to make the argument so watertight that, logically speaking, no other conclusion could follow from the premisses. As Wright, however, indicates, if that were to be the case, we would have to change the nature of the argument radically. Up to this point we have been concerned with the issue of the weight of the evidence: in logical terms this is an inductive argument. When, however, we modify the argument in such a manner that the conclusion necessarily follows from the premisses, the argument has lost its evidential character. When this occurs, the supporting evidence is linked to the conclusion on the basis of semantic considerations: either implicitly or explicitly, the conclusion is already contained in the premisses in such a case. This type of argument is called a deductive argument. Examples in which the conclusions are explicitly contained in the premisses are clearly rather trivial as the following example, where s_5 has been added, clearly illustrates.

s_1: Shortly after the assassination Lee Harvey Oswald was noticed in the book depository from which the shots had been fired.

s_2: Oswald's palm print was found on a rifle left close to the window from which the shots had been fired.

s_3: An eye witness identified Oswald as the assassin.

s_4: According to the ballistic tests conducted, it was found that the fatal shots could have been fired from the rifle (in s_2).

s_5: Lee Harvey Oswald assassinated President Kennedy.

C: Lee Harvey Oswald assassinated President Kennedy.

It is clear that the conclusion is explicitly contained in the premisses. Obviously, no one would ever present an argument of this nature. It does, however, illustrate the structure of a deductive argument and the source of its conclusiveness. It also indicates the extent to which deductive arguments are semantic in nature: if one were to support the premisses and deny the conclusion, one would be contradicting oneself. More interesting deductive arguments are those in which the conclusions are implicitly contained. As an example we may use an illustration related to the previous examples:

s_1: President Kennedy was shot by Marina Oswald's husband.

s_2: Lee Harvey Oswald was Marina Oswald's (only) husband.

C: President Kennedy was assassinated by Lee Harvey Oswald.

The aim of the above example has been to illustrate the principle of degrees of inductive support and the notion of adequate support. At the same time it has been possible to show that inductive and deductive arguments are radically different. This difference will now be explored in a more systematic manner.

Induction and deduction

It is important that we re-emphasize that in our analysis of inferences — the inferential relationship between premises and conclusion — we are not interested in the epistemic status (the truth or falsity) of the premises. For the sake of our argument it is necessary that we accept that all premises are true — in other words, that the evidence is reliable. If we accept that the premisses are true, the question that arises is how much support do they provide for the conclusion. In the Kennedy example, two possible answers to this question were distinguished: inductive support in which the premises provide gradual support (from little to a lot) for the conclusion, or deductive validity (as a rule we will not use the expression deductive "support") in which the truth of the conclusion is either implicitly or explicitly contained in the premisses. If is, therefore, possible to formally define induction and deduction in the following manner:

Definition of induction:

In an inductive argument, genuine supporting evidence (as expressed in the premisses) can only lead to highly probable conclusions. In other words, in an inductive argument supporting statements merely lend gradual support (from a little to a lot) to the conclusion(s).

Definition of deduction:

In a deductive argument, true premisses necessarily lead to true conclusions; the truth of the conclusion is already either implicitly or explicitly contained in the truth of the premisses.

The following simple examples of deductive and inductive arguments may be presented:

Deductive: All mammals have hearts
              All horses are mammals
              _____

              All horses have hearts

Inductive: All horses that have been examined had
              hearts
              _____

              All horses have hearts

The use of similar evidence in both these examples illustrates the important differences between inductive and deductive arguments. In both examples it is accepted that the supporting evidence is true. In the deductive argument, however, the conclusion is already implicitly contained in the premisses, and the conclusion is, therefore, no more than an explication of the premisses. In the inductive argument, however, the premisses provide a good deal of inductive support for the conclusion. The conclusion is highly probable. However unlikely this may appear, the possibility still exists that a type of horse may be discovered which does not have a heart. In the inductive argument, the conclusion, therefore, does not follow of necessity. The differences between induction and deduction are summarized in the following manner by Salmon (1973: 14):

DEDUCTIVE	INDUCTIVE
I. *If all of the premisses are true, then the conclusion must be true.*	I. *If all of the premisses are true then the conclusion is probably true, but not necessarily true.*
II. *All of the information or factual content in the conclusion was already contained, at least implicitly, in the premisses.*	II. *The conclusion contains information not present, even implicitly, in the premisses.*

In the examples that follow, we intend paying attention to less trivial examples of inductive reasoning.

EXAMPLES OF INDUCTION

In Marais' (1985) study (the article appears as Appendix 2 in the Afrikaans edition of this book) of the semantic dimensions of modes of address (more specifically the Afrikaans *u* and *jy*), Marais found that there were interesting associations relating to the respective use of the terms *u* and *jy*. One of the major aims of the research was to test Brown's theory that *u* and *jy* were respectively associated with power and solidarity. The first paragraph under discussion can be represented in the following manner:

s_1: The series of highly significant differences in group means of means of ratings of *u* and *jy* indicate that the two personal pronouns cannot be regarded merely as alternative forms that are arbitrarily exchanged by the sender and the receiver in the encoding and decoding processes.

s_2: The significant systematic differences were an indication that *u* and *jy* gave rise to different sets of associations — at any rate, as far as the sample was concerned.

s_3: To the extent that power and solidarity were in fact represented by the semantic differential scale, the analyses indicated that *u* is associated with power to a greater extent than *jy*, and that as far as solidarity is concerned *jy* is associated with this construct to a greater extent than *u*.

C: The preceding may be regarded as confirmation of Brown's theory regarding personal pronouns and their relationship to power and solidarity.

This is a good example of the manner in which inductive inference can be employed to confirm hypotheses or theories. In studies of this nature, the theory or model serves as a frame of reference which is used to guide the manner in which data are collected and analyzed in a clearly structured manner. When the eventual findings are in agreement with the theory or model, one would be in a position to say that the findings constitute inductive support of the theory or model. The example with which we started this chapter was, therefore, also an example of a situation where a specific theory (Smelser's theory of collective behaviour) was further confirmed by means of new empirical data. Clearly, this does not mean that a particular theory (Smelser's theory or Brown's theory on personal pronouns) can now be regarded as conclusively confirmed; it is rather the case that the new findings have increased the probability that the theories may be true.

A specific category of inductive argumentation is known as enumerative induction. As indicated by the use of the term enumerative, the inductive argument in this case is based upon a frequency count of the observed cases. The simplest example would be found in the case where, if I were to remove all the marbles from a jar and I were to identify all of them as green, I would then arrive at the conclusion that all the marbles in the jar are green:

s_1:   The first marble is green
s_2:   The second marble is green
  ⋮
  ⋮
  ⋮
s_{20}:   The twentieth marble is green

C: The twenty marbles contained in the bottle are green.

In this case the conclusion was arrived at on the basis of having counted all twenty marbles in the bottle. Assume that five of the marbles were red and the remaining 15 were green. In that case we would have been able to arrive at the following conclusion:

C: 75 % of the marbles are green and 25 % are red.

It is possible to provide less trivial example as we did in earlier examples:

s_1:   The average divorce rate in South Africa was 12 per 1000 persons during 1984

s_2:   The average divorce rate in Holland was 8 per 1 000 during 1984

s_3:   The average divorce rate in the USA was 10 per 1 000 during 1984

s_4:   The average divorce rate in England was 8,5 per 1 000 during 1984

114

C: The average divorce rate in South Africa during 1984 was higher than that in Holland, the USA, and England.

In the case of enumerative induction, the conclusion is merely a summary of the premisses. Good examples are the numerous public opinion polls that are conducted. If a researcher were interested in determining public opinion towards abortion, and were to pose the question "What is your attitude towards abortion?" to a sample of 1 000 people, the following results may have been obtained: 250 indicated that they were strongly opposed to abortion, 500 were opposed, 150 were in favour, and 100 were strongly in favour. The following conclusion could then have been drawn on the basis of the data:

C: 25% of those who were questioned were strongly opposed to abortion, 50% were opposed, 15% were in favour, and 10% were strongly in favour.

If the researchers were in a position where they could claim that the sample is representative of the population as a whole, they would also be able to claim that the percentages do not only reflect the attitudes of the sample (descriptive statistics), but that they represent the attitudes of the total population (inferential statistics). In a case of this nature, the validity of the inference is, to a large extent, dependent upon the representativeness of the sample. This issue will be dealt with later in the chapter under the heading external validity.

EXAMPLES OF DEDUCTION

As we indicated in the preceding section, deductive arguments are characterized by the essentially semantic nature of the inferential relationship between the premisses and the conclusion. In other words, the conclusion is based upon the meanings of the central concepts in the specific statements. The following is a well-known example:

s_1:   All humans are mortal

s_2:   Socrates is human

C: Socrates is mortal

In this case s_1 and s_2 are regarded as true by definition, and C necessarily follows from the statements. Although it may appear from this example as if deductive arguments cannot be of much use in the research process, in view of the fact that, strictly speaking, no new knowledge content is transferred to the conclusion in a deductive argument, it will be shown that there is a definite function for deductive inference in research.

Where inductive inference is used to arrive at conclusions on the basis of new empirical evidence, deductive inference is mainly used during the phase of hypothesis formulation. The aim in a research project is frequently to test an existing theory or model. This usually means that testable hypotheses (also called research hypotheses) are derived from the theory, that data are collected, and that the researcher determines whether or not the data support the research hypothesis (in experimental designs where null-hypothesis designs are employed, the aim of the research is to falsify or reject the null hypothesis). The formulation of the research hypothesis (and also the null hypothesis) from existing theory is a deductive process.

The following theory on conflict potential is presented in the form of three statements:

s_1:   Conflict potential in a complex segmented society (as in South Africa) increases if two unequally stratified interest groups are differentiated by both colour and class differences.

s_2:   The potential for mass conflict is reduced by increased inter-group mobility, and if socio-economic integration is promoted.

s_3:   Increased occupational mobility promotes mobility between social classes.

If one were to accept these statements as the core of a theory on conflict potential, and if one were further to accept that South Africa is a complex segmented society, then the following conclusion may be drawn:

C: An increase in occupational mobility among the members of the politically and economically deprived Black communities in South Africa, will lead to a decrease in conflict.

It is now possible to reformulate the conclusion as a research hypothesis and to make it the theme of a long-term research project. If the hypothesis were to be confirmed in the long term, this confirmation would provide inductive support for the theory of conflict potential. The development of the conclusion from the premisses s_1 to s_3 was, however, based upon deductive inference.

Obviously, theories are not the only source that can be used to derive hypotheses. A clearly formulated generalization, such as the following, may also be used as the frame of reference of a research hypothesis:

s_1:   Increasing levels of welfare have a negative influence on rates of population growth in the Third World OR higher levels of welfare in Third World countries usually results in lower rates of population growth.

If one were also to assume that the majority of the members of the Black community in South Africa display the typical socio-economic and demographic characteristics of Third World people, the following conclusion can be drawn:

C: Increasing levels of welfare among the members of the Black community in South Africa will result in a decrease in the population growth rate of that group.

We once again have the situation that C deductively follows from premiss s_1 and the assumption that we made that the basic pattern of living of Blacks in South Africa resembles that of Third World inhabitants. C may now be used as the research hypothesis of a project. If the data that are collected were to support the hypothesis, it would provide inductive support for the generalization concerning the relationship between welfare and population growth rates.

It is, therefore, clear that induction and deduction have to be regarded as complementary modes of reasoning. In those disciplines in which clearly articulated theories and models offer explanations for particular phenomena, the deductive derivation of new research hypotheses from existing frames of reference could well form the first step of an investigation. The subsequent collection of evidence offered in support of the research hypothesis, would obviously display a typically inductive pattern. Schematically, this may be represented in the following manner:

Theory → deductive inference leading to → research hypothesis (hypotheses) → collection of empirical evidence → inductive → confirmation of hypothesis → indirect support of the initial theory.

At the beginning of the chapter we referred briefly to the differences that exist between research in which a deductive strategy is followed and research in which use is made of an inductive strategy. Following our discussion of deduction and induction, it ought to be clear that this distinction is based upon the differences that are to be found between deductive and inductive inference. In research in which use is made of a deductive strategy, the basic pattern that we presented schematically in the previous paragraph is followed. In research of a more inductive nature, however, (compare the majority of studies in which historical analysis is used, as well as textual analysis, exploratory studies, and so on) the study usually ends with a more explicit hypothesis or theory, or merely with an interpretation. These findings are derived from the data in an inductive manner.

Threats to inferential validity

It is evident that the most important threats to inferential validity are associated with the nature of the inference between premiss and conclusion.

(1) As far as deductive inferences are concerned, the question is whether the conclusion does, in fact, follow from the preceding premisses. Is the con-

117

clusion explicitly or implicitly (and this is the more difficult case) contained in the premisses?

(2) As far as inductive inference is concerned, the question that has to be asked is whether the premisses offer relevant and adequate inductive support for the conclusion.

The question that now arises is: "What are the most important measures that the researcher can take to ensure that he or she complies with the requirements of inferential validity?" For the simple reason that the inferential process is a cognitive process, it is extremely difficult to formulate stringent rules of inferential validity. The nature of deductive inference has obviously been formalized in great detail in deductive logic. Apart from the possibility of following a formal course in deductive logic, the best alternative appears to be to determine which hypotheses are in fact implied by means of a thorough conceptual explication (compare chapter 3) of the concepts of the theory or model that is being tested.

As we indicated at an earlier stage, the requirement of relevance in inductive inference is usually fairly easy to establish. It is, however, a good deal more difficult to establish when sufficient evidence has been collected for a particular point of view or interpretation. Conceivably, Wright's (1982) suggestion represents the best approach. According to him the researcher should constantly ask him or herself whether an alternative conclusion could not have been arrived at on the basis of the available evidence. As long as an alternative, or equally plausible, conclusion can be arrived at with the same data, the researcher does not have adequate evidence for the conclusion.

We demonstrated how the collection of additional evidence against Lee Harvey Oswald progressively excluded alternative conclusions. It is obviously not always possible to attain the same level of comprehensiveness in empirical research. Researchers may, at times, be aware of alternative interpretations of their findings but may, nevertheless choose a specific conclusion because they are convinced that that interpretation does, in fact, represent the best and most plausible of the competing interpretations. Good research, therefore, means that researchers do not attempt to obscure or ignore alternative interpretations of findings, but rather that they clearly indicate the reasons for having preferred a given conclusion.

Attaining inferential validity is evidently one of the more difficult validity considerations in social sciences research. This phase requires systematic and critical thinking to a greater extent than any of the other phases of the research process.

External validity

Before finally setting aside the theme of inferential validity, we shall briefly pay attention to the criterion of external validity. As we indicated in Chapter 2, (see diagram on p. 49), it is customary to distinguish between internal and external validity in research. As far as internal validity is concerned, we have paid fairly detailed attention to its most important dimensions which comprise theoretical validity, measurement validity, reliability, and inferential validity. In our discussion of inferential validity we have, however, only paid attention to the requirement of valid inference with regard to the data collected from the sample that was studied. In those cases, however, in which the researcher wishes to make inferences about the population from which the sample was drawn, (in other words studies of more general interest) the question that arises is whether the conclusions are externally valid.

The term external validity is used as a synonym for generalizability. It is for this reason that we referred to external validity within the context of research of a more general interest. Typically, this research would proceed along the following lines: a target population of people or situations or periods would be defined as clearly as possible. For example, all first year psychology students at universities who use English as the language of instruction. Following this, samples representative of this population would be drawn and studied. At the conclusion of the study the aim would be to apply the findings based upon the sample to the defined population or, in other words, to generalize the findings to the defined population. From this brief exposition of the issue of external validity it is sufficiently clear that the greatest threat to external validity is to be found in the extent to which the sample is representative of the population. The subjects included in the *sample* could, for example, be more highly motivated, older, more conservative, more intelligent, or more urbanized than the population, and these factors would all have a negative influence on the external validity of the findings. Cook and Campbell (1979: 73-74) distinguish three threats to external validity.

SELECTION EFFECTS

The way in which the sample is selected can have a significant effect upon the generalizability of the findings. This effect is particularly evident in experimental studies in which ethical considerations frequently compel the researcher to use volunteers as participants. In a classical study on the *volunteer subject* Rosenthal and Rosnow's (1969) findings indicated that volunteer subjects were frequently more highly educated, more intelligent, of a higher professional status, and displayed lower levels of authoritarianism than did non-volunteer experimental subjects. A number of studies have been published since the appearance of the Rosenthal and Rosnow study in which the selection effects on psychological research have been indicated where a large proportion (some authors claim that it is as high as 90%) of the studies have been conducted exclusively with psychology students as participants.

CONTEXT EFFECTS

Is it reasonable to expect that the causal relationships that were established in a factory would also apply in an office environment? Are the findings that were obtained in a military camp also applicable to a university residence? The setting within which research is conducted can have an important bearing upon the generalizability of the findings. More specifically, it ought also to be obvious that findings which are based upon laboratory conditions cannot simply be made applicable to natural environments.

PERIOD EFFECTS

The effect associated with the time at which research is conducted is obviously not only to be found in studies of universal interest. Nonetheless, it is likely that they have the most far-reaching consequences in this case.

Is it, for example, possible to regard a study that was conducted on a specific day or during a given month and year as valid for all time? Studies of a socio-political and economic nature are evidently particularly sensitive as far as the time of the year and the specific year during which they are conducted are concerned! Events such as elections and assassinations, and conditions such as economic recessions, all influence people's attitudes, convictions, and perceptions.

Selection effects have a direct bearing upon the representativeness of the sample. Context and period effects are more closely associated with the representativeness of the circumstances under which the research was conducted. As far as the former is concerned, the standard answer to the problem in the social sciences is to be found in the principles of sampling design. Because of the fact that external validity is such a difficult, but at the same time, important consideration in social scientific research, a considerable amount of attention has been paid to the development of measures by means of which sampling may be optimally done. The basic principle is that of random sampling. If every element in the population has an equal opportunity of being selected as part of the sample, the chances are that much greater that the sample will, in fact, be representative of the defined population. By the very nature of things, the ideal of random sampling is not always attainable, and as a result non-random techniques have to be employed. In situations of this nature it is, strictly speaking, not possible to accept that the eventual sample is representative of the defined population, and there must then necessarily be some doubt concerning the generalizability of the findings.

The most important guideline concerning context and period effects is that of variation. The researcher ought, as far as possible, to vary the circumstances, design, period, and so on. It is only by the use of repeated measurement under different circumstances and during different periods that it is possible to control for these effects.

The problems associated with sampling design are discussed in detail in the more technically oriented methodology texts. For this reason we conclude with these remarks.

A TYPOLOGY OF RESEARCH DESIGNS

In chapters 2 to 5 we discussed the problems associated with research design from the point of view of the most important validity considerations. The notion of validity was divided into internal and external validity. Under the rubric of internal validity we emphasized theoretical validity (conceptualization), measurement validity (operationalization), reliability (data collection), and inferential validity (analysis and interpretation). We also briefly referred to external validity as generalizability. In summarizing these four chapters, we shall present a classification of research designs which is based upon the most important distinctions that were drawn. Our aim is not to discuss each type of design in detail, but rather to illustrate the most important similarities and differences between the major types of design.

The first distinction that may be drawn is associated with the nature of the sources of the data that are used: Are new data collected or are existing or available data used? Available data are found in documentary sources (books, texts, letters, diaries, census statistics, newspaper reports, and so on) or in physical sources (records, tape recordings, video recordings, films, paintings, sculpture, architectural style, and so on).

New data are primarily collected by means of direct observation of human behaviour or by means of indirect observation (interviewing, the completion of questionnaires, applying psychological tests, the use of projective techniques, and so on). On the basis of this distinction, experimental, quasi-experimental, survey, and ethnographic or field designs would be classified as research in which new data are collected. Existing data are primarily employed in historical analysis, content analysis, discourse analysis, and the construction of life histories.

In chapter 2 we drew a second distinction between those studies with a more general interest, and those with a more contextual interest. As we indicated, this distinction in research strategy is also associated with the three divisions that we proposed in terms of the aims of research, namely exploratory, descriptive, and explanatory studies. Studies with a general interest tend to be explanatory-descriptive, while those with a contextual interest tend to be more descriptive-exploratory. In this manner experimental and quasi-experimental studies tend to be focussed on general-explanatory findings; surveys are more general-descriptive, and ethnographic or field studies are contextual-descriptive (and also exploratory). As far as the analysis of existing sources of data is concerned, quantitative content analysis tends to be focussed on generalizable findings (both explanatory and descriptive), while historical analysis, text analysis, and case studies (life histories) are primarily of a contextual nature — interpretative, descriptive, and exploratory.

Bearing these distinctions in mind, it is possible to classify research designs in the following manner: (We consistently use the most prototypical categorization of a research design. More variations are obviously possible than are indicated in the table.)

TABLE 5.1

	RESEARCH GOAL	COLLECTION OF NEW DATA	ANALYSIS OF EXISTING DATA
RESEARCH STRATEGY	EXPLANATORY	EXPERIMENTAL and QUASI-EXPERIMENTAL DESIGNS (Emphasis on experimental control, structured direct & indirect observation)	
GENERAL INTEREST	DESCRIPTIVE	SURVEY DESIGNS (Emphasis on structured indirect observation, questionnaires & interviews)	(1) SECONDARY ANALYSIS — census data (2) QUANTITATIVE CONTENT ANALYSIS — newspaper reports, speeches, etc.
	EXPLORA-TORY	SURVEY DESIGNS (pilot studies)	
	EXPLANA-TORY (VERSTEHEN)		(1) QUALITATIVE CONTENT ANALYSIS OR DISCOURSE/ ASSERTION ANALYSIS (2) HISTORICAL ANALYSIS (What was the cause of x?)
CONTEXT-TUAL INTEREST	DESCRIPTIVE	FIELD DESIGNS or ENTHNOGRAPHIC DESIGNS (Emphasis on unstructured direct and indirect observation)	(1) QUALITATIVE CONTENT ANALYSIS or DISCOURSE ANALYSIS (2) HISTORICAL ANALYSIS (What happened?)
	EXPLORATORY	FIELD DESIGNS or ETHNO-GRAPHIC DESIGNS (Emphasis on the use of informants, elite figures)	

Suggestions for further reading

1. Two books on informal logic in which central concepts such as argument, evidence, inference, and others are treated in an elementary fashion, are those by Wright (1982) and by Scriven (1976). Similarly, the book by Salmon (1973) is an elementary introduction to logic.

2. The first comprehensive discussion of the concept *external validity* and *threats to external validity* appeared in Campbell and Stanley (1963). Cook and Campbell (1979) subsequently presented a more detailed discussion. Good discussions of this concept may also be found in Smith (1975) and in Denzin (1978).

3. For a general introduction to different types of research designs the following texts may be consulted: Bogue (1981), Drew (1980), Kazdin (1980), Leedy (1980), Nesselroade and Baltes (1979), Selltiz *et al.* (1965), Smith (1975), and Spector (1981). A few of the texts that are available on the topic of experimental design are: Chapin (1974), Christensen (1980), Das (1979), Finney (1974), Keppel (1973), and Myers (1979).

Introduction

Concepts

Connotation and denotation
Variables

Dichotomous, polytomic and continuous
Variables
Independent and dependent variables

Statements

Definitions

Theoretical definitions
Operational definitions

Hypotheses

Conceptual frameworks

Typologies
Models
Theories

Paradigms

Normal science

Components of paradigms
Functions of paradigms

Scientific revolutions
Paradigms in the social sciences

Resumé

Suggestions for further reading

CHAPTER 6

CENTRAL CONSTRUCTS IN THE RESEARCH PROCESS

INTRODUCTION

In the preceding chapters on research design, we have emphasized the dynamics of the decision-making process in social sciences research, and the considerations that need to be taken into account in order to maximize the validity of the findings of a given project. In this chapter we turn our attention to those components of research which are found in any research project: concepts, definitions, hypotheses, models, theories, typologies, and paradigms. Our emphasis is, therefore, upon the analytical "tools" of the researcher; the instruments by means of which he or she is able to make sense of the phenomenon that is being investigated. The constructs with which we shall deal constitute at the same time the frame of reference of any investigation (research simply cannot take place in the absence of concepts, statements, and conceptual frameworks), and the products of the research process (research leads to the development of new theories and models).

The constructs that we discuss form an hierarchical order that may be represented in the following manner:

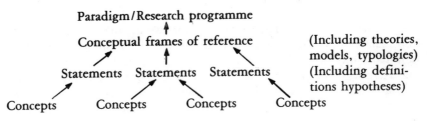

125

The schematic representation also gives an indication of how the discussion in this chapter will be ordered.

CONCEPTS

Concepts may be defined as the most elementary symbolic constructions by means of which people classify or categorize reality. Concepts are the "pigeon holes" into which we sort our unstructured empirical experiences. Concepts are, therefore, the primary instruments by means of which humans come to grips with reality.

From a different perspective, concepts may be regarded as those symbolic constructions by means of which people make sense of, and give meaning to, their life worlds. A concept is a symbol of meaning. Let us now pay some attention to the meaning of *meaning*.

Connotation and denotation

Ever since John S. Mill drew a distinction between the two constitutive elements of meaning, namely *connotation* and *denotation*, in his *System of logic* (1852), it has become common practice to distinguish between them. Subsequent to Mill, Frege suggested that the terms *sense* and *meaning* could be used to refer to these elements. Copi defines the differences between connotative and denotative meaning in the following manner:

In one sense the meaning of a term consists of the class of objects to which the term may be applied. This sense of meaning, its referential sense, has traditionally been called extensional or denotative meaning. A general or class term denotes the objects to which it may be correctly applied, and the collection or class of these objects constitutes the extension or denotation of the term... The collection of properties shared by all and only those objects in a term's extension is called the intension or connotation of the term (1972: 125).

General or class terms have both connotative and denotative meaning. In this manner, the connotation of the term *skyscraper* includes those characteristics that are common and distinctive of buildings of a certain height. The denotation of *skyscraper* is the class of phenomena which would, for example, include the Empire State Building, the World Trade Centre, and the Carlton Hotel.

It is also necessary to distinguish between the two uses of the term *connotation*, namely the subjective and the conventional. The subjective connotation that a specific person attaches to a word refers to the particular class of characteristics that he or she believes are characteristic of objects or phenomena that are denoted by that word. It is obvious that the subjective connotation of a word will vary from one person to the next. The specific connotation that a person would attach to words such as *freedom* and *justice* would be closely associated with that person's mindset and experiences.

Although a person would, therefore, employ common terms such as *beautiful* and *ugly* in his or her interpersonal communication, and would usually understand what other people mean when they use the terms (and would be understood by others when he or she uses these words), it is clear that the user would attach specific idiosyncratic connotations to these terms: it is indeed the case that beauty is in the eye of the beholder. The *conventional* connotation of a word is the commonly assumed meaning of that word: the meaning that has implicitly been agreed upon for the sake of communication. People agree to use words in a specific manner to ensure that communication and conversation between them is possible.

When this distinction between subjective and conventional connotation is applied to the social sciences, we find the following. To some extent each researcher employs scientific concepts in an idiosyncratic manner (subjective connotations) that is associated with specific theoretical preferences, training, interests, and so on. Nonetheless, researchers within the same discipline and, more specifically, within the same paradigm or research tradition, tend to share specific conventional connotations. Because concepts have, at least to a certain extent, specific meanings within a given conceptual framework (theory, model), it is obvious that researchers from the same paradigm are likely to be able to communicate with relatively greater ease than would be the case between researchers from different schools or paradigms. In the remaining part of this chapter we shall consistently refer to conventional connotation when the term *connotation* is employed.

In chapter 3 we referred to the fact that the core concepts of the social sciences tend to be highly abstract in nature. Some of these concepts originated not in the concrete world of everyday intercourse, but rather in highly abstract theory. A good example is the term *alienation* which was discussed in some detail in chapter 3. Concepts of which the meanings are determined by theory from the outset, are also called *theoretical concepts* or *constructs*. An implication of this is that the ontological status of such constructs is often in dispute. One may ask: Do such constructs denote or refer to real entities or structures? If a specific term is developed entirely within the framework of a specific theory, does it have an existence independent of that theory? Can entities or structures such as the *id, ego,* and *superego* (Freud), *cognitive dissonance* (Festinger), *labelling* (Becker), *anomie* (Durkheim), and so on be said to exist, or are they merely fictitious creations of highly imaginative social scientists? This is not the place to discuss this highly philosophical problem. It is sufficient that we take note of the very real denotative problem of a large number of concepts in the social sciences. The obvious solution to the problem is to operationalize constructs in a rigid and accurate manner — an ideal which, as we have indicated in an earlier section, is far easier said than done!

127

An important observation that follows from the discussion in the preceding paragraph is that the denotations of theoretical concepts are largely, if not entirely, determined by their connotations. For the simple reason that concepts of this nature did not develop, and were not given meaning, in the concrete world of everyday experience, but resulted within the theoretical space of a conceptual framework, the denotation is primarily dependent upon the connotation. For example, the phenomena that are classified under *alienation* are largely determined by the connotations that are associated with the concept in theories of alienation. In contradistinction, the denotations of everyday *concrete* concepts such as dogs, cars, trees, furniture, sun, books, tables, and so on are reasonably fixed. The consequence is that the conventional connotations that are attached to these concepts are also reasonably fixed. The relationship between the connotations and denotations of concepts may be summarized in the following manner:

(i)   In the case of highly theoretical concepts or constructs, the denotations of the concepts are largely determined by the connotations that are attached to them within the framework of the theory concerned.

(ii)   In the case of more concrete concepts associated with everyday experience, the denotations frequently determine the (conventional) connotations that are attached to the concepts.

Another far-reaching implication of the discussion so far is that concepts (and specifically theoretical concepts) frequently have more than one connotation. Because, for example, there are several theories of alienation, it is clear that this concept has a number of connotations. The result is that different social scientists frequently interpret and categorize the same phenomenon in different ways.

A good example of the manner in which individuals define the reality of their social environment in different ways is to be found by comparing Karl Marx's conceptualization of social stratification with that of Max Weber. According to Marx, social stratification (the unequal ranking of socially defined positions in society) is the consequence of the capitalistic system of production in which the haves and the have nots are differentiated into two permanently antagonistic classes. He argued that all class-differentiated societies are characterized by a mutually antagonistic relationship between a minority of *non-producers* (who dominate the means of production) and a majority of *labourers* (who do not own any property, but who produce the surplus production which forms the basis of the wealth of the first class. In modern capitalistic society this antagonistic relationship is manifested as a class struggle between the capitalists and the proletariat (mainly industrial workers in the urban industrial centres). While Marx viewed the stratification process as the consequence of private property or, stated differently, as a result of economic power — or the absence thereof — Max Weber identified other determinants of stratification. He distinguished between three broad dimensions or hierar-

128

chical systems of stratification to indicate the economic, social, and legal-political facets of society. This scheme produces three main stratification structures: class, status, and power. Each of these three hierarchical systems is manifested in a specific group context namely classes, status groups, and political parties.

Weber defined *class* primarily in terms of economic considerations (an individual's position in the market in relation to the resources in society, especially property); *status* was seen as an expression of social honour and prestige; and *power* was associated with a person's political bargaining position. It is, therefore, clear that Weber viewed social stratification as a multidimensional phenomenon that involved more than Marx's class dichotomy. He also indicated that a person need not necessarily be placed at the same level in each of these three hierarchical systems. A person who achieved a high class and political (power) position could, for example, have a low ranking as far as social prestige is concerned.

Because concepts *provide access* to empirical experience, different social scientists adhering to different theories of the same construct will often study different phenomena. This is the problem that Kuhn indicated with his *incommensurability thesis*. According to him, the fact that scientists operate from different conceptual frameworks makes communication between them impossible and excludes any comparison between theories. As far as we are concerned, this point of view is too radical for two reasons (Kuhn also, incidentally, toned this down at a later stage): On the one hand, this would apply only to highly theoretical concepts — a good deal of overlap is to be found between more concrete concepts. On the other hand, it is certainly the case that even the more abstract theories include certain lower level terms (compare our discussion of Marx's theory in chapter 3) which would imply a degree of overlap in meaning between theories.

Variables

We shall conclude this section with a brief discussion of the concept *variable*. A common practice amongst social scientists is to refer to the characteristics of the research object that is being investigated as *variables*. (Strictly speaking, this is an abbreviated form of *characteristics that are variable*). Examples of variables that are commonly used in investigations include: gender, income, socio-economic class, productivity, unemployment, education, mobility, anxiety, religious affiliation, political preferences, intelligence, and achievement.

There are a variety of classification principles in terms of which different types of variables may be distinguished. We shall only discuss two in this section.

DICHOTOMOUS, POLYTOMIC AND CONTINUOUS VARIABLES

Real dichotomous variables that can only assume one of two values, that is whether a given characteristic is either present or absent, are, for example, male-female, alive-dead, employed-unemployed. Variables that can assume a variety of values are referred to as polytomic. Examples would include religious affiliation (Muslim, Christian, Jewish), and political affiliation (Nationalist, Conservative, Progressive, Democratic, etc). The majority of variables can, however, at least in theory, assume a continuum of values, for example, intelligence, authoritarianism, anxiety, and introversion. Variables of this nature are usually measured by means of a scale that permits a wide (actually unlimited) spectrum or continuum of possible values.

INDEPENDENT AND DEPENDENT VARIABLES

The distinction between independent and dependent variables refers to the basic cause-effect relationship between specific events or phenomena. The independent variable refers to the antecedent phenomenon and the dependent variable to the consequent phenomenon.

In an experimental situation the researcher, by definition, is able to control the independent variables which he or she systematically manipulates in an attempt to isolate the actual causes of specific phenomena. For example, a researcher who wishes to determine which factors are contributory in determining scholastic performance could compare the efficacy of two methods of instruction. This would be done by regarding the two methods of instruction as independent variables. For example method A is the first independent variable, and method B is the second independent variable. By means of systematic manipulation of these conditions, and eventual statistical analysis (analysis of variance), the researcher would be able to determine which method is the most effective in increasing scholastic performance as measured on a given test.

Quite often researchers wish to determine the influence of specific variables upon others, but find themselves in a situation where they are not able to manipulate the independent variables. A useful example relates to the situation where the researcher wishes to determine the influence of gender, home language, or intelligence on scholastic performance. These variables cannot be experimentally manipulated (they are also referred to as characteristic or organismic variables) and in such cases the researcher would seek to control the variables by means of statistical procedures.

This concludes our brief discussion of concepts and variables — the most basic building-blocks of all knowledge. But these ''building-blocks'' need to be ''cemented'' into more meaningful constructs, i.e. statements, in order to become truly part of the edifice of science.

STATEMENTS

In chapter 1 statements were defined as sentences that make a specific knowledge claim concerning an aspect of reality. Statements, it was said, are sentences in which a demonstrable epistemic claim is made. It follows from this that statements have to be either true or false. The epistemic claims that are made in statements are either correct or not.

For the purposes of this book, two types of statements are discussed — definitions and hypotheses. As we discussed the nature and structure of definitions in chapter 3, we shall merely summarize the main points here.

Definitions

Definitions can be defined as statements by means of which the meaning (connotation and denotation) of concepts is specified. An important classification of definitions is based upon the distinction drawn earlier, between connotative and denotative meaning.

THEORETICAL DEFINITIONS

Where the connotative meaning of a concept (the general intention or ''idea'' that it incorporates) is more closely specified, we usually refer to the theoretical or connotative definition. This means that the relationships between a given concept and related concepts within a specific conceptual framework (model or theory) are brought into focus. In other words, the context within which a concept is used virtually delimits its connotation. Let us look at an example from the physical sciences: In theories developed during the eighteenth century *heat* was defined as a type of liquid (our concept of electrical current can still be traced back to this view). Nowadays, however, *heat* is defined as a form of energy. This shows that concepts have different connotations depending upon the currently accepted theory within which it occurs and from which the definition is derived. The same variation in meaning applies to different theoretical (i.e. high-level abstract concepts) concepts such as energy, gravitation, space, and time. This is even more true of concepts in the social sciences. The definition of *culture*, for example, would differ between materialist-evolutionist, idealist, and structural- functionalist frames of reference. The same applies to other concepts such as violence, aggression, intelligence and so on.

A theoretical or constitutive definition of a concept, therefore, derives from the conceptual framework or theory within which it is used. Because conceptual frameworks differ (for example, a conflict approach and a consensus approach to social phenomena), considerable variation exists between the connotations of concepts. In addition, one has to bear in mind that connotation usually also determines the denotative content of concepts.

People therefore, depending upon the frame of reference to which they subscribe, actually delimit and classify social phenomena differently. Depending upon one's frame of reference, an individual may either be classified as a deviant or merely as a member of a minority group. Similarly, the same event may be classified as a legal procession, an illegal demonstration, or racial unrest by different researchers depending upon their frames of reference.

In this context, one may also consider the variation of meaning or relativity of meaning of concepts such as conservative, liberal, progressive, justice and freedom.

OPERATIONAL DEFINITIONS

In an attempt to find some kind of counter measure to the problems associated with meaning variance, researchers tend to emphasize the explication of the denotation of concepts. In other words, what exactly is being referred to, or what does the concept indicate? One technique that is used for this purpose is operational definition.

An operational definition of a concept describes certain operations (usually some type of measurement) under which the use of the concept is valid. In other words, an operational definition presents specific conditions for the appropriate use of a specific concept — conditions that state that the execution of certain operations will result in specific results.

In his book *Foundations of behavioral research* Kerlinger presents the following hypothetical example from psychology:

Let us build a "small theory" of underachievement to illustrate these notions (constitutive and operational definitions). Suppose an investigator believes that underachievement is, in part, a function of pupils' self- concepts. He believes that pupils that perceive themselves "inadequately", who have negative self-percepts, also tend to achieve less than their potential capacity and aptitude indicate they should achieve. He further believes that ego-needs (which we will not define here) and motivation for achievement (call this n-ach) are tied to underachievement. Naturally, he is also aware of the relation between aptitude and intelligence and achievement in general. A diagram to illustrate this "theory" might look like this.

The investigator has no direct measure of self-concept, but he assumes that he can draw inferences about an individual's self concept from a figure drawing test. He operationally defines self-concept, then, as certain responses to the figure-drawing test. This is probably the most common method of measuring psychological and educational constructs. The heavy single line between cl and Cl indicates the relatively direct nature of the presumed relation between self-concept and the test (The double line between Cl and the level of observation indicates an operational definition.)

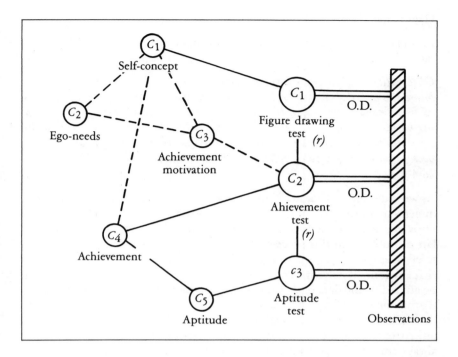

A single solid line between concepts — for example between the construct achievement (c4) and the achievement test (C2) — indicates a relatively well-established relation between postulated achievement and what standard achievement tests measure. The single solid lines between Cl and C2 and between measures C2 and C3 indicate obtained relations between the test scores of these measures... (coefficient of correlation r).

The broken single lines indicate postulated relations between constructs that are not relatively well established. A good example of this is the postulated relation between self-concept and achievement motivation. One of the aims of science is to make these broken lines solid lines by bridging the operational definition — measurement gap (1973: 33-34).

At the beginning of our discussion of statements we indicated that statements always have to be either true or false. It is, however, clear from the examples that we have presented that it is rather strange to talk about definitions in terms of them being true or false. Because theoretical and operational definitions are embedded in theories and models, it is customary rather to refer to the theoretical validity of theoretical definitions, and the measurement validity of operational definitions (compare chapter 3).

Definition always concerns delimiting the meaning (connotative and denotative) of concepts. The validity of a definition is, in the final analysis, dependent upon the accuracy of the manner in which it is delimited.

Hypotheses

In his book *Conjectures and refutations* Popper makes the following important statement:

Observation is always selective. It needs a chosen object, a definite task, an interest, a point of view, a problem... For the animal a point of view is provided by its needs, the task of the moment, and its expectations; for the scientist by his theoretical interests, the special problem under investigation, his conjectures and anticipations, and the theories that he accepts as a kind of background: his frame of reference, his "horizon of expectations" (1974: 46-47).

As we indicated in Chapter 1, the teleological dimension is one of the basic dimensions of research. No research is conducted aimlessly, without any frame of reference or eventual goal. A first step in the research process is to formulate a problem. In this process, the researchers are guided by what Popper refers to as their *horizon of expectations*. Quite correctly, Popper emphasizes that any form of naive inductivism — the assumption that the researcher can be guided by the data or that the data speak for themselves — is misleading. At the one end of the spectrum, in exploratory and unstructured research, the researcher is led by general notions, expectations, anticipations, and so on. At the other end, in explanatory or descriptive research, the project is always embarked upon with clearly formulated hypotheses.

An hypothesis is a statement in which an assumed relationship or difference between two or more phenomena or variables is postulated. An hypothesis is a statement in which, for example, it is postulated that there is a relationship between intelligence and scholastic performance or that an increase in unemployment results in an increase in crime. Since it has become customary to use the term *hypothesis* largely within the context of postulated relationships between empirical phenomena, one could refer to this type of hypothesis as a *research hypothesis*. Stern (1979), on the other hand, suggested that the expression *central theoretical thesis* be used rather than hypothesis when referring to more theoretical investigations. The distinction between hypothesis and central theoretical thesis does not, however, indicate a fundamental difference between the nature or the structure of the construct involved. At most, it can serve to indicate the particular context within which a given *hypothesis* is embedded.

In general, there are two ways in which hypotheses are generated. On the one hand, hypotheses are derived from existing theories and models in a given discipline as in the case of deductive or hypothesis-testing investigations. All the existing theories and models in the market of intellectual resources (cf. chapter 1) constitute a potential source of new hypotheses. In this manner, Smelser's theory of collective behaviour constituted the conceptual framework for the formulation of research hypotheses in the study of the unrest in Reiger Park (chapter 5). Joubert's construction of a typology of value orientations is also a good example of the manner in which a more theoretical hypothesis or central thesis was developed directly from the model postulated by Parsons (Appendix 2).

On the other hand, it is possible to generate hypotheses inductively from observations and experience. In unstructured or semi-structured research, the researcher is likely to perceive new relationships — relationships that can be formulated in the form of hypotheses. In reading a certain text or documents, the researcher frequently notices implicit themes or structures that are, in some way, related to the more obvious themes and, in this manner, is led to the formulation of a new hypothesis. In his investigation into the philosophy of science of Francis Bacon, Mouton (1987) noticed that Bacon would consistently illustrate an idea relating to scientific progress with religious analogies. Further investigation led to the conjecture that Bacon's notion of scientific progress was, in an important sense, a secularization of the millenialistic notions of a future reign of peace. This supposition was subsequently elaborated and various *hypotheses* concerning the origin of Bacon's theories of scientific advancement, objectivity, and methodology eventually became the central object of the investigation.

Within the framework of quantitative research in which hypotheses are tested, it has become customary to refer quite specifically to the statistical hypothesis and the null hypothesis. A statistical hypothesis is a statement in statistical terms in which the statistical relationship between phenomena is postulated. For example, that the means of A are larger than those of B $(\mu_A > \mu_B)$, or that the correlation coefficient is larger than 0,30 ($r > + ,30$). A statistical hypothesis is a prediction of the nature of the outcome of the statistical analysis of the quantitative data in an investigation.

It is not possible, however, to test the statistical hypothesis in its original form. It has to be tested against something else. This *something else* is the null hypothesis. The null hypothesis is a statistical statement in which it is postulated that no relationship or no difference exists between the variables that are being studied. In terms of the examples in the previous paragraph, the associated null hypotheses would postulate that the means of A and B do not differ, or that $r = 0$. Kerlinger describes the null hypothesis in the following terms: *The null hypothesis says, "you're wrong, there is no relation; disprove me if you can"* (1973: 202). Particularly in experimental investigations, it is customary to structure the research in such a manner that an attempt is made to disprove or falsify the null hypothesis. If the null hypothesis were then shown to be false, the researcher is able to accept that a significant relationship exists between the variables that are being studied.

Assume that the aim of an investigation is to assess the relative merits of two methods of instruction. Further assume that the researcher formulates a statistical hypothesis to the effect that the mean scores on method A will be higher than the mean scores on method B ($\mu_A > \mu_B$). The usual format of this type of hypothesis is:

$$H_1 : \mu_A > \mu_B.$$

Assume that the findings indicate that the mean for method A is 68, and that for method B is 61. One would be inclined to regard this as a confirmation of the statistical hypothesis. This assumption may, however, be quite erroneous as the possibility that the differences may be attributable to chance factors which had not been eliminated. The appropriate strategy is to include this element of chance in the design of the research by formulating what may virtually be referred to as a chance hypothesis or, more conventionally, a null hypothesis. According to the expectations associated with chance factors, μ_A ought to be equal to μ_B.

This null hypothesis is then represented as:

$$H_0 : \mu_A = \mu_B.$$

The refutation of H_0 now becomes the aim of the study. Stated differently: the researcher attempts to refute the statement that the difference between the means of the two methods are the result of chance factors. If the data were to indicate that the null hypothesis is in error and that the obtained differences are significant (a term that is statistically defined), the researcher would assume that the statistical hypothesis has been confirmed.

In summary, it is clear that the single most important characteristic associated with a good hypothesis is its testability. As far as research hypotheses are concerned, the requirement is that they should be empirically testable: one should be able either to confirm or refute them. As far as theoretical hypotheses are concerned, it would also apply that it ought to be possible to identify it either as a tenable or an untenable hypothesis by means of logical and conceptual argumentation. A prerequisite for any form of testing is clear and unambiguous concepts. Particularly in the case of research hypotheses, it is essential that the concepts that are used must possess single references or denotations to identifiable phenomena in reality.

CONCEPTUAL FRAMEWORKS

Concepts are structured in certain types of statements (definitions, hypotheses, or observation statements) according to specific syntactic rules. Although we have, on a number of occasions in the preceding sections, emphasized that scientific knowledge consists of scientific statements, and that researchers aim at generating valid scientific statements, it is evident that statements are not entirely independent. When statements are arranged according to regulative interests or orientations and are integrated into conceptual frameworks, we find the familiar *structures* of science: typologies, theories, and models. The nature of the conceptual framework is determined by the regulative function that the framework has to fulfil.

On these grounds, it is possible to distinguish between three types of conceptual frameworks: *typologies* that basically have a classifying or categorizing function, *models* that, apart from classification, also suggest new relationships heuristically, and theories that, apart from the preceding functions (classification and heuristics), also fulfil an explanatory and interpretative function. It will, however, become evident that the borders between models and theories are often extremely vague.

Typologies

A typology may be defined as a conceptual framework in which phenomena are classified in terms of characteristics that they have in common with other phenomena. **Classification** is one of the more basic functions of conceptual frameworks. The history of the physical sciences has produced a number of well-known classifications or taxonomies: Mendeleev's classification of the elements, Linnaeus's classification of the different species of animals, and so on.

Similarly, classifications, or more accurately typologies, are to be found in every discipline in the social sciences: people are classified as introverts or extroverts, societies are classified as democratic or totalitarian, attitudes as conservative or progressive, values as inclusive or exclusive (compare Joubert's typology in Appendix 2), literary texts as epic, dramatic, lyrical, and so on. Himes (1980), for example, classifies the interest groups that are involved in a conflict situation as *participants, establishments,* and *neutrals.* Each of these main types is then further classified. Participants, for example, include three main types: *organizational participants, nonmember participants*, and *coalitional participants.*

From these examples, and particularly if one were to make a careful study of Joubert's typology, it is possible to summarize the major characteristics of a typology as follows:

(1) The basic unit of a typology is the *type* or (to employ Weber's terminology) the *ideal type.* In a description of the typical characteristics of a phenomenon, the common or outstanding is emphasized and the trivial or incidental is eliminated. The identification of the typical therefore clearly involves a process of abstraction. Starting with the concrete level of experience we move to a higher level of abstraction in which the common is emphasized at the expense of that which is specific.

(2) The consequence of abstraction is that no type is ever an exact reproduction of all the characteristics of a phenomenon. Because abstraction involves *selection*, the relationship between the type (construct) and the phenomenon (that is typified) is one of approximation.

(3) The criteria of good classification, and for that reason also of typologies, are (i) exhaustiveness and (ii) mutual exclusiveness. As far as possible,

137

a given type should include all possible relevant characteristics that are associated, in a single classification (exhaustiveness). In addition, the different types that comprise the typology should, as far as possible, be mutually exclusive — any overlap between categories ought to be eliminated through a process of further refinement.

In his detailed discussion on the construction of typologies McKinney (in Doby et. al., 1954) summarizes it in the following manner:

(1) *The constructed type is not a homogeneous universe as that concept is ordinarily understood. The type certainly has classificatory significance but it cannot be equated with "class" because it has a configurational significance totally lacking in the "class" as homogeneous universe.*

(2) *The constructed type does not refer to the most common form of a phenomenon, but to the most significantly representative form. For instance, it makes sense to talk about the "economic man" despite the fact that it is doubtful that the "rationality" imputed to him is the most common form of economic behavior.*

(3) *The constructed type is not a stereotype in that the stereotype often lacks an empirical referent, and is an unplanned, affectual exaggeration that is not empirically "useful" because of a lack of explicit criteria that make it comparable to concrete cases* (1954: 147).

Typologies fulfil different functions in different types of research. As Joubert indicated in his article (Appendix 2), the construction of a typology of value orientations was regarded as the first step in a process that would ultimately culminate in the systematic collection of data. Typologies, as is the case with all conceptual frameworks, therefore serve as a frame of reference for observation and data collection. This function involves not only that the data collection process is guided by it, but also that the eventual data analysis procedure is facilitated. As far as the latter is concerned, it offers a framework for analysis because possible commonalities between phenomena have already been systematized in the typology. Typologies can also serve a limited heuristic function when they result in the formulation of new hypotheses. The model is, however, the primary conceptual framework that has a heuristic function.

Models

The term *model* is probably one of the most ambiguous in the vocabulary of the social scientist. A variety of factors have led to the situation where model and theory are frequently used as synonyms. The discussions in the literature of the philosophy of science about the differences between models in the physical and social sciences have unfortunately merely confused the issue.

It is generally accepted that theories and models bear a number of important similarities (compare Achinstein, 1968, and Gorrell, 1981). Both these authors

138

maintain that the differences between models and theories are largely differences of degree. Although it is not always essential that a rigid distinction be drawn between model and theory, the differences between these two constructs will be emphasized here.

In the process we shall argue that the **heuristic** function is the most common characteristic of models, while the explanatory function is usually attributed to theories.

The fundamental relationship between model and analogy is discussed by Giere:

The use of models in science can be described in general terms as follows. There is a type of system, such as atoms, about which not much is known. However, there are other systems such as solar systems, about which a lot is known. In 1900 there were already good theories of solar systems (e.g. Newton's). Someone then suggests that maybe the unknown type of system is like the known one in certain important respects. This in turn suggests questions that one should ask about the unknown system: How fast are the electrons moving around their orbits? Are the orbits circular or elliptical? and so on. The model also suggests ways of answering the questions ... So it is clear that models as the basis of analogies do play an important role in scientific research — that is, in the creation of new theories (1979: 79).

In this case an established theory of the planetary system was used as the source for the construction of a model of the relatively unknown phenomenon of atoms. We encounter the same situation in the social sciences where models of political dynamics (Easton's systems theory model), or models of problem solving (Popper's evolutionary theory) have their origin in the biological sciences. This analogical relationship does not, however, only exist between the better-known and the less well-known (the new) model, but also between the model and the real-life phenomena of which it is the model. As Kaplan (1964: 265) indicated, this has led to models also being known as *scientific metaphors*. By investigating a specific phenomenon, the researcher reveals certain similarities or relationships, and systematizes these (in a simplified form) as a model of that phenomenon. One could claim that the model is an 'as if framework' in which a model of X would claim that X is structured in the manner suggested by the model. We can illustrate this *as if character* of models very clearly by means of one of the well-known models in the field of communication science, i.e. Shannon and Weaver's (1948) model of the communication process.

In this model certain aspects of the communication process are highlighted, namely information and the accuracy of information transfer. One of the impediments to reliable communication is *noise*, that is, undesirable signals that have a negative influence on reliability.

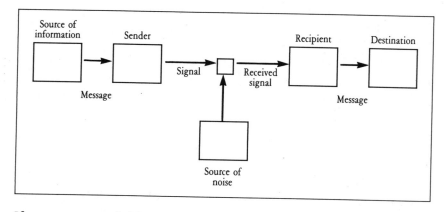

If we were to regard this model as typical, it is possible to indicate the differences that exist between it and typologies on the one hand, and theories on the other. As we have indicated, a typology is a conceptual framework in which phenomena are classified in terms of constructs or ideal types. A typology, therefore, presents no more than a static image or a cross section of a specific class of events. In a model, on the other hand, an attempt is made to represent the dynamic aspects of the phenomenon by illustrating the relationships between the major elements of that phenomenon in a simplified form. In Shannon and Weaver's model it is not merely a matter of identifying the major elements of the communication process (sender, message, recipient, noise and so on) but an attempt is also made to specify the relationships between the source of information, the sender, the recipient and the destination. In the following discussion, we shall indicate that a theory goes one step further by also suggesting an explanation of the systemic relationships between the phenomena.

The key issue to bear in mind when either studying or using models, is that they do not pretend to be more than a partial representation of a given phenomenon. As Kaplan quite justifiably indicates: *the model is a particular mode of representation, so that not all its features correspond to some characteristic of its subject matter* (1964: 284). A model merely agrees in broad outline with the phenomenon of which it is a model. Certain characteristics of the phenomenon, irrelevant for the model, are conveniently excluded, while the most obvious aspects are emphasized. The value of this simplification is that it draws the attention of the researcher to specific themes. In Shannon and Weaver's model the issue of the accurate transfer of a message and the role of noise in this process are emphasized. It is this guiding function of models that is referred to as the heuristic function (literally *heuristic* means to discover or to reveal). The model is, therefore, used to suggest new areas of research because certain relationships and dimensions are emphasized to an unusual degree.

We can conclude with Gorrell's summary of the different characteristics of models. Gorrell, incidentally, consistently uses the term *precursive theoretical models*. The reason for employing this terminology is that Gorrell wishes to indicate that most models in the social sciences (in contradistinction to those in the physical sciences) are characteristically precursors to subsequent theories. The term *theoretical* serves merely to distinguish the model from physical or scale models. He emphasizes four characteristics of precursive theoretical models:

(1) Models identify central problems or questions concerning the phenomenon that ought to be investigated.
(2) Models limit, isolate, simplify, and systematize the domain that is investigated.
(3) Models provide a new language game or universe of discourse within which the phenomenon may be discussed.
(4) Models provide explanation sketches and the means for making predictions.

As far as (1) is concerned, Gorrell (1981: 130 *et seq.*) refers to Harre's discussion of this issue: *According to Harre, there are four types of questions that a precursive theoretical model might generate.* They are:

1. *Existential questions: "Are there elementary information procedures?" The attempt to answer these questions generates directions for experimental procedures.*
2. *Descriptive questions about the hypothetical mechanism: "Is human thinking composed of elementary information processes?"*
3. *Causal questions: "Is hysteria caused by repressed experience?" The power of a hypothetical mechanism to produce the phenomenon is queried.*
4. *Questions about modal transformations: "Is a slip of the tongue really an admission of guilt?"* (Harre, 1970: 55).

In summary, this function is part of the heuristic properties of precursive theoretical models since the model provides questions, pointers and directions for inquiry which might, if pursued, lead to a better understanding of the domain under investigation.

As far as the second characteristic of precursive theoretical models is concerned, Gorrell (1981: 132) maintains that: *The precursive theoretical model generally simplifies and systematizes the domain under investigation by virtue of positing certain assumptions about the structural, causative or functional nature of the modellandum, reference to which is intended to remove some puzzles or explain something about it. The simplifying and systematizing power derives, in short, from the quasi-theoretical structure of the model and the attribution of certain properties and relationships to aspects of the modellandum which are deemed significant in understanding the nature and behavior of the modellandum.*

In the third place, models provide new definitions of scientific concepts.

The precursive theoretical model generally provides a universe of discourse or way of talking about certain structural and behavioral aspects of the object or phenomena under investigation. It does so by introducing new terms (e.g. "schizophrenic", "extrovert", "id") and implicitly or explicitly specifying their meanings. It also does so by using terms of ordinary language or well-established and familiar theoretical language (from other fields) in slightly new or different ways in describing the modellandum (Gorrell, 1981: 132). Gorrell refers to this as the meaning-constitutive function of models.

The fourth function of models is to provide explanatory sketches of a phenomenon. Although Gorrell uses the term *explanatory* sketch to indicate that models do not, as yet, provide complete explanations of phenomena, it is our opinion that the boundary between model and theory becomes far too tenuous if this distinction were to be entertained. In terms of our distinctions at the beginning of this section, the explanatory function is usually associated with theories. It is obviously the case that the model, by suggesting relationships between variables, does explain the order or pattern of that phenomenon in a superficial manner. The mere fact that a given phenomenon is brought into a set of relationships with other phenomena by means of that model, does, to some extent, explain the phenomenon. As we shall indicate in the next section, however, theories constitute more comprehensive levels of explanation.

Theories

A well-known definition of a theory is that offered by Kerlinger: *A theory is a set of interrelated constructs (concepts), definitions, and propositions that present a systematic view of phenomena by specifying relations between variables, with the purpose of explaining and predicting the phenomena* (1973: 9).

In this definition the specific characteristics of a typology (*set of interrelated constructs*) and a model (*specifying relations between variables*) may be recognized. In addition to the classifying and heuristic functions of typologies and models, theories may be distinguished on the basis of the fact that they are also aimed at explaining and predicting phenomena or events.

Different views of scientific explanation are encountered in the literature on the philosophy of science: Hempel's deductive-nomological model, Salmon's statistically-relevant model, Dray and Von Wright's rational model, and the more recent realistic models of explanation (see Bhaskar, Keat & Urry). For our purposes it will be sufficient to emphasize the following:

(1) An explanation is usually an answer to a why question, or, stated differently, a phenomenon is explained when one indicates why it has occurred. This implies that explanations are always explanations in terms of causes

or in terms of reasons (compare our discussion on causality in Chapter 2).

(2) Causal explanations or rational explanations (in terms of reasons or motives or aims) can be either universal or contextual. In the first case the explanation occurs in terms of some *physical law* or *generalization*. In the second case the phenomenon is explained in terms of the specific contextual factors that obtain. An example of the first is Smelser's theory of collective behaviour (chapter 5) in which a universal relationship is postulated between certain determinants and collective behaviour. According to this theory, the presence of the specific determinants (provided they occur at a given intensity) will generally result in the occurrence of uninstitutionalized collective behaviour. Examples of more contextual explanations are usually to be found in qualitative studies where the aim is to explain a given phenomenon of human behaviour in terms of the distinguishing, and even unique, circumstances associated with a single case or with a small number of cases.

(3) To a greater or lesser extent scientific explanation entails that a given (observable) phenomenon or event is associated with an inferred or underlying mechanism or structure. In the Reiger Park riots the observable collective behaviour is also explained as the specific consequence of underlying structures or mechanisms (for example structural strain, generalized beliefs). This characteristic of scientific theories, which is emphasized in realistic perspectives of explanation, is indubitably one of the most noticeable characteristics of theories. Irrespective of whether the theory offers an explanation which may be generalized or whether it applies to individual behaviour only, some underlying mechanism or construct will inevitably form the basis of such an explanation. An example of the first type is to be found in Weber's well-known explanation of the rise of modern capitalism in terms of what he referred to as the Protestant *ethic*. An example of the second is Freud's explanation of the hallucinations and visions of psychotic patients in terms of the so-called *primary process* — a process of the id in terms of which an individual will attempt to alleviate tension by construing an image of an object that will reduce the tension.

(4) Because theories explain phenomena by identifying specific causes of the phenomena, the relationship between the theory (an explanation) and the phenomenon or phenomena that it explains (the so-called explanandum) is much more specific than the relationship between a model and the phenomenon to which the model relates. Since a model is deliberately used to simplify and abstract, it is typified as an 'as if framework'. A theory, on the other hand, postulates real relationships between real phenomena or variables and, for this reason, it must be empirically testable. Where the criterion of a good model is situated in its heuristic potential (rather than its accuracy), the criterion of a good theory is associated

with its ability to explain: the ability to explain actual relationships between phenomena. Obviously, in theories we are concerned with high levels of abstraction: this is one of the consequences of using constructs as principles of explanation. It is, nonetheless, essential that the constructs which are employed are sufficiently explicated, and eventually operationalized, so that it becomes possible to deduce testable hypotheses that may either be supported or rejected on the basis of empirical data. A good example of this characteristic of theories is reflected in the discussion of the theory of alienation in Chapter 3. In that section we indicated how the theory of Seeman, which includes a range of theoretical constructs such as meaninglessness, isolation, normlessness, and so on, was made measurable through the process of operationalization.

The most important characteristics of typologies, models, and theories, and the relationship between them, are summarized in the following diagram.

	TYPOLOGY	MODEL	THEORY
Function(s) (with distinguishing functions in bold)	**classifying categorizing**	classifying categorizing	classifying categorizing
		heuristic discovering	heuristic discovering
			explanatory

PARADIGMS

Thus far, we have discussed the most important constructs of the research process, namely concepts, statements, and conceptual frameworks. Throughout our discussion we have concentrated on the so-called propositional elements of the system of scientific knowledge, i.e. scientific statements in one form or another. As we emphasized in Chapter 1, certain recent developments in the philosophy and sociology of science have led to a re-emphasis of the sociological dimension of research. Apart from the purely propositional elements (from statements to theories) of science, and the decision-making stages (from formulating the problem to interpretation) involved in the generation of these constructs, there is another important element of the practice of science that requires attention. In the first chapter of this book we briefly referred to the sociological dimension of science. Here we shall focus on the paradigm concept as the clearest manifestation of the social nature of science.

In the modern sense of the term, the origin of paradigm is to be fund in Thomas Kuhn's 1962 book called The structure of scientific revolutions. The concept is best understood against the background of the problem that Kuhn addresses, namely the nature of growth and development in the sciences — especially the physical sciences. According to Kuhn, the history of the physical sciences displays a clearly discernible pattern of periods of so-called normal science followed by scientific revolutions; these are, in turn, followed by a period of normal science, and so on.

Normal science

Kuhn maintains that, if we look at the history of the physical sciences, it is always possible to identify the theories or theoretical systems that can be regarded as the origin of a given science. In this manner Ptolemaios' theory of astronomy, the Aristotelian theory of motion, Lyell's geological theory, Franklin's theory of electricity, Newton's theory of optics, Stahl's phlogiston theory, and Darwin's theory of evolution, represent the origins of various disciplines. In the periods preceding the general acceptance of such a theory, we almost invariably find that there were a number of competing theories or points of view. These periods are characterized by an absence of unanimity regarding which of the competing theories ought to be accepted as the correct one. In the field of optics, for example, before Newton's work in the latter part of the seventeenth century, there were proponents of the theories of Aristotle, Epicurus, and Descartes who all claimed that their theory was able to explain the fundamental nature of light.

When, however, a specific theory is developed at a given stage which appears able to offer satisfactory solutions to real empirical problems we have, according to Kuhn's usage, entered the phase of normal science. While the pre-paradigmatic phase is characterized by lengthy debates that tend to be rather methaphysical or sphilosophical in nature, i.e. questions concerning the real nature of the phenomena that are studied in a given discipline, we find that once the period of normal science has been entered, these fundamental questions are set aside, and specific theoretical or empirical issues are tackled. Normal science is, therefore, research that is based upon certain scientific achievements, achievements that are acknowledged and accepted by a given scientific community as the basis for further research. Kuhn refers to these achievements as paradigms. *By choosing (paradigms), I mean to suggest that some accepted examples of actual scientific practice — examples which include law, theory, application and instrumentation together — provide models from which spring particular coherent traditions of scientific research* (1970: 10).

Normal science may, therefore, be defined as the practice of scientific research within, and from, the frame of reference supplied by a dominant paradigm, i.e. from a collection of mutually accepted achievements (theories, exemplary solutions, predictions, laws, and so on). In this sense, a paradigm is primarily a model for conducting normal research. We shall now turn our attention to (1) the different components of a paradigm, and (2) to its most important functions.

COMPONENTS OF PARADIGMS

If we were to analyze various traditions in the history of science, for example Newtonian mechanics, Darwinian biology, and so on, we would, according to Kuhn, find that the researchers in those periods made a variety of commitments to components of the paradigm concerned.

(i)   In the first place, the scientists commit themselves to a specific theory or law, or to a set of theories or laws. *The most obvious and probably the most binding (commitment) is exemplified by the sorts of generalizations we have just noted. These are explicit statements of scientific law and about scientific concepts and theories. While they continue to be honored, such statements help to set puzzles and to limit acceptable solutions* (1970: 40). The specific theory (or theories) undoubtedly forms the core of a paradigm — as Newton's law of gravity and the three laws of movement constitute the core of the Newtonian paradigm.

(ii) In the second place, the researcher espouses a given methodology or set of research techniques that are dictated by the paradigm. *At a level lower or more concrete than that of laws and theories, there is, for example, a multitude of commitments to preferred types of instrumentation and to the ways in which accepted instruments may legitimately be employed* (1970: 40). In this context, Kuhn refers to the varying role of experimental methods in the history of physiology.

(iii) In the third place, scientists commit themselves to particular metaphysical assumptions and preconceptions. In this context, Kuhn refers both to the assumptions concerning the research object (that which ought to be studied), and to the assumptions concerning the manner in which it ought to be researched (criteria for an acceptable view of science). These assumptions obviously overlap with (ii) because they contain certain methodological implications. *The nest of commitments proved to be both metaphysical and methodological. As metaphysical, it told scientists what sort of entities the universe did and did not contain: there was only shaped matter in motion* (Cartesian ontology — JM). *As methodological, it told them what ultimate laws and fundamental explanations must be like: laws must specify corpuscular motion and interaction, and explanation must reduce any given natural phenomenon to corpuscular action under these laws. More important still, the corpuscular conception of the universe told scientists what many of their research problems should be* (1970: 41).

146

(iv) In conclusion, there are certain assumptions that the scientist makes as a scientist. *Finally, at a still higher level, there is another set of commitments without which no man is a scientist. The scientist must, for example, be concerned to understand the world and to extend the precision and scope with which it has been ordered. That commitment must, in turn, lead him to scrutinize ... some aspect of nature in great empirical detail* (1970: 41).

Kuhn talks about the network of commitments of each researcher, and calls them *conceptual, theoretical, instrumental* and *methodological* commitments. In summary, it would be possible to classify them into three major categories:

- theoretical-conceptual commitments: commitments to the accuracy or truth of the theories and laws of the particular paradigm;
- methodological-technical commitments: commitments to the criteria regarded as scientific and of the methods and instrumentation by means of which a given view of what is scientifically valid may be realised;
- ontological commitments: assumptions concerning the nature of the research object.

FUNCTIONS OF PARADIGMS

In this section we pay attention to the dynamics of normal science or, stated differently, to the manner in which the acceptance of a paradigm enables the research community to conduct normal research.

A group of scientists commit themselves to a particular paradigm, because they regard that paradigm, in comparison with other competing paradigms, as the most promising. According to Kuhn, it is for this reason that normal science has to be regarded as an actualization of that promise — *an actualization achieved by extending the knowledge of those facts that the paradigm displays as particularly revealing, by increasing the extent of the match between those facts and the paradigm's predictions, and by further articulation of the paradigm itself* (1970: 24). In an important sense, normal science may be viewed as a mopping-up operation. This mopping-up operation consists primarily of three functions, and all these functions may be defined in terms of a major problem-solving task:

(1) Establishing appropriate facts;
(2) Matching facts and theory;
(3) Articulation of the theory.

As far as (1) is concerned, it should be noted that a fruitful paradigm provides clues concerning which empirical and theoretical problems are appropriate and relevant for further problem-solving activities. The paradigm, therefore, serves a selection function because it is used to identify relevant problems. As far as (2) is concerned, during normal science, researchers tend to conduct

147

that type of research in which the predictions made under the theory can be verified by the facts. The major task is that of solving problems relating to matching theory and facts. Concerning (3), a good deal of time and attention is spent in the articulation and further refinement (definition, conceptualization, and so on) of the theory, or theories, of the paradigm.

The fundamental aim during normal science is to solve problems. *Bringing a normal research problem to a conclusion is achieving the anticipated in a new way, and it requires the solution of all kinds of complex instrumental, conceptual and mathematical puzzles. The man who succeeds proves himself an expert puzzle-solver, and the challenge of the puzzle is an important part of what usually drives him on* (Kuhn, 1970: 36).

It was Kuhn himself who referred to the analogy between normal science and building a jigsaw puzzle or filling in a crossword puzzle. Further explication of this analogy explains what Kuhn had in mind, and it also illustrates the *relationship* between the paradigm, as an embracing framework, and normal science. In the same manner as the person who is doing a crossword puzzle is constrained by the existing structure (the number of squares), the paradigm, to all intents and purposes, defines the problem area for the researcher — what he or she should research, and also how it ought to be done. A good and fruitful paradigm will, however, literally provide clues (as in a crossword puzzle) concerning possible solutions in the form of model solutions, theoretical predictions, and so on. Finally, the paradigm also determines — as contained in the ontological, theoretical, and methodological commitments — what would be regarded as valid solutions. As the crossword puzzle determines the parameters of the solution — not more than five letters across and four letters down — the paradigm determines what may be regarded as acceptable solutions and what may not.

In previous studies of the history of science, a good deal of emphasis has been placed on those *sparks of genius* that have led to scientific discoveries or on those *flashes of insight* into some theoretical problem. Kuhn, however, emphasizes a far more pedestrian aspect of research, namely the long process of trial and error that is involved in the search for solutions. Of course, this does not imply that the researcher is unmotivated. *What then challenges him is the conviction that, if only he is skilful enough, he will succeed in solving a puzzle that no one before has solved or solved as well* (1970: 38).

In conclusion one may state that normal science is a highly successful and highly cumulative enterprise. During normal science, the researcher does not strive to discover new theories. The researcher's task is rather to solve those problems that have already been identified as well as he or she can, and to match the existing theory with the facts as closely as possible by further refinement and articulation of that theory. In spite of all this, we all know about noteworthy discoveries in the history of virtually every discipline which resulted in the whole history of that discipline being changed. Kuhn pays attention to these radical renewals and discontinuities in history when he deals with scientific revolutions.

Scientific revolutions

A radical break in the normal course of research has its origins in a growing awareness of the existence of a contradiction or an anomaly, i.e. *with the recognition that nature has somehow violated the paradigm-induced expectations that govern normal science.* When new empirical facts are discovered that are not predicted by the paradigm, or that are entirely unexpected in terms of paradigmatic expectations, we are confronted by an anomaly. Not until the paradigm has been adapted to such an extent that the new fact may be accommodated, and the unexpected becomes the expected, does the anomaly disappear. Becoming aware of the existence of an anomaly does, therefore, not necessarily lead to the rejection of a paradigm. Normal research is specifically a process of continuous problem solving. The question is therefore: What distinguishes an anomaly from the normal type of problem with which a researcher is confronted every day? Kuhn's answer is: When the paradigm cannot be adapted to accommodate the particular problem, we are probably faced with an anomaly. The same would obviously apply to the situation where theoretical problems are generated that cannot be accommodated by the paradigm.

When, therefore, the research community is confronted by (1) insoluble empirical and theoretical problems, and (2) these problems affect the core of the community's commitments to the existing paradigm, then, according to Kuhn's view, we are faced with a crisis within that discipline. In the short term, the crisis situation is usually dealt with by means of a variety of *ad hoc* measures, but in the long run, a crisis invariably results in the rejection of the inadequate paradigm. This step, which is known as the scientific revolution, can, however, only take place if an alternative paradigm is available. Once an alternative of this nature is available, parts of the research community will reject the existing paradigm in favour of the new one, until the stage is reached where the majority support the new one. Once this stage has been attained, we have once again entered a phase of normal science. The whole process may be represented in the following manner:

Problems $\rightarrow$ anomalies $\rightarrow$ crisis $\rightarrow$ revolution $\rightarrow$ normal science

↑ alternative ↑

Scientific revolutions may be defined as those discontinuities or non-cumulative episodes in the history of a discipline in which an existing and inadequate paradigm is replaced by a new one. Examples of this are to be found in the rejection of the Ptolemaic system in favour of the Copernican system, the Aristotelian theory of movement in favour of Galileo's paradigm, and subsequently that of Newton, and Stahl's phlogiston paradigm in favour of the new paradigm of Lavoisier and Priestly.

Paradigms in the social sciences

Kuhn's use of the term *paradigm*, and the supporting theory of paradigms has had a major impact on the philosophy and methodology of the social sciences. Following Kuhn's historical analysis of the physical sciences, a veritable flood of studies in which similar meta-analyses of the social sciences were undertaken, appeared in the 1970s. Typically, the following questions were addressed: Where are the boundaries between paradigms? Which paradigm is currently the dominant one in a given discipline?

Quite often the conclusion was reached that a given discipline accommodated a variety of competing paradigms. In this manner one would find structural-functionalism, symbolic interactionism, ethnomethodology, systems theory, Marxism, Neo-Marxism, and so on in sociology. In psychology one would, for example, be able to identify psycho-analytic, systems theoretical, behaviouristic, and phenomenological paradigms. In a similar manner it would be possible to quote a variety of examples from each discipline (see also Suggestions for further reading).

A typical strategy in publications in which the aim is the identification and discussion of paradigms in the social sciences, is to compare the natural and social sciences using Kuhn's theory of paradigms as a point of departure. Almost inevitably, the conclusion is then reached that the social sciences are still in a pre-paradigmatic phase of development because of the fact that there is no discipline in which there is a single dominant paradigm. The conclusion is reached that all these disciplines remain at a phase of relative immaturity. As far as we are concerned, this strategy is unacceptable because the concept paradigm is used out of context. Kuhn attaches the concept very strongly to the function of problem solving: a function that has a clear and specific meaning in the natural sciences. Even a fairly superficial study of the *traditions* and *schools* in the social sciences would readily indicate that *problem solving* is not as central an epistemic goal in the social sciences as it is in the natural sciences. Goals such as an in-depth understanding, explanation, analysis, and interpretation are more common. It is, therefore, quite obvious that the social sciences will not compare favourably with the natural sciences as long as a typically natural science standard is used as yardstick for such comparisons. For this reason, it is only acceptable to use the concept *paradigm* in a more metaphorical sense when it is applied to the social sciences than one would do in the case of natural sciences.

The model of the practice of the social sciences in Chapter 1 is, as we indicated at that stage, an attempt to make some of the components of Kuhn's paradigm concept (as well as some of the other aspects of his paradigm theory) applicable to the social sciences.

RESUMÉ

The aim of this chapter was to present a cross-sectional account of the research process. Where we paid attention to the different decision-making phases of the research process in Chapters 2 to 5, in this chapter we moved our focus to those typical *structures* or constructs that (1) guide the decision making, and (2) which are themselves produced, developed and refined, in the research process.

Social science is intrinsically a process in which researchers give meaning to the reality in which they find themselves. They systematize, classify, categorize, simplify, abstract and conceptualize, with the aim of gaining a clearer conception of, and insight into, social reality. In the process of giving meaning to experiences and observations, social scientists create the typical constructs of social science — those constructs that we have discussed in this chapter.

Suggestions for further reading

1. Although a relatively old source, McKinney's chapter in Doby *et. al.* (1954) remains one of the best discussions on the construction of typologies. That chapter also has an extensive reference list. A more recent discussion may be found in Rudner (1966).

2. There is no doubt that Gorrell's (1981) discussion of *model* in the social sciences is the best available. Botha (1984) also presents a broad overview of the general literature in this field.

3. The orthodox positivistic point of view relating to theories is thoroughly discussed in Feigl (1970), Hempel (1965), and Rudner (1966). For a more recent post-positivistic interpretation, one may consult Nicholson (1983), and Keat and Urry (1975).

4. Kuhn's paradigm concept is thoroughly discussed in Masterman (1970). For general introductions to Kuhn's point of view, you may consult Chalmers (1982), Koningsveld (1980), Newton-Smith (1981), and Suppe (1974). The best overview of Kuhn's impact on the social sciences is to be found in Gutting (1980).

Introduction

The spectrum of the social sciences

Terminology

Science and research

    A research model
        Concepts
        Hypotheses
        Observation

    A comparison between qualitative and quantitative approaches
        Concepts
        Hypotheses
        Observation

Example

    Confidentially speaking ...
        Example A
        Example B
            Concepts
            Hypotheses
            Observation

Implications

    Width
    Height
    Depth

Conclusion

Suggestions for further reading

CHAPTER 7

PERSPECTIVES ON QUALITATIVE AND QUANTITATIVE RESEARCH

INTRODUCTION

Of the many characteristics which people have attributed to the scientist, a critical and inquisitive attitude is probably the most noticeable. The scientist refuses to accept things at face value — at least in his or her own field of specialization. It has been said while art is characterized by the suspension of disbelief, science is characterized by the suspension of belief (belief in this case implying a blind acceptance without any argument). This implies that the scientist will also adopt a critical and evaluative stance with regard to his or her own approaches and methods of work. It would, therefore, also necessarily follow that in the social sciences, where the boundaries are less clearly drawn (for example between them and the arts), where an unusually wide and diverse spectrum of activities is included (ranging, for example, from philosophy at the one extreme to psycho-physiology at the other) one is likely to encounter a continuous debate on the nature and essence of research.

This debate is frequently characterized by a cyclic pattern in which issues that were heatedly debated at some time in the past, and which are left more or less on their own for a period of time, may once again become the focus of attention, resulting in further debate, analysis, and speculation. Some of the types of disputes and questions that frequently figure in discussions on research methodology in the social sciences are:

- Is it possible to *measure* social phenomena?

153

- How do scientist study *underlying* dynamic social *processes?*
- How *scientific* (and also *objective*) is research in which it is not possible to build in adequate inter-subjective controls?
- How is it possible simultaneously to regard both History and, for example, Social Demography as sciences?
- Is Theology a science?

Questions like these and variations on them tend to appear at regular intervals wherever the status of the social sciences is considered. As a matter of fact, some of these questions are to be found in the original publications of the sociologist Comte and the psychologist Wundt — two of the fathers of the social sciences. Recently there has been a strong tendency for these questions to emerge once again.

In a sense the questions that we listed above have in common the fact that they all relate to the relative merit of qualitative and quantitative approaches in social scientific research. Such questions are of considerable importance because they compel the scientist to reflect on the nature and essence of research and science; and in the social sciences these issues are of paramount importance.

THE SPECTRUM OF THE SOCIAL SCIENCES

The question of the value of either qualitative or quantitative approaches to research in the social sciences has led to a debate which is unique to the social sciences because they are characterized by a considerable spectrum of divergent, and frequently conflicting, approaches. In this regard, we need merely refer to two sets of examples:

Example 1: Dreams as psychic events or phenomena could be studied by psycho-analytically oriented researchers who would analyze the symbolic content of the dreams as repressed material. At the other extreme, the same phenomena could be studied by a group of psychologists who would investigate the wave patterns of cortical electric activity by means of EEG apparatus. These two approaches are clearly distinct.

Example 2: A contemporary historian might analyze a political speech holistically within the context in which it was delivered. A communication psychologist, using the same speech, might, on the other hand, conduct a detailed analysis of eye movements, hand movements, and tone of voice for each predetermined time unit of the speech, while a specialist in linguistics might display a greater interest in the syntax or in the audience's comprehension of key terms. The interesting issue is that the three scientists are all interested in the meaning and impact of this speech.

These, and similar examples, lead to the question of whether all these approaches to the same object can be regarded as (scientifically) justifiable and tolerable. Stated differently, are we really dealing with scientific research in these examples?

This question is the subject of the present chapter. We shall deal with a number of perspectives relating to qualitative and quantitative research. Our point of departure will consistently be that science is a relatively open system which must necessarily comply with the systemic characteristic of equifinality — the idea, that the same goal may be attained through different methods. We first pay attention to terminological problems. We then present a general definition of research and the characteristics of research that may be derived from this description. This leads to a brief description of a research model which is used as frame of reference for this chapter. Following this, qualitative and quantitative approaches are compared with one another within the framework of this model, and a few examples are discussed in greater detail. In conclusion we refer to certain implications of the preceding discussion.

TERMINOLOGY

Although the terms *qualitative* and *quantitative* are fairly commonly used, there is a good deal of confusion about the exact meaning of these terms. One therefore finds that some authors are likely to classify all research that does not contain statistics as qualitative, while others may be more inclined to specify that research in which specific methodologies or approaches such as hermeneutics, ethnomethodology and phenomenology are used must be regarded as qualitative and, at the same time, that approaches such as positivism are quantitative by definition. The question which arises is, however, whether the terms *more* and *less* are not in essence quantitative terms when one bears in mind that the notion of ranking, as in *more* and *less*, is an integral part of the number system that we use. From this it would follow that one does not necessarily have to use numbers to have a quantitative approach. Another difficulty that complicates the identification of qualitative and quantitative approaches is the point of view that research is a process that consists of various stages or phases, and that each phase is characterized by a different type of approach. Do dyed-in-the-wool empiricists not become qualitative when, in the interpretation of their research findings, they extrapolate beyond the direct statistical analyses and data? This situation is further complicated by the fact that researchers who have not had any training in statistics sometimes behave in what may be described as a reactionary manner by condemning anything that contains any statistics whatsoever.

For the purposes of this analysis the *quantitative approach* may be described in general terms as that approach to research in the social sciences that is more highly formalized as well as more explicitly controlled, with a range that is more exactly defined, and which, in terms of the methods used, is relatively close to the physical sciences. In contradistinction, *qualitative approaches* are those approaches in which the procedures are not as strictly formalized, while the scope is more likely to be undefined, and a more philosophical mode of operation is adopted.

SCIENCE AND RESEARCH

It would be possible to become embroiled in virtually endless arguments about the relative merits of either including or excluding certain elements in various definitions of science and research. As many of these issues have been addressed in other sections of this book, we shall simply present the following definitions which are in agreement with definitions that have been discussed elsewhere.

What is science?

Science may be defined as that system of concepts, theories, findings, and methods that is accepted by a number of scientists. (Compare the preceding chapters).

What is research?

In keeping with the definition that was presented in chapter 1, research may be defined as a collaborative activity by means of which a given phenomenon in reality is studied in an objective manner, with a view to establishing a valid understanding of that phenomenon.

The manner in which the concepts *science* and *research* were used in the preceding section, indicates that *science* refers to the *system of scientific knowledge*, while *research* refers to the *process by means of which* a system of this nature is established. Research is, therefore, a specific way of conducting an investigation and, in this context, it is interesting that the French word *recherche* refers to both research and the work done by a detective. It is important to note that this definition of research does not specify a *specific* method or group of methods that are regarded as scientific.

Although a definition of social scientific research therefore involves neither a preference for, nor a rejection of, either qualitative nor quantitative approaches, it is possible to distinguish between what is scientific and what is not by applying the criteria that are intrinsically part of the definitions. It is, however, necessary to employ a model of scientific research if we are to provide an overview of the distinctions and similarities between the qualitative and quantitative scientific approaches. We shall present such a model in brief outline in the following paragraphs.

A MODEL OF RESEARCH

The three essential components that are present in all research are *concepts,*

156

hypotheses, and *observation*. (It is of course true that some psychologists maintain that these elements are part and parcel of human behaviour in general). In the previous chapters concepts and constructs were described as the most elementary symbolic constructions by means of which human beings are able to classify and categorize their experiential worlds. In other words, concepts are collective nouns that are used to label units of experience.

In very general terms, hypotheses may be described as suppositions, expectations or statements concerning anticipated results. As we indicated earlier in this book, it is customary to distinguish between different types of hypotheses, but that distinction is not an important element in the present discussion.

In general terms observation may be defined as that form of behaviour by means of which a researcher is able to register information from his or her environment. Clearly, it can assume a variety of forms which may vary from physiological measurements to reporting dreams.

We indicated in Chapter 1 how scientific statements differ from everyday pre-scientific statements. We shall discuss the same theme here, with the difference that we shall indicate that each of these components is situated on a continuum on which varying degrees of the scientific character are represented. In figure 7.1 below, there is a schematic representation of this in terms of concepts, hypotheses, and observation.

FIGURE 7.1

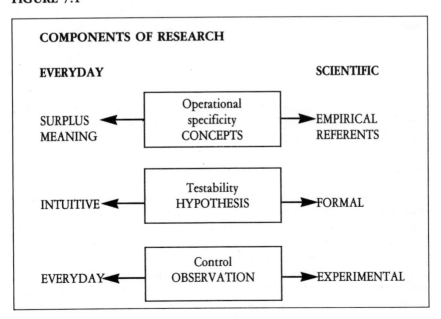

A number of comments will serve to clarify the issues raised in figure 7.1. The figure originally appeared in Marx (1963).

Concepts

The criterion *operational specificity* refers to the extent to which a concept has been explicitly defined so that its meaning becomes unambiguous. In science it is customary to strive towards a situation where the conditions with which a phenomenon has to comply before it is awarded a specific label such as "construct" or "concept" - are explicitly described in advance. In everyday life, however, concepts are usually employed with a variety of meanings. A single example: in everyday life a mother would, at some stage, tell a child lying on her lap that she loves him or her. In all likelihood the child would react by telling the mother that he or she also loves her. One would, nonetheless, know that two different meanings have been conveyed, and that science ought to be able to draw a distinction between the two. Murray, for example, described the first type of love as *nurturance* and the second as *succorance*.

Hypotheses

It is not a unique scientific phenomenon that people have specific suppositions about the manner in which different phenomena are related. One need do no more than analyze one's own shortcomings, read a newspaper, or listen to a political speech to realise how often suppositions, expectations, assumptions, and so on concerning relationships between phenomena are expressed. The distinguishing question here is, however, the extent to which these suppositions, or rather hypotheses, are testable — in other words, the extent to which such an hypothesis may be proven to be either right or wrong. In everyday life and in the arts the testing of such hypotheses occurs in an intuitive manner on the basis of incidental experiences. Obviously, science cannot be allowed to function in such a random manner, and consequently hypotheses in scientific research are formulated in such a manner that they may be submitted to strict testing and, more especially, that they may be rejected on the basis of research findings.

Observation

In our contact with our environment and in the manner in which we register information from the environment, we are dependent upon some form of observation or other. When we have to distinguish between scientific observation and everyday observation, it is necessary to establish the extent to which these observations were made under controlled conditions. In everyday life a person who lives in Johannesburg may reach the conclusion that Pretoria drivers are reckless and poorly disciplined on the basis of a few unfortunate experiences. It is highly unlikely that a member of the public will control

158

such an observation by comparing it with the accident statistics, traffic offences, and so on. In contradistinction to this ad hoc observation, we would find that scientific observations have to be very closely controlled. The best example is to be found in experimental work in which the scientist places a subject under artificial conditions in a laboratory. In science, observation can assume many guises. One approach is to virtually become a member of a group and to use specific criteria and dimensions for recording the day to day existence of traditional communities (participant observation). Another approach is to make use of pre-tested questionnaires to determine the expectations of economists regarding the economic climate of a country.

It is important to note that the three sets of criteria — *operational specificity*, *testability*, and *control* — actually represent three continua. In other words, one cannot refer to an absolute category at the one extreme that can be described as science, with an opposed separate category that would be described as commonplace, the arts, and so on. We are dealing here with differences of degree that can range from the ideal type and the perfectly pure science at the one extreme, to the other extreme that is completely incidental, subjective, and ad hoc. It is for this reason that one can imagine a situation where an article in a newspaper concerning a political event could well be a more meaningful and valid version of the actual events than a scientific political analysis of the same material. In the same manner, it is conceivable that Picasso's rendition of the bombardment of the Spanish civilian population at Guernica during the Spanish Civil War is a more accurate representation of the human disorganization and suffering than a description by a historian or a sociologist could be. Nonetheless, it is possible to indicate the relative degree of compliance with the spirit of science by employing these three criteria.

With the aid of those parts of the different continua that we may describe as more or less scientific, it is possible to identify the most important similarities and differences between qualitative and quantitative approaches to research. In the following paragraphs we shall pay attention to this comparison of the two types of models.

A COMPARISON BETWEEN QUALITATIVE AND QUANTITATIVE APPROACHES

Against the background of our brief discussion of the research model, it is possible to use the same mode of operation to arrive at a comparative analysis of the qualitative and quantitative approaches. In line with the representations in figure 7.1 in which that which is typical of the physical sciences was placed at the extreme right of the three continua, we shall place the more quantitative approach on the right of the continuum in the discussion that follows, while qualitative approaches are placed on the left.

Concepts

In figure 7.2 below, qualitative and quantitative approaches have been characterized in terms of the element referred to as construct or concept. Obviously, it has to be borne in mind that we are not interested in discrete categorizations but rather in different placings on this continuum.

FIGURE 7.2

<table>
<tr>
<td colspan="2" align="center">CONCEPTS
(Operational specificity)</td>
</tr>
<tr>
<td>QUALITATIVE</td>
<td>QUANTITATIVE</td>
</tr>
<tr>
<td>Surplus meaning: in other words, the concept can be interpreted in a number of ways.</td>
<td>Unambiguous meaning: in other words, new words with a unique meaning could even be created.</td>
</tr>
<tr>
<td>Sensitizing concepts; meaningful sketches.</td>
<td>Precisely identified terms.</td>
</tr>
<tr>
<td>Intuitive experience for labelling.</td>
<td>Can be operationalized in terms of measuring instruments.</td>
</tr>
<tr>
<td>Reasonable degree of connotatively rich meaning.</td>
<td>Strives towards complete denotative meanings.</td>
</tr>
</table>

For the qualitative researcher *concepts* and *constructs* are meaningful words that can be analyzed in their own right to gain a greater depth of understanding of a given concept. It is a frequent occurrence that qualitative researchers will conduct an etymological analysis of a concept as part of their description of a phenomenon. Such researchers will then interpret the phenomenon on the basis of the wealth of meaning of the concept. Quantitative researchers, on the other hand, are likely to choose concepts, or even to create words, in such a manner that no more than a single meaning can be attached to the word that they choose. It is also essential that such researchers would have to specify from the outset how they intend making that (abstract) concept *visible*. In other words, they would have to provide an explicit operational definition of the concept. An operational definition is a description of the actions that are required ultimately to measure the concept. A simple example of an operational definition would be to say that disarmament (= concept) is the score that people attain on a Likert scale that measures attitudes to disarmament. In sharp distinction to this, qualitative researchers are more inclined to allow themselves to be led by meaningful sketches or by intuition.

In the preceding discussion we have indicated that the concepts in qualitative studies are frequently likely to be connotatively richer, while those in quantitative studies will be denotatively more specific.

Hypotheses

As we indicated at an earlier stage, hypotheses may be regarded as the guiding elements in research. By means of an hypothesis the researcher indicates what he or she is aiming at. In the case of a theoretically oriented investigation, the hypothesis is likely to be presented in the form of a central thesis — but it does not loose its character of being a brief summary of what the researcher is trying to *prove*. In figure 7.3 we have summarized some of the most noticeable differences in the utilization of hypotheses between qualitatively and quantitatively oriented researchers.

FIGURE 7.3

HYPOTHESES	
QUALITATIVE	QUANTITATIVE
Frequently undeclared or merely stated in the form of a general research goal.	Stated explicitly, at least in the form of a research question.
Emerging from the development of the investigation.	Ought to be formulated beforehand.
Can often not be rejected.	Can be rejected.

As indicated in figure 7.3, quantative researchers are far more concerned with ensuring that the hypotheses have been formulated before the investigation is embarked upon. They will also ensure that the hypotheses are formulated in such a manner that they may be rejected or falsified, and, to a large extent, the whole study revolves around the hypotheses. Researchers in the qualitative mould, on the other hand, tend to be far more vague about what their intentions are and, as a rule, they will provide no more than a general research aim in their introductions. This aim is usually not formulated in such a manner that it is falsifiable. In other cases, the central thesis or hypothesis tends gradually to emerge and it can frequently be described as the result of the investigation.

The matter of the presence or absence of an hypothesis or central thesis is a rather thorny issue. One would, for example, be able to say that an investigation which has as its aim ... *to present an overview of* ... does not really require any further explicit hypotheses. One should, however, bear in mind that it hardly ever occurs that such a comprehensive overview of whatever phenomenon is presented that the researcher cannot be accused of having been selective. In some way or another, the researcher does make choices and one could infer from this that there must be some conjecture or hypothesis that the researcher was trying to confirm. Another difficult issue related to the absence of hypotheses or central theses is associated with ethical issues.

A research report is usually a logically integrated unit that was constructed over a period of time and which resulted in certain conclusions. The ethical implications of the case where the researcher formulates an hypothesis or central thesis once the research has been concluded, which is then incorporated at the beginning of the report, are fairly obvious.

As we shall indicate at the end of this chapter, qualitative research tends to deal with highly complex problems. It would, therefore, be unfair to expect that investigations of this nature would include simplistic empirically-based hypotheses. All the same, it would appear that the complexity of investigations of this nature could be accommodated within the structure of a central thesis which would also serve a useful guiding function.

Observation

Observation was described as that process by means of which researchers establish a link between *reality* and their theoretical assumptions. It can assume a large variety of guises, ranging from jotting down subjective experiences to psycho-physiological measurements of certain body functions. The most conspicuous differences between qualitative and quantitative observation are represented in figure 7.4

FIGURE 7.4

OBSERVATION	
QUALITATIVE	QUANTITATIVE
Subjectifying and personally experienced.	*Objectifying*
Researcher involved with events/ phenomena.	Researcher remains aloof.
Spontaneous and fortuitious examples.	Pre-planned observation.
Occurs in a *non*-structured manner.	Observations may even be scalable.
Open to make it possible to record unexpected events.	Usually with inventory previously drawn up; expected observations placed in categories in anticipation.
Contextualizing, i.e. the context taken into account.	Context controlled as far as possible.
Participant observation as example.	Interaction Process Analysis (Bales) as example.

The differences between the ways in which qualitative and quantitative researchers conduct their observations or, stated differently, the manner in which they collect their data, can be reduced to two issues.

In the first place, quantitative researchers are usually characterized by their inclination to impose a system upon a phenomenon — whether this be a set of categories for a content analysis, a structured interview schedule, or response categories in a questionnaire or a psychological test. The researcher attempts to transpose a certain structure onto a phenomenon. Compared with this, the qualitative researcher's point of view is that the phenomenon should "speak for itself" or, stated differently, that the phenomenon as it exists should reveal itself and that the researcher will register it.

Secondly, the qualitative researcher tends to become more involved with the phenomenon, while the quantitative researcher adopts a more distanced stance. At times the qualitative researcher is prepared to be part of that which is being studied. One finds examples of this in participant observation in which, for example, the sociologist or anthropologist lives as part of the group or community that is being studied. A more radical example is to be found in phenomenological investigations in which the researchers undergo psychotherapy or engage in systematic introspection with the aim of subsequently describing and analyzing their experiences — and therefore observations — from within.

In a certain sense, quantitative researchers tend to study a phenomenon as outsiders. They assume that if they were to become part of the process being investigated, they would become too involved in the "object" and, therefore, view the phenomenon from a too egocentric point of view. In rather stark contrast with the activities of the participant observer in the field of qualitative research, the quantitative researcher would rather make use of a structured, *objective*, standardized observation technique such as Bales's Interaction Process Analysis. Frequently the quantitative researcher has some difficulty in accommodating response patterns in his or her system of observation where these were not anticipated. In comparison, the qualitative researcher has the openness to observe forms of behaviour as and when they occur.

In summary, the differences between qualitative and quantitative approaches could be reduced to differences in structuring, control, and scope. Qualitative approaches are relatively more open and broader in the way in which they tackle problems than are quantitative approaches. At the same time it is important to emphasize the parallels and areas of overlap between these two approaches.

EXAMPLES

We shall now, by means of two examples, discuss the differences that are to be found between qualitative and quantitative approaches regarding the same research themes. The examples relate to "looking behaviour", or more appropriately "eye contact". As considerations of space do not allow the complete examples to be accommodated here, we shall have to rely upon summaries of these. In our discussion, we shall merely present an indication of the most important differences between them; the reader can compare the two examples more thoroughly by employing the research model that we outlined earlier.

Confidentially speaking...

This example consists of brief summaries from two different research traditions on the topic of interpersonal perception. Example A is a summary of Sartre's analysis of interpersonal perception derived from a summary originally prepared by Van Leent (1965). According to Van den Berg, this is one of the best phenomenological analyses yet undertaken and it is, therefore, a good example of qualitative research. Example B is a summary of a typical experimental investigation into interpersonal perception, and is typical of the research conducted by well-known empiricists such as Argyle, Exline, and Jaspars.

EXAMPLE A

In this study, Sartre was intensely involved with an attempt to determine the most deep-seated meaning of gazing or glances. To achieve his aim he neither conducted laboratory experiments, nor did he get involved with opinion surveys in his attempts to determine how people experience this phenomenon or for that matter, what the extent of their experience in this regard may have been. He actually set about trying to interpret everyday occurrences and people's largely unconscious experiences at this level. Stated differently, Sartre provided a description of what occurs in real life when an individual is aware of the fact that he or she is being looked at. To attain this end, he makes use of examples of which the following is probably the most striking (our translation of Van Leent's Dutch summary, 1965: 154):

Imagine, he said, that I were peeping through a keyhole. I am entirely an eye, having totally lost myself in what I am able to see in the other room. My consciousness consists entirely of looking, absorbed by the act of looking as ink is absorbed by blotting paper. I have become entirely transcended, myself — my body that is standing in front of the door, my inquisitive inner being — having reached out to the scene which I have "joined". My attitude is nothing less than a connection between a means — the keyhole — and a goal — the scene while my inquisitiveness merely exists in the fact that there is something to be seen behind the door that cannot be missed. At that stage I am not aware of my own existence," or as Sartre would have it, "my being escapes from me although I am in fact, this escaping of my own being": "un pur neant."

Then I suddenly hear a footstep behind me in the passage and feel someone looking at my back. At that moment, the world beyond the keyhole dissolves, while I freeze into a being that is standing bent over next to a door. The gaze of the Other returns me to myself, makes me an object among objects and destroys my transcendence, my subjectivity, my freedom. I am no longer master of the situation, and am ashamed of what I am. Under the gaze of another I am merely what I am — just like an inkwell on a table, I am standing in front of the door, just as a tree is bent by the wind, I am bent in front of a keyhole by my inquisitiveness. Shame in its purest form is not a question of feeling as if one were an unacceptable object, but simply that one is an object, in other words, to recognize oneself in that degraded and frozen being that I am in the eyes of the other.

Sartre then proceeds to discuss the option that the person who has been peeping has. Those individuals who basically have a Devil-may-care attitude may attempt to strike an attitude of "invulnerability" and to look at the other person in such a manner in turn that he is turned into an object, while the one who peeped regains his freedom. The options that exist in such a situation, and for that matter in all situations as far as Sartre is concerned, are that one turns another person into an object or that one runs the risk of being turned into an object oneself.

Sartre's fundamental analysis of interpersonal perception is based on examples similar to the preceding one.

EXAMPLE B

Social psychologists are primarily interested in the nature of relationships between people and, for this reason, it is not at all surprising that a number of investigations concerning eye contact and interpersonal perception have been conducted within this discipline. Eye contact is, after all, one of the basic elements upon which relationships are based. Although there are many variations of the manner in which this phenomenon is investigated in social psychology, the following is rather typical of the approach adopted in a number of experiments: A great deal of care is taken to establish exactly what the subject focuses on during the experiment, usually by means of fairly complicated closed-circuit television or camera arrangements. By making use of some sophisticated technical arrangements, it is possible to determine with an accuracy level of one square millimetre what an eye is focussed on at any given moment during the course of the experimental treatment. In social psychological experiments the distance between two or more people will also be rigidly controlled because it has been established in previous research that physical distance is an important dimension in communication. The angle

*at which people are placed towards one another would also be carefully con-
trolled. Depending upon the exact nature of such an experiment, the instructions will be presented in a standardized form. If the experimenter were
for example, interested in a person's subjective experience of eye contact,
the experiment could be designed to include a subject (actually a collabora-
tor) who has been instructed to stare into the eyes of one of the other subjects during a simulated conversation without the subjects knowing about
the instruction. The duration will be carefully controlled and systematically
varied. At the conclusion of the experimental treatment, the naive subject
will typically be asked to complete a questionnaire in which he or she is required to respond to items relating to issues such as the pleasantness-
unpleasantness, and other related dimensions of the experience. It is also possible that the subject's reactions to the eye contact situation could have been
assessed by means of galvanic skin reaction. Following this the social psychologist will employ statistical analyses in which eye contact, distance, gender,
and so on are included as either treatment or classification variables, and by
these means he or she would arrive at interpretations about the nature of
interpersonal perception.*

*It is, therefore, evident that in laboratory situations of this nature, a great
deal of effort is expended to ensure that the physical circumstances and the
situations to which the subjects are exposed are controlled as carefully as possible, and that attempts to attain high levels of accuracy for actual levels of
eye contact under circumstances that have been carefully and systematically
varied are, to a large extent, the core of the matter.*

Concepts

Even from these brief summaries we are in a position where it is possible to
identify the manner in which concepts were dealt with. Sartre uses the term
le garde which could perhaps, within the context of Sartre's work, best be
translated as *disembodied* gaze. According to this analysis, a disembodied
gaze is not an attribute of the eye, but rather relates more closely to an individual's awareness that he or she is being observed. In this analysis Sartre
is virtually toying with concepts — he bases the meanings with which he en-
dows them upon intuitive experience and thereby creates the opportunity
for a wealth of connotative meanings.

In quantitative studies concepts are less ambiguously defined and used in
a more specific manner. In this case the experimenter is dealing with eye contact. Bear in mind that Sartre chose to ignore the role of the eye as a sense
organ in his analysis. Concepts in quantitative investigations such as that
described, can be operationalized to the extent that it is possible to express
them in terms of the actual number of seconds of actual eye contact as determined by means of relatively complicated camera arrangements.

Hypotheses

In the case of Sartre's study it is difficult to find any trace of explicit hypotheses or theses that were formulated in advance. In the example that we have dealt with, he analyzes and describes the behaviour of human beings; he does not attempt to test specific hypotheses. In contrast, hypotheses, or at the very least, clearly defined goals, are always to be found in empirical investigations of looking behaviour. One such hypothesis, for example, states that excessive eye contact is anxiety provoking.

Observation

To reach his goal, Sartre uses an imaginary example which involves the reader as a participant. What he presents resembles a natural, spontaneous, and chance situation. The quantitative researcher, on the other hand, constructs a situation in which eye contact may be measured by means of pre-structured instruments such as watches, questionnaires, electronic instrumentation, and so on. Nothing is left to chance, and the context within which the observation occurs is strictly controlled.

In conclusion: In addition to the differences in approach between qualitative and quantitative researchers that have been illustrated in the preceding examples, it is also possible to demonstrate yet another typical difference between qualitative and quantitative research by means of the same set of examples. Generally, it may be observed that qualitative research tends to be reported in a more fluid, rich, and redundant style. Research reports of quantitative investigations, on the other hand, tend to be written in a rigorous, parsimonious, and impersonal style. Stated differently, qualitative research reports are often written in a more gripping style. From a linguistic point of view, quantitative reports are probably written in a barren style — if these qualitative remarks may be justified!

IMPLICATIONS

As we indicated earlier, the examples reported above are situated at different positions on the respective continua. There can be no doubt whatsoever that the qualitative investigation can be classified as scientific research. In fact, an investigation such as that by Sartre may justifiably be regarded as one of the milestones in the field of interpersonal perception. Even intuitively — if we were to be a trifle phenomenological — it is clear that such a study cannot possibly be confused with art, as for example in literature, although art forms are frequently employed in investigations such as these as part of the data that is used.

In spite of the fact that both the qualitative and quantitative approaches are regarded as scientific, it is also the case that they operate at different levels.

The different levels can probably best be indicated by using the classification developed by Van Leent. According to Van Leent the "scientific space" consists of three dimensions that he refers to as a breadth dimension, a height dimension, and a depth dimension. For an application of this model see Marais (1979).

Breadth

On the breadth dimension, the social scientist attempts to describe a phenomenon exhaustively. All aspects of the research, such as for example theory and empirical research, are approached on as broad and all-inclusive a basis as possible. Examples of this type of research are to be found in survey research, effect studies in the media, and so forth. Approaches to theory development on this dimension would, for example, include the construction of typologies (compare Appendix 2).

Height

The height dimension is characterized by systematically constructed theory that is derived from an empirical base and is expanded at successive levels of increasing abstraction. In this case the researcher concentrates on a detailed investigation of a single variable and would tend to attempt to explain phenomena in terms of causal relationships. Because *explanation* is the core of the matter here, it is evident that the research design would be some variant of the different experimental designs. While nuisance variables are controlled as stringently as possible, the supposed cause is systematically manipulated so as to determine its effect on the key variables. Usually, but not invariably, one would refer to such studies as laboratory experiments. In the field of theory construction the researcher tends primarily to follow a hypothetico-deductive approach (compare Appendix 3).

Depth

The third dimension is characterized by attempts on the part of the researcher to penetrate to the innermost nature of phenomena. Ultimately, the problem that is examined along this dimension is the very essence of human existence. Here researchers attempt to establish what semiologists refer to as the null-degree of a phenomenon — in other words, its most fundamental aspect. Questionnaires and other pre-structured measuring instruments cannot be used for this purpose. In the final analysis, this activity concerns an attempt to understand the very essence of the phenomenon (compare Appendix 1).

Van Leent identified a number of requirements with which studies on each of the three dimensions have to comply. Unfortunately there is not enough space to deal with these issues in sufficient detail. We have, however, identified them briefly in the diagrammatic representation on Van Leent's classification that appears in figure 7.5.

In this figure we have made a distinction between the dimensions in terms of the quantitative and qualitative approaches. Typically, research conducted along the breadth dimension, as well as that conducted along the height dimension, would require quantitative approaches to research. In terms of research design requirements, the breadth dimension would typically necessitate survey research, while the height dimension would typically require experimental designs. In comparison, any attempt to penetrate to the essence of a phenomenon can only be made by means of qualitative approaches.

One should, however, exercise some caution here, as the preceding discussion was not intended to convey the impression that it is really possible to classify individual research projects exclusively along one of the dimensions. It is probably closer to the truth that the majority of investigations are, to some extent, a mixture of these dimensions. An analysis of the interactions between the dimensions would, however, constitute a major assignment.

One of the major conclusions that we may draw from the preceding discussion, is that research approaches are, to a large extent, determined by the nature of the subject matter and by the research goals. When the goal of an investigation is to provide a representative view of a phenomenon, the most appropriate approach would be a quantitative one. Similarly, if researchers are interested in explaining the causal relationships between phenomena, they would generally have to make use of one of the quantitatively-oriented experimental designs. Should researchers, however, be interested in understanding the essential elements of a phenomenon, they would be forced to employ qualitative methodologies. What is, however, of the utmost importance, is that researchers should adhere to certain conditions and requirements on each of these dimensions if they wish to proceed in a scientifically acceptable manner.

CONCLUSION

At the beginning of this chapter we indicated that social science research is characterized by apparently divergent approaches to research. Anyone who has had more than coincidental contact with the social sciences, is bound to have been struck by the remarkable level of intolerance that exists between the adherents of different research approaches. At times one gains the impression that the validity of one individual's approach can only be substantiated by being able to demonstrate that the approach of another is invalid. The point of view put forward in this chapter is that the phenomena which are investigated in the social sciences are so enmeshed that a single approach can most certainly not succeed in encompassing human beings in their full complexity. It would, therefore, be quite futile to behave as though one approach should be canonized and another excommunicated. By adopting a point of view of convergence and complementarity (possibly inter-paradigmatic overlap) we may eventually be in a position to understand more about human nature and social reality.

FIGURE 7.5

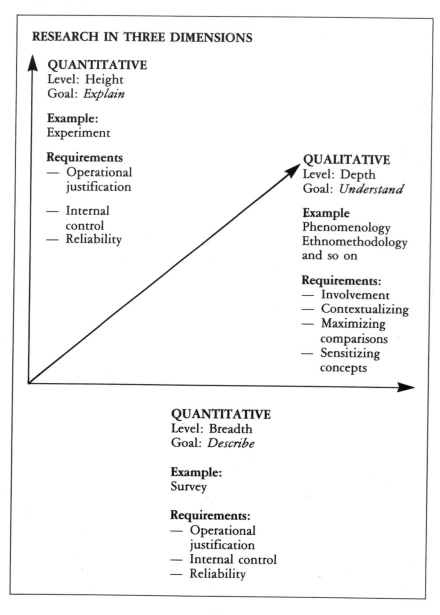

RESEARCH IN THREE DIMENSIONS

QUANTITATIVE
Level: Height
Goal: *Explain*

Example:
Experiment

Requirements
— Operational
   justification
— Internal
   control
— Reliability

QUALITATIVE
Level: Depth
Goal: *Understand*

Example
Phenomenology
Ethnomethodology
and so on

Requirements:
— Involvement
— Contextualizing
— Maximizing
   comparisons
— Sensitizing
   concepts

QUANTITATIVE
Level: Breadth
Goal: *Describe*

Example:
Survey

Requirements:
— Operational
   justification
— Internal control
— Reliability

Suggestions for further reading

1. A similar introductory exposition of these problems is to be found in Mouton (1983a). The foundations of the distinction between qualitative and quantitative research are in the philosophy of science also discussed in Hughes (1980) and Mouton (1984a).

2. Excellent texts on qualitative research are readily available nowadays. Some of the most important are included in the following list: Bogdan and Taylor (1975), Bruyn (1966), Burgess (1982 and 1984), Filstead (1970), Glaser and Strauss (1967), Gorden (1980), Johnson (1975), Lofland (1971), McCall and Simons (1969), Schwartz and Jacobs (1979), and Smith and Manning (1979). A good introduction to the phenomenological approach in psychology is to be found in Kruger (1979).

PART 2

Goals of this chapter

Introductory remarks on how to write a
research proposal

Types of research proposals

Initial preparations

Form and content of research proposals

Characteristics of successful proposals

Examples of extracts from research proposals

Suggestions for further reading

CHAPTER 8

GUIDELINES FOR WRITING A RESEARCH PROPOSAL

GOALS OF THIS CHAPTER

Research proposals or research tenders are such important planning and information documents that we have decided to devote a separate chapter to the issue. We have three goals in mind for this chapter.

In the first instance, we shall present a brief indication of what ought to be included in research proposals — our primary aim here is to provide hints and guidelines on how to write a research proposal.

In the second place, we shall try to foster a critical attitude towards the manner in which research proposals are formulated by making use of three examples — in this case our aim is to increase the reader's sensitivity for certain important requirements with which research proposals have to comply.

In the third instance, we also aim to provide further references by means of which the reader will be able to trace manuals and guides which deal with this topic, as the standards that are set for research proposals that are accepted are constantly becoming more demanding.

INTRODUCTORY REMARKS ON HOW TO WRITE A RESEARCH PROPOSAL

Research proposals are closely tied to the whole issue of planning a research project. It may well be regarded as something that develops naturally from

175

the process of planning a project and, seen from this point of view, it is not all that difficult to write a research proposal. For the researcher who has done a thorough job of planning his or her research, it may virtually appear as if the proposal flows onto the paper without any undue effort on his or her part. That is, however, merely part of the whole issue. Apart from the fact that the research proposal is a planning document in which the researcher indicates what he or she plans to do, and how he or she plans to set about it, the proposal is also, in the majority of cases, a sales document. The proposal is used as a source of information, and serves as the basis upon which decision makers decide whether the project ought to be approved or not and, whether the funds that have been requested are to be granted. It is, therefore, quite clearly of considerable importance that the proposal should convey a favourable impression of the project and of the researcher. It is necessary that the decision makers gain the impression from the proposal that the researcher is a wise planner, and that he or she knows how best to utilize his or her skills, time, and money. It is also necessary that they should believe that the researcher plans to tackle a project that is really worthwhile. If the decision makers are not experts in the field in which the project is to be conducted (and this is quite often the case), the project has to be presented to them in such a manner that they will believe that it is a project that simply has to be approved, and that they would be willing to take this step.

From the preceding, the reader may have gained the impression that there is a specific recipe for writing research proposals. Unfortunately, there is nothing like a prizewinning recipe. There are simply too many kinds of research proposals to make this a viable proposition. Nonetheless, it is possible to make certain preparations to ensure that one is, at least, heading about the typical issues that have to be attended to in a research proposal. One could also refer to the striking characteristics of some successful proposals, and look at examples of good and poor proposals. The more practically oriented a reader should be in a position to compile a list of questions while reading this chapter that he or she would be able to use as a checklist for testing a proposal when in the process of finalizing it. In conclusion, one must never forget the complexity associated with the variety of themes that are to be found in research proposals, requests for research grants and research tenders, if one wishes to avoid running the risk of oversimplification in dealing with the matter. By consulting the references that are listed at the end of this chapter, the reader will be able to find more detailed information on the topic.

In the same manner that it is possible to refer to the art of living, or to the art of writing or painting, one may, according to some authors, refer to the *art of grantsmanship*. Any researcher who wishes to apply him or herself to gaining bursaries or grants, will have to realize that research proposals have to be prepared with a great deal of care. This chapter is intended for the beginner who has not yet learnt the art of writing successful research proposals but who wishes to acquire this art in due course.

TYPES OF RESEARCH PROPOSALS

Depending upon the type, it is possible that research proposals and applications for research grants can differ quite considerably. There are, for example, a number of different types of research grants that are made by an organization such as the Human Sciences Research Council such as *ad hoc* grants, grants for contract projects, for senior researchers, for larger research projects, and for the establishment of research units. It is also possible to submit research proposals to certain government departments for financial or other support. Organizations in the private sector, such as the mining houses and other large corporations, are at times prepared to support meritorious projects that are submitted to them. A final type of research proposal that should be mentioned here is that which is prepared by a prospective Master's or Doctoral student.

In the case of each of the preceding types of research proposals, there are usually instructions in which the requirements with which the research proposal or application for a grant has to comply, are spelled out. It is of the utmost importance that the requirements that are indicated in such instructions be complied with in the finest detail by an applicant who would wish his or her application to succeed. The length of any proposal will probably be positively correlated with the amount of money that is at stake, and also with how complicated or extensive the proposed research project is.

INITIAL PREPARATIONS

The preparations that are required before a research proposal is submitted, are likely to vary from one case to the next. In the case of a research proposal in which the work is to be undertaken in a foreign country and that has to be funded by some organization in that country, it would, for example, be of the utmost importance to make a thorough study of the culture surrounding the awarding of research grants in that country. Fortunately, literature on this topic is available as indicated in the reference list at the end of this chapter.

Before the researcher is in a position to submit his or her research proposal as a polished document, a good deal of work would have gone into it. He or she would have obtained the most recent information and established the current requirements for the submission of such proposals by means of correspondence, a telephone call, or even a personal interview. The applicant would also have established quite clearly that the project that he or she wishes to undertake is, in fact, one that falls into the category of projects supported by the funding organization concerned. By the time that the proposal is written, the wise researcher would have cleared out the merits and feasibility of the project with experts in the field. The strengths and weaknesses of the project would have been exposed to critics and possibly even to representatives of the potential funding organization.

The final formulation of the proposal is tackled with the greatest possible care. It is necessary to present a well-considered exposition that is scientifically justifiable, and which also presents a clear picture of the scope of the project and the manner in which it is to be conducted. Those reading and evaluating the proposal must be in a position where they will be able to gain an overall impression: The rationale of the project appears to be in order; it would also appear to be possible to conduct the project, it appears likely that the results of the project will be worthwhile, and, in general, the project appears to be in capable hands.

FORM AND CONTENT OF RESEARCH PROPOSALS

There are no absolute rules as far as the form and content of a research proposal are concerned. The nature of the material that is included and the most effective and appropriate information to present, always depends upon the nature of the project and the attitude of the funding organization.

As far as the sub-sections of the proposal are concerned, it is however, possible to refer to certain issues that are usually dealt with in such proposals. Whatever the specific labels may be that are given to the sub-section, the main aim is to answer the following eight questions adequately:

What do you wish to do?
Why do you wish to do it?
How do you intend to do it?
Who are you going to involve in getting it done?
Where are you going to do it?
What is your time schedule like?
How much will it cost and how do you intend using the money?
What fundamental contribution is likely to be made by the project?

In the application form for a research grant or in the accompanying information sheet that is provided, one often finds that sub-sections such as the following are mentioned, and that they have to be included in the research proposal:

(i)   a brief introduction in which the general aim of the research is indicated, as well as the importance of the project conducted by the specific researchers with his or her experience, is indicated;

(ii)   specific aims in the project and an indication of possible research hypotheses or central theoretical arguments or theses that will guide the investigation;

(iii)   a description of the scientific method that will be followed, and an indication of the proposed time schedule;

(iv)   the budget, with an indication of the direct and indirect costs that are to be incurred and, in those cases where items appear that are likely to give rise to critical enquiries, the provision of special explanations;

(v)   in conclusion, a specific indication of the possible value of the research results (and the extent to which it is likely to be possible to implement them) as seen from different points of view;

(vi)   important supporting documents such as a *curriculum vitae* of the researcher, a copy of a letter written by someone occupying a high-level position in which the importance of the research is emphasized, and proof or written approval that the project may be conducted on a specific target group, if such approval is necessary, should be provided as appendices.

CHARACTERISTICS OF SUCCESSFUL PROPOSALS

In the literature on research proposals there are frequent references to proposals that have succeeded and those that have not. Two useful books to consult in this regard are *Grant proposals that succeeded* (V. White Ed.) and *The individual's guide to grants* (J.B. Margolin). The point of departure in publications of this nature is that a good deal of competition exists between applicants for research grants. It, is however, evident that the requirements that are set for the proposals that are funded are high, as indicated in the following references.

In her book which we referred to above, Margolin presents a list (pp. 214-215) of characteristics which are usually typical of good research proposals. Such a proposal:

- bears a research idea that is really worthwhile and it takes account of pertinent problems in the community;
- makes it quite clear that the applicant has a particularly suitable approach to the problem and that he or she has developed a plan of action that is likely to succeed;
- creates a feeling of confidence on the part of the sponsor that the researcher is likely to succeed;
- indicates that the research falls within the area in which the sponsor is interested, and also that the proposed research is likely to constitute a good investment for the sponsor given his specific aims;
- provides an indication of the probable results of the proposed project — results that would justify the anticipated expenditure in time and finance associated with the project.

179

Some of the characteristics that are mentioned by White in her book *Grant proposals that succeeded* relating to successful proposals include the following (see pp. 35, 37, 78, 141):

- If it is at all possible, the applicant should indicate that the proposed project is likely to be a unique undertaking. This may be achieved by indicating why the specific researcher and the specific research context are ideally suited;

- attention should be paid to issues of detail in such a manner that it is clear that the applicant has considered the entire project, and that the application is complete in all respects;

- a thorough discussion of the methodology ought to be presented which indicates that the applicant is a careful and responsible scientist;

- the proposal should display a sensitivity for the research sponsor's agenda and primary goals;

- in a proposal for a major project, certain milestones should always be indicated to make it possible to control progress, and to facilitate the eventual evaluation of results;

- a proposal, and this applies particularly to a lengthy one, should be neatly presented and should be as easy to read as possible; a long proposal, say one which consists of ten pages or more, should preferably also contain an abstract and a table of contents.

Conclusion

From the preceding discussion it is possible to compile a brief checklist of the most important considerations for the design of a research proposal. These considerations are formulated as guidelines in much the same manner as we shall do in the next chapter.

GUIDELINE 1
The relevance of the proposed project for the sponsor and discipline should be spelt out in an unambiguous manner.

GUIDELINE 2
The rationale or motivation for the project must be clearly explained.

GUIDELINE 3
The specific aim and goal of the project should be explained.

GUIDELINE 4
The methodology or scientific approach of the design and execution of the project should be spelt out in a fair amount of detail.

GUIDELINE 5
The feasibility of the project as far as time, finances, and human-power are concerned must be adequately motivated.

GUIDELINE 6
The extent to which the eventual results may possibly be implemented should be indicated (if applicable).

GUIDELINE 7
The academic record of the applicant should be provided to convince the sponsor/university that the researcher possesses the necessary background and qualifications to conduct the project.

GUIDELINE 8
The general style in which the proposal is presented should be brief, clear and legible, and all irrelevant and unnecessary information should be avoided.

EXAMPLES OF SELECTIONS FROM RESEARCH PROPOSALS

In this section three selections from research proposals are presented. Each case is followed by brief notes, and/or questions. To illustrate the points which we have made, it appears more appropriate to present the information in this manner rather than to present complete examples of different types of research proposals.

In selecting these examples, an attempt was made to include cases from different areas of the social sciences. In practice each of the three examples actually falls within more than one discipline, for example sociology and education in the case of example 1, anthropology and sociology in the case of example 2, and linguistics and demography in the case of example 3.

Example 1

Project title

The socialization of urban white secondary school pupils as far as their attitudes and perceptions towards intergroup relations in South Africa are concerned.

Aims of the project

To analyze the role of the secondary school as a socializing agent in the formation of certain attitudes and perceptions relating to specific aspects of intergroup relations among urban white secondary school pupils in South Africa.

Motivation for the project

The manner in which the relations between specific established South African ethno-historic and socio-somatic groups are defined by the politically dominant white population segment is primarily determined by the socializing agents found in the white community. Differing views concerning the role of race and colour as determinants of social stratification in the plural South African society can often be associated with the effects of differential socialization. This differential socialization is, to a considerable extent, a function of the different approaches of race, colour and intergroup relations to which pupils are exposed at school. Research of this nature can be of considerable value in promoting sound intergroup relations, especially as such research can identify the negative socialization processes which may be eliminated by means of various corrective procedures. In the context of perceptions of intergroup relations, the socialization process of students in South African secondary schools plays an important role in the manner in which the conflict, which has been built into the problems of intergroup relations in South Africa, may be accommodated. In this regard, the proposed project complies with the overall aims of the national project.

Research hypotheses

(i)   In the formation and internalization of attitudes towards, and perceptions of, intergroup relations in South Africa amongst young urban white adults, a significant proportion results from the socialization processes which occur within the secondary school context.

(ii) Differential perceptions of intergroup relations amongst young urban white adults is to a significant extent the function of differential socialization which takes place within the secondary school context.

Brief description of the research design (for example experiment, survey, literature study) with the most important detail for example samples

The investigation will be based upon known theories concerning (a) the socialization of young adults, (b) the relationship between perceptions of intergroup relations, and the accommodation of conflict within deeply segmented societies. From an empirical point of view, the investigation will largely be based upon a sample survey. A random sample of 1 500 white urban matriculants is envisaged. The empirical study will be preceded by a theoretical orientation and a study of the appropriate published research data. Bearing in mind the aims of the project, the empirical analyses will be structured in such a manner that the primary explanatory variables involved in the process of different socialization will be identified. In this context variables such as language, church membership, gender, age, language medium of school, size of school, choice of school subjects, and other structural-functional variables of the school, will be taken into account.

Data collection procedure

Relevant data will mainly be collected by means of a random sample survey. A structured questionnaire will be designed for the survey and will be applied to 1 500 white urban matric pupils. Field-workers will be trained specifically for this purpose.

COMMENTS REGARDING EXAMPLE 1

In the first instance, you should pay attention to the language used in this example and specifically the difficulty level of the language which is used. It is most decidedly not the most elementary form of language usage imaginable. For a large number of university students in the social sciences, the language usage in the proposal may be a trifle too difficult for a cursory reading. On the other hand, the proposal was not intended for students. The research proposal that we have dealt with was written by an experienced research specialist. The proposal was aimed at the panel of judges who were also all highly qualified researchers in the social sciences. He was aware of the fact that the specific group of readers would be able to understand his subject terminology, and that the level of his language usage would not be regarded as excessively complicated by them. Pay attention to the fact that he is quite able to deal with this relatively complicated language usage as if it were his natural idiom. It is most certainly not an attempt by an inexperienced researcher to write in such a manner that he will be regarded as highly literate. The description of the project also complies with the most important guidelines which we discussed earlier on. The aim of the project, the rationale, the exact research hypotheses, and the data collection methods are clearly described. The manner in which he discusses the proposed project is clear and to the point while, at the same time supplying enough detail to make it perfectly clear how he intends approaching the problem, and how he proposes to set about the actual task.

In conclusion the applicant also describes the manner in which his project will fit into the larger research programme from which he is requesting sponsorship.

Example 2

Project title

Attitudes and stereotypes within the context of popular culture.

Aims of the project

See motivation and hypotheses below.

Motivation for project

In the outline of the National Programme which has been supplied, not enough provision is made for an investigation of outlook on life. This is obviously necessary for an explanation of relationships between groups if one were to intend understanding the manifestations of conflict.

Research hypotheses

That outlook on life and perception of reality will exert an important influence in the explanation of reciprocal racial and ethnic stereotypes:

(i) The outlook on life and perception of reality is precipitated amongst other things in language, which may serve as an explanatory background for stereotyping.

(ii) To use outlook on life and perception of reality as a point of departure and explanatory background for stereotyping regarding the different factors of group relations.

Brief description of research design (for example experiment, survey, literature survey) with essential details, for example sample

(i) Literature study. The approach will be linguistic, anthropological and sociological.

(ii) Random samples and the utilization of the questionnaire method and direct observation.

(iii) Interdisciplinary co-operation, synthesis and recommendation.

Data collection methods

Questionnaire technique supplemented by semi-structured interviews, participant observation, and literature study concerning cultural contact situations, outlook on life and the importance of language as the conveyer of certain views.

COMMENTS CONCERNING EXAMPLE 2

Seen against the background of the guidelines which were formulated earlier on, and in comparison with example 1, which has been discussed, the following questions may well be asked:

(i) Did the explanation of the background and the description of the programme receive enough attention in example 2?

(ii) Does the reader get a clear impression of exactly what is planned for the research project, for example

- how large will the samples be?
- where will the questionnaire survey take place?
- who will do the field-work?
- in which manner do the different disciplines play a role in the project? (Compare interdisciplinary co-operation and the approach will be linguistic, anthropological and sociological.)

(iii) The formulation of the research hypotheses is extremely vague, mainly because central concepts such as outlook on life and perception of reality, and stereotyping are not clearly defined. Strictly speaking, not one of the so-called research hypotheses complies with the requirements which are set for the formulation of research hypotheses: no clear relationships between the variables are specified. Also pay attention to the fact that two of the paragraphs begin with the word "that": is the relationship between the two paragraphs clear and why does the third paragraph begin with the word "to"?

(iv) Do you find it acceptable that the person who drew up this research proposal provides more detail under the heading Data collection procedures and what the extent of the literature survey will be than, for example, under the heading Research design?

(v) If you were obliged to decide about the allocation of the funds for such an applicant, would you be prepared to support his application for an amount of, say, R15 000?

Example 3

Title of project

Atlas of language communication in South Africa.

Statement of problem

Ten major languages are currently spoken in South Africa. The extent of the usage of these languages (in other words: the extent to which they are spoken, read, written and understood) has not yet been determined on a regional basis. For the sake of communication campaigns, and the provision of services in which language plays a role, particularly in urban areas, it is important to obtain comprehensive knowledge concerning the complete language situation within each region.

Considerable levels of population migration during the past two decades, and an increasing interest in regional development, has increased the need for accurate information concerning the language situation within each region in South Africa.

Aims

(i) To compile maps of the major languages of the total population based on the census and other statistics for 1960, 1970 and 1980.

(ii) To study language movements of the past two decades and to analyze the implications of these movements.

Nature of the research

A researcher of the Institute for Languages and the Arts of the HSRC will analyze the results of various census surveys in conjunction with other institutes of the HSRC. The related statistics such as those concerning readership and the utilization of the mass media, will also by analyzed. A research assistant will compile language distribution maps with the assistance of cartographers who are not attached to the HSRC. The sociolinguists of the HSRC, in collaboration with other experts, will subsequently make recommendations for future language planning.

Advantages

(i)   An atlas of language communication in multi-lingual South Africa will become available for the first time.

(ii) Accurate information concerning the language profile of each region will become available to regional planners and those who provide related services.

(iii) The project will provide material for language planning as well as for projection for future language situations.

COMMENTS CONCERNING EXAMPLE 3

When one compares the language usage and style of presentation in example 3 with that of example 1, it is clear that the formulation in example 3 is brief but, nonetheless, adequate. In example 3 the project proposer had to stay within certain clearly defined parameters as far as the length of the project proposal was concerned, and it is for this reason that the document is presented in a pithy manner.

The authors of the research proposal (example 3) had to convince the decision makers of the following issues in their brief proposal:

(a) the priority and actuality value of the proposed research (compare statement of the problem and advantages), at this time in South Africa;

(b) the feasibility of the research (compare aims and nature of research) as a type of research investment which ought to be made;

(c) as far as both (a) and (b) are concerned the proposal is clear enough. The data sources (central statistics for 1960, 1970 and 1980) are clearly described, and the eventual utility and implementability of the findings are also clearly explained (advantages for future language planning).

Suggestions for further reading

For those who are interested in further reading matter concerning the considerations which have to be borne in mind in the compilation of research proposals, there are primarily six books that may be consulted. Each of these books also contains an extensive list of references which may be consulted by those who really wish to make a study of this aspect. The six books are Beasley (1982), Coleman (1980), Davitz and Davitz (1977), Margolin (1983), White (1975) and White (1983).

Introduction

The context of reporting

Theoretical guidelines

Metatheoretical guidelines

Methodological guidelines

> Research problem
> Research design
> Data-collection
> Analysis
> Interpretation

Technical guidelines

Suggestions for further reading

CHAPTER 9

GUIDELINES FOR WRITING RESEARCH REPORTS

INTRODUCTION

This chapter aims at identifying the essential elements of good project reports. Different researchers will obviously deal with these elements in their own way, but it is important that all researchers should account for the specific elements as explicitly as possible. Each research report should be a scholarly document and it should therefore comply with general standards of social sciences research. The exposition of criteria (theoretical, meta-theoretical, methodological and technical) which follows, can in fact be regarded as a summary of the most important methodological considerations discussed in Chapters 1 to 7.

THE CONTEXT OF REPORTING

Recent studies in the sociology of science (Kuhn, Barnes, Hägstorm, Knorr-Cetina, Ravetz, *et al.*) emphasize the *social* nature of scientific praxis. The best known view is probably that of Thomas Kuhn in which the social structure of scientific research, as embodied in his *paradigm* concept, constitutes the core of his conception of science. Kuhn emphasizes that scientific research is embedded in a context of social structures, values and rules, giving new meaning to tradional concepts such as scientific progress, truth, objectivity, validity, etc. Methodological criteria are not without context: their contents are *inter alia* determined by expectations, demands and commitments of the research community concerned.

Reporting does not therefore occur in a vacuum. It is not only a one-way communication from a researcher to a financing institution/contractor. The nature of scientific communication is determined by the unique nature of science. In a recent study Böhme defends the view that *argumentation* constitutes the unique context of science and in this way determines the nature of scientific communication.

> *In contrast to most other types of communication scientific communication, however, is argumentation: the coherence of communication is the coherence of an argumentative context. This thesis may seem trivial, but that it is not so is shown by the fact that scientific communication is frequently understood to be an exchange of information.. Even the communication of pure measurement results usually is the adducing of empirical evidence for a hypothesis or even is itself an empirical hypothesis for which theoretical arguments have to be brought forward in the publication* (1975, 206).

Böhme compares the act of scientific communication (as distinct from the research process) with the traditional context of validation/justification. Scientific communication (reporting) is an act of validation; an act in which the scientist argues for a specific view, hypothesis or finding relative to the position taken by other scientists. The logic of reporting is the logic of validation. It is the act of advancing arguments or reasons (empirical or theoretical) in support (refutation) of a specific hypothesis/finding.

In view of the above introductory remarks, it follows that it is the responsibility of the scientist to prove that the research he or she is reporting complies with the methodological requirements (reliability, validity, objectivity, accuracy, etc.) applicable to his discipline. The social structure of research implies that there is not only one acceptable methodological, theoretical or metatheoretical (even ideological) paradigm in the social sciences. The meaning of objectivity is, for example, different in the quantitative and qualitative traditions, whereas methodological guidelines vary on the continuum of empirical to theoretical research. The researcher should, however, still indicate the central argument or hypothesis of his or her research in the report and give reasons (arguments) why it is scientifically acceptable. In the report his or her metatheoretical assumptions, as well as theoretical and methodological preferences and commitments should therefore be clearly indicated in order that the scientific acceptability of the research can be evaluated on internal grounds.

In order to systematize the various types of guidelines relevant to the writing of a report, the following categories of guidelines are distinguished below: theoretical, metatheoretical, methodological and technical guidelines.

THEORETICAL GUIDELINES

It is generally accepted that no meaningful scientific research can exist in isolation. Although individual studies or projects are written and published, they always form part of a particular theoretical framework. Knowledge in a given field of research should logically form part of a series of interdependent preceding studies as well as of some theories/models that exceed the boundaries of those used in the particular framework.

Given the importance of the *argumentative* context of scientific research, it follows that a literature survey should not merely describe existing theories in a mechanical way: one or more theoretical views should be integrated with the logic of the research objective/task. For example, the researcher should be able to answer the following questions:

- How does the central theme of the investigation relate to other research and existing theories?

- Is an explanation given in the (introduction to the) study of the way in which the basic argument of the research has been integrated in the wider framework of relevant theory and research?

GUIDELINE 1

The research project should be integrated into a wider framework of relevant theory and research which is reflected in a review of the literature.

The primary constituents of theories are undoubtedly the concepts in which the researcher categorizes reality as it is observed. Scientists do not always attach the same meaning to concepts. In addition, the social scientist, in contrast to the natural scientist, usually employs general or everyday terms for his or her concepts and constructs. It is mainly for the above-mentioned two reasons that concepts with more than one meaning are sometimes used by researchers in a somewhat individualistic way. This happens more frequently when the research deals with problems in which the researcher is personally involved. These considerations form the context of the second guideline.

GUIDELINE 2

All central/important concepts/constructs should be defined explicitly.

METATHEORETICAL GUIDELINES

It is generally accepted in philosophy of science today that no scientific finding can be *conclusively* proved on the basis of empirical research data. In different stages of the scientific research process and for different reasons the researcher is compelled to make assumptions justifying specific theories, methodological strategies, etc. that are not tested in the specific study. One important category of such assumptions is metatheoretical (or metaphysical) assumptions underlying the theories/models/paradigms that form the definitive context of the study.

The argumentative (and public) nature of scientific communication demands that this often tacit dimension of scientific practice should be made explicit.

More effective scientific communication and, in the long run, better research, is promoted by the explication of the metatheoretical assumptions underlying the use of one theory rather than another and one methodological approach than another.

GUIDELINE 3
The scientist should clearly explicate the metatheoretical assumptions (or commitments, (pre)suppositions, beliefs) applicable to his or her research.

METHODOLOGICAL GUIDELINES

The quality of research findings is directly dependent on the accountability of the research methodology followed. For this reason, researchers should fully describe the way in which their research has been planned, structured and executed in order to comply with scientific criteria.

The most important steps in the research process, viz statement of the research problem, research design, data collection, analysis and interpretation should be incorporated in the specification of methodological guidelines.

Research problem

In empirical research the *research hypothesis* directs the investigation while the *central theoretical thesis* serves this purpose in theoretical research. In addition, it is necessary that core concepts in the statement of the problem should be clearly defined and (in empirical research) also be operationalized.

GUIDELINE 4
The research hypothesis/central theoretical thesis should be clearly formulated.

Research design

A research design is an exposition or plan of how the researcher decided to execute the formulated research problem. The objective of the research design is to plan, structure and execute the project concerned in such a way that the validity of the findings are maximized.

Three aspects are usually included in the research design, namely the aim of the research, data/information sources and considerations of validity and reliability.

The *aim of the research:* The researcher should in the first place state what the aim of the project is: exploratory, descriptive, explanatory, analytical or predictive. Other variations of the aim are hypothesis-generating as opposed to hypothesis-testing. The methodological requirements relating to the different objectives naturally differ.

GUIDELINE 5
The research report should specify the aim/objective(s) pursued.

Data/information sources: A variety of data sources are available for social sciences research: physical sources, documentary sources, indirect and direct observation. The use of questionnaires, interviews, scales, tests, etc. is included in indirect observation. Irrespective of the sources of his data, the researcher should also report on the

- nature, credibility and relevance of the sources (especially in the case of documentary sources),

- representativeness of the sources. In empirical research in which individuals are studied, representativeness refers to the problems related to sampling. In these cases the researcher is required to provide adequate information on the techniques of sampling, the demographic characteristics of the sample, etc.

GUIDELINE 6
Information should be provided on the nature, credibility, relevance and representativeness of data and information sources.

Reliability and validity: In the research design stage researchers should already consider the different factors which could prevent them from making valid inferences. In theoretical research this problem emerges as a problem of objectivity: the selection of only those views and arguments supporting the researcher's views, insufficient supporting evidence/reasons for the final conclusion, implicit prejudice, etc. In empirical research the researcher should take a variety of confounding variables into account which could threaten the final validity of his findings. The aim of a research design is after all to control for systematic bias, confounding variables and experimenter effects by means of various measures.

> GUIDELINE 7
> The research report should include information on the ways in which reliability/validity and objectivity of the data/information have been controlled.

Data-collection

Against the background of considerations regarding data collection in the design stage, the researcher should report on the methods and techniques of data collection, the time when the project was executed , and the events at that time which could have had an influence on the data collected, the controls used to ensure that the process of data collection yielded reliable data, etc.

> GUIDELINE 8
> The research report should detail relevant information on the methods (and context) of data collection.

Analysis

Analysis includes both qualitative (for example historical and conceptual analysis) and quantitative approaches. It is generally accepted that empirical data can be analysed in different ways. Different approaches to such analysis can sometimes lead to different findings. A few examples are the different ways in which large data sets can be reduced (for example by various types of factor analysis), the different methods of stratification, the statistical control of variables (for example analysis of covariance), bivariate and multivariate approaches, etc. Since different approaches can often have more or less the same validity, the researcher must give reasons for specific choices.

> GUIDELINE 9
> The procedures used for analysis should be described in full.

Interpretation

In theoretical as well as empirical research, the report should be concluded with an interpretation of the findings against the background of the original research problem. Criteria of objectivity require that the interpretation should not be selective, but that data should be reported in full. A valid conclusion is one in which the data (empirical) or reasons/evidence (theoretical) provide both *sufficient* and *relevant* grounds for the conclusion.

GUIDELINE 10
The interpretation and conclusions should be provided within the framework of the original research problem and design and should include all the relevant information/data.

TECHNICAL GUIDELINES

Diverse factors determine the technical editing of a report. The nature and extent of an investigation will obviously determine the length, etc. of the report. The most important aspects which should be taken into consideration when a report, article or dissertation is edited, are:

- the format: the length of the text (A4 or A5) and line-spacing;
- the length;
- the number of copies;
- the reference style;
- the necessity for acknowledgements; and
- the summary.

The precise nature and content of each of these factors will depend on the context of the report. Articles submitted to journals usually have to comply with the conventions of the journal in question. Universities also have strict rules regarding any thesis or dissertation submitted to them, while organizations such as the Human Sciences Research Council have their own set of criteria for research reports. The only guideline which can therefore be formulated, is the following:

GUIDELINE 11
The research report should comply with the technical guidelines (format, length, number of copies, reference style and summary) laid down by the organization or journal concerned.

Suggestions for further reading:

Besides the references which were given at the end of Chapter 8, the following publications could also be consulted: Allen & colbrunn (1975), Allen & Colbrunn (1976), Anderson & Haugh (1978), Bailey (1981), Balian (1983), Blustein & Geary (1981), Ceely, *et al.* (1978), Coggins (1977), Draper (1978), Graves & Hoffman (1965), Noland (1970), Phillips & Hunt (1976), Russo (1980), Sanderlin (1983), Sternberg (1977), Sussams (1983), Taylor (1974), Warren (1972) and Wiles (1968).

PART 3

APPENDIX 1

A SOCIOLOGICAL ANALYSIS OF MEDICAL ENCOUNTERS OF AGED PERSONS AT AN OUTPATIENT CENTRE: A QUALITATIVE APPROACH[1.]

Monica Ferreira

1. INTRODUCTION

The medical encounters of aged persons at outpatient departments of general hospitals can be seen to constitute a sociological problem. From time to time there are reports in the media of depersonalising treatment received by elderly persons at these centres. Critics claim that the aged are handicapped in the care that they receive through these facilities, which is criticised for being impersonal, discontinuous and insensitive to the needs and capacities of older patients.

There is a substantial body of literature pertaining to health care provided at outpatient departments. Most of these studies, however, are of a positivistic, quantitative nature, planned and constructed from the point of view of health professionals and service providers. Few studies have been undertaken from the point of view of patients, a perspective which would suggest studies with a qualitative approach.

To evaluate whether the service and treatment provided for elderly persons at an outpatient centre are adequately responsive to the real needs of these persons, and how the elderly patients perceive this, an investigation was undertaken from a patient perspective within a qualitative theoretical and methodological framework.

2. THEORETICAL ORIENTATION

Medical sociology studies the provision and utilisation of health care services, as well as the behaviour of individuals in health care settings, within the overall context of medical systems in societies. In this study the traditional approaches of medical sociology were reviewed and found to be inappropriate for the investigation. It was considered necessary, therefore, to construct a more humanistic[2] theoretical perspective to view the elderly patients' perceptions of their medical encounters at an outpatient centre.

2.1 Traditional approaches in medical sociology

The traditional approaches in medical sociology have been largely positivistic and quantitative, dealing more at a functional or structural level than on an interactional level. Among these are the structural-functional approach of Parsons (1951) and the structural approach of Freidson (1961, 1970, 1973).[3] Themes that have commonly been investigated in earlier studies are cultural and social class factors in the treatment of illness (Koos 1954; Kosa, Zola 1957); utilisation rates of medical services (Koos 1954; Blum 1960); differing lay and professional perspectives (Baumann 1961; Davis 1963); the doctor-patient relationship (Parsons 1951; Freidson 1961, 1970, 1972); communication between patient and doctor (Apple 1960; Duff, Hollingshead 1968), and the concept of an illness career (Suchman 1965).

Most of the traditional approaches have derived from the model of illness behaviour implied by the Parsonian concept of the sick role (Parsons 1951) — a classic description of a set of expectations most commonly accepted by sick people. These expectations are that (i) the sick person understands that he is exempted from performance of his normal roles; (ii) he is not held responsible for his condition and it is accepted that he cannot cure himself; (iii) it is his responsibility to get better as soon as possible, and (iv) he must therefore seek competent technical help and co-operate with medical agents.

Parsons' formulation of the sick role concept has been severely criticised. Basic inadequacies of the postulates appear to be the assumption that all sick individuals will behave in a similar manner (Twaddle 1969), and that the postulates represent only the physician's point of view (Freidson 1961, 1971, 1972; Bloom 1963). The formulation has also been criticised for its limited applicability to chronic illnesses (Kassebaum, Baumann 1965; Callahan *et al.* 1966). For the chronically ill, the issue of getting well is irrelevant and the patient is often expected to take a more active, independent role in dealing with the illness than Parsons describes.

In addition Dingwall (1976) criticises the traditional approaches for failing to view illness and illness behaviour as social action. He suggests that it is in their concern with precise measurement and quantification that these studies are guilty of a positivistic bias, leaving the absolutist claim of service providers and their predominantly pragmatic motives largely unquestioned. Consequently he proposes that some of the shortcomings of the traditional approaches might be overcome by microsociological studies as an alternative methodology.

Recently other sociologists have also questioned the passivity model of the patient. These studies, which are essentially microsociological, include the studies of patient impetus (Davis, Horobin (eds.) 1977). In addition, contemporary observational studies characterise medical encounters as negotiated occasions in which all parties strive to achieve their separate ends via a variety of strategies (Balint 1957; Roth 1963; Katz *et al*. 1969; Stimson, Webb 1975).

Microsociological studies are represented by various phenomenological schools, most notably interactionism and ethnomethodology. As such they are characterised by attention to meaning and interpretation and by denial of the social structure in the macrosociological sense. These studies customarily provide for a dialectical construction of social reality. Hence, microsociological studies require a qualitative approach which provides for an understanding of the actor's definition of the social situation and the meanings which he finds in it.

2.2 Statement of the problem

A microsociological approach within the field of medical sociology seemed particularly well-suited for a study of elderly persons seeking health care at an outpatient centre who are likely to be medically indigent and suffering from chronic diseases typical of aging (Shanas 1962: 34). In particular this approach would enable an understanding of the effects of medical treatment and the patient role on the individuals' perception of self.

Problems that elderly persons who attend outpatient centres purportedly experience are difficulties with transportation to and from the centre; long waits to clerk in, see the doctor and collect prescriptions; impersonal consultations with different doctors on each occasion, and abruptness and impatience from hospital staff. The experience and perception of these difficulties by elderly patients may create psychosocial problems for them in the form of feelings of depersonalisation. This has implications for the self-definitions of these persons, in their perception of their capacity to cope with the exigencies of seeking medical treatment at a centre and simultaneously retain favourable self-images.

The situation of elderly persons seeking health care at an outpatient centre was therefore seen to constitute a sociological problem inasmuch as elements of depersonalisation might inhere in the service and care. The primary hypothesis of the study was that elderly persons who seek medical care at a particular outpatient centre experience feelings of alienation and conflict during medical encounters which are depersonalising to their self-image.

Chronic diseases are incurable and irreversible and call for a special model of patient care in the treatment.[4] This applies even more so in treating the chronic illnesses of the aged. The model of patient care generally operative at outpatient centres is the classical model, deriving from the treatment of acute diseases, which stresses the need for the patient to be obedient to medical authority and is based on an expectation of cure. The role of the patient is a passive one. Ideally, chronically ill persons should be treated through a rehabilitative model, in which a cure is not expected and the patient is required to take a more active role in his treatment (Field 1967; Safilios-Rothschild 1970). A subhypothesis of the study was that the model of patient care at the outpatient centre therefore neglects the psychosocial needs of elderly, chronically-ill patients.

The decision to conduct the study from a patient perspective consequently called for a qualitative approach whereby the perceptions and interpretations of the elderly patients of their medical encounters would be given primary importance.

2.3 A theoretical framework for the investigation

The study was concerned with the symbolic meanings that elderly patients give to medical encounters at an outpatient centre. A perspective was thus required for viewing the dialectic between the patient and the social structure of the organisation. Symbolic interactionism appeared to provide such a perspective. According to this perspective the individual is viewed as a conscious actor in his world, who perceives situations and events in terms of his own meanings and definitions of the situation which themselves arise from social interaction with others. Human beings are seen to interpret and define each other's actions instead of merely reacting. Responses are not made directly to the actions of another, as positivistic theories propose, but to the meanings attached to such actions. Human interaction is assumed to be mediated by the use of symbols, by interpretation and by imputing meaning to actions and the actions of others. The symbolic interactionist perspective thus approaches society from the viewpoint of the individual's constitution of meaning in interaction with other individuals.

In seeking treatment at an outpatient facility, elderly persons enter a situation in which they are confronted by differing definitions of their "selves" by others with whom they interact.[5] A "self" has both cognitive and emotional elements: the cognitive element constitutes the self-concept, the individual's definition of himself; the emotional element constitutes self-esteem, which is how the individual feels about his self-concept in comparison with some ideal. Social interaction functions in developing self-esteem as much as it does in developing the self-concept. A positive self-concept is a prerequisite for an individual's personal happiness and daily functioning.

According to symbolic interactionistic theory, the self is established, maintained and altered in interaction with others. Other persons' reactions will affect the self-concept. Specifically the amount of respect and concern that significant others show to a person will be perceived by him as a measure of his own worth,[6] while devaluing judgments expressed by others will affect the maintenance of his self-esteem. An important goal of the study was therefore to determine whether the nature of the interaction during medical encounters at the centre was threatening to the self-images of the elderly patients.

Symbolic interactionistic theory also allows for the conceptualisation of the social situation within which the action takes place.[7] This perspective considers that behaviour can only be understood when viewed in its whole context. The term "definition of the situation" implies that a situation is not only as it exists in its verifiable form, but also as it seems to exist (Timasheff, Theodorson 1976: 170).[8] Interaction between individuals thus takes place in specific situations to which they bring interpretations which are their definitions of the situations. These definitions then direct the interaction process and constitute the reality of the actor.

Goffman's (1959) concept of the "presentation of the self" refers to how actors attempt to present themselves in the best possible way.[9] In constructing interpretations of particular social situations, individuals in effect seek to "manage" the image of themselves that they give to others. If the selves that are presented are negatively evaluated, the self-images of the persons become degraded.

Several themes common in symbolic interactionist theories had particular relevance for the study. These were (i) the emergence of the self in interaction with others (the study was based on the perceived value judgments of "others" at the centre by the subjects of themselves); (ii) the interaction process (within medical encounters) being a potentially emergent event, and (iii) the perspective always returning to that of the actor (the acting elderly patient).

Symbolic interactionism thus provided a humanistic theoretical perspective for the investigation and firmly grounded it within a qualitative framework.[10] Instead of viewing the elderly patients as mere responding organisms, the perspective afforded a more social-psychological approach to their experiential states, giving the perspective of the elderly individuals primary importance. It also posited a fundamental link between patients and the social structure at the centre which rested on the role of symbolic and common meanings. The perspective thus permitted an expanded treatment of how elderly patients are linked to, shaped by and in turn create this social structure.

3. METHODOLOGICAL STRATEGY

Symbolic interactionism has no explicit methodology of its own. For the empirical investigation this perspective was therefore coupled with the methods of Weber's (1949) verstehende approach. These methods aim at an "empathic understanding" of the emotional structure of a situation, as seen through the eyes of those concerned. The approaches of symbolic interactionism and verstehen are compatible inasmuch as the subject matter of both is typical social action from the viewpoint of the acting individual.

In operationalising the study however, the methods of the verstehende approach were found to be rather limited in their capacity to describe the social action at the centre. Empathic understanding alone did not seem able to reveal all the significant aspects of the patient world[11] at the setting. It therefore seemed necessary to develop a broader methodological base within the overall qualitative paradigm, in which the premises of the verstehende approach could be retained and the perceptions of the elderly patients and the articulation of the patients within the setting could be examined.[12]

3.1 The qualitative research paradigm

The qualitative paradigm is based on induction, holism and subjectivism.[13] A qualitative research strategy is inductive in that the researcher attempts to understand a situation without imposing pre-existing expectations on the setting. Qualitative research designs begin with specific observations and build towards general patterns. Categories or dimensions of analysis emerge as a researcher comes to make sense of and organise patterns that exist in the empirical world which he is studying. He then begins to focus on testing and elucidating what appears to be emerging. The qualitative researcher thus develops analytical, conceptual and categorical components of explanation from the data itself.

Holism is the assumption that the whole is greater than the sum of the parts, and that context is essential for understanding a situation. The qualitative approach therefore aims to gather data on numerous aspects of a situation, and to construct a complete picture of the social dynamic of the particular situation or setting. An important assumption of the qualitative paradigm is understanding a situation from the perspective of participants in the situation. The qualitative approach is subjective in that the focus is on the experiential states of actors and their perceptions of a situation.

In the qualitative paradigm individuals are conceptualised as active agents in constructing and making sense of realities that they encounter. There exist no clear-cut response sets to situations. A major methodological consequence, therefore, is that the qualitative study of people in situ is a process of discovery: the researcher must find out what is happening, in those people's terms. In short, the qualitative method advocates an approach to examining the empirical world which requires the researcher to interpret the real world from the perspective of the subjects of his investigation. This calls for an emphasis on natural observation and field work in the collection of data in the natural setting of the subjects.

The qualitative method is implemented as follows: To understand the complex processes that precipitate human interaction, it is necessary to obtain information that is relevant to various attitudinal, situational and environmental factors in the world of those being investigated. For an accurate interpretation, the researcher needs intersubjective, personal knowledge. This knowledge is embedded in the complex network of social interaction. The task of the qualitative methodologist is to provide a framework within which subjects can respond in terms of their own meanings. Methods such as participant observation and in-depth interviewing allow him to "get close to the data" (Lofland 1971) and to obtain first-hand knowledge.

Lofland (1971: 3-4, 7) outlines four elements which are necessary in undertaking a qualitative study: (i) intensive immersion in a sector of social life to gain "intimate familiarity" with what is going on; (ii) focusing on and depicting the situation that the scrutinised actors are dealing with; (iii) focusing on interactional strategies and tactics of participants to cope or deal with the situation, and (iv) assembling and analysing an abundance of qualitative data of situations, events, strategies, action, people and activities to convey the reality of the place represented in its mundane aspects.

The commitment to get close, and to be factual, descriptive and quotive, is thus a commitment of the qualitative researcher to represent participants in their own terms and to give a living sense of day-to-day talk, activities, concerns and problems in such a way that the audience is at least partially able to project itself into the point of view of the people depicted. For this reason qualitative researchers prefer to record data in the language of the subjects.

3.2 Research design

To understand the stresses impinging on elderly persons in a typical social situation in which they interact, it is necessary to see the "world" through their eyes. An assessment of how stressful circumstances at an outpatient centre might be for elderly patients required that the perceptions that they had of themselves in relation to the world around be reconstructed as faithfully as possible. The actual data in the study were at an experiential level, revolving around the self-awareness, self-perceptions and self-conceptions of the subjects, their experience of the social environment at the centre and their relevant social perceptions in general.

To operationalise the study a design was constructed for observing the articulation of the subjects and the setting as social action. For this purpose the triangulation strategy of Denzin (1970, 1978) and the analytical units schema of Lofland (1971) were incorporated in the research design.

The triangulation strategy of Denzin (1970, 1978) refers to the combination of multiple methods of observation which direct a researcher to utilise several different tools in the observational process. The rationale for this is that no method alone can adequately treat all problems of discovery and testing. Since each method has restrictions, by combining several methods in the same study the restrictions of one tool are often the strengths of another. Denzin (1978: 101-103) proposes that the greater the triangulation in a research design, the greater the confidence a researcher may have in his findings. Glaser and Strauss (1967) similarly argue that different people in different positions may offer very different information about the same subject as the "facts". Denzin (*ibid.*) suggests that a triangulation strategy should embrace (i) multiple data sources, whereby the researcher goes to as many concrete situations in a setting as possible to form an observational base; (ii) multiple methods, whereby any and all techniques that can better unravel the processes under study are used, and (iii) multiple perspectives, whereby participants' accounts of their behaviour are compared with alternative theoretical schemes. A combination of these strategies was used in the investigation.

Lofland (1971: 13) suggests that qualitative research activity is concerned with certain analytical units. These he lists as (i) acts, which are temporally brief; (ii) activities, which are acts of longer duration and constitute significant elements of participants' involvements in a setting; (iii) meanings, which are the verbal production of participants that define and direct action; (iv) participation, which is the holistic involvement in or adaptation to the situation or setting of participants; (v) relationships, which are the interrelationships between participants considered simultaneously, and (vi) the setting, which is the entire setting under study. Lofland (1971: 87) proposes that these analytical units should be focused on in an inquiry to gain "intimate familiarity" with the setting, the participants and the problem. Each of the analytical units of Lofland were employed during observations and in the analysis.

Some methodological issues which surfaced in the design were the following:

(i) Gaining access to the setting

Gaining access to medical settings to do research is notoriously difficult. Ethical issues involved in the confidentiality and sanctity of the medical consultation between doctor and patient are particularly stressed by the medical profession. In this study it was feared that the hospital administrators might not permit the researcher access to the centre to undertake the investigation. This might have occurred through a lack of understanding on the part of the administrators of the nature of the research; the relevance of the research towards potential solutions to the problem, or apprehension about the use to which the findings might be put. It was thus considered necessary to first secure the co-operation of the administrators by fully discussing the aims of the research with them beforehand in order to allay any such fears and avoid misunderstanding.

(ii) Units of analysis

Because of the ethical issue concerning the confidentiality of doctor-patient interactions, it was decided not to seek access to consultations. This left a problem, however, of how to convert the social activity of consultations into a researchable phenomenon. It was decided to focus analytically on the entire encounter process. The nature of the interaction between patients and doctors would be extrapolated from subjects' retrospective accounts of consultations.

In terms of the analytical units schema of Lofland (1971), focus would therefore be on the setting of the encounter process; the relationships of the subjects with their doctors; the participation of the subject in the interaction with their doctors and in the entire setting, and the meanings that the interaction had for the subjects. The acts and activities of the subjects, as they were reported by the subjects or observed, would be viewed as ''managed'' social activity. This would provide a view of the strategic nature of the subjects' actions, in terms of the presentation of their selves, and would facilitate an appraisal of the extent to which they were able to ward off possible insults to their self-images.

(iii) Problem of ''measurement''

The measurement of the degree to which the self-images of the subjects had been degraded, or the phenomenon of depersonalisation, presented a methodological problem both in terms of definition and quantification. The term ''depersonalisation'', which may differ in the abstract and the concrete senses, fails to specify covert feelings and overt actions that accompany the process. It was decided to base the observational parameters on the broader rubric of ''patient satisfaction'', defined as the degree to which the expectations that elderly patients have of the health care which they receive, and what they feel to be important in the process of care, are met.

No research study can avoid the problem of bias and this issue was particularly salient in the present study. Firstly, the choice of the problem area and the methods meant that one side of the medical interaction (in this case the patient) would be emphasised at the expense of the other (the doctor and the organisation). Secondly, a large part of collective life is problematic to define because of its essentially oral tradition and because even its formally stated written tradition is subject to different perception and interpretation by actors variously distributed in the social structure (Cicourel 1964: 221). Thirdly, some features of social action are difficult to measure by means of the methodological tools available to the sociologist.

An assumption of the study was that an individual has a subjective conception of his or her self which constitutes self-image. The researcher set out to evaluate, by way of empathic understanding of explicit or implicit indications of the subject, whether the self-image had been insulted.

(iv) Sampling

The population attending the outpatient centre is extremely large, unknown in size, transient and mobile, with elderly patients dying, becoming temporarily immobile or too ill to visit the centre, too infirm to continue utilising the facility, or changing to another health care agency for a time. Since the population was unknown, a probability sample could not be drawn.

Denzin (1978: 99) proposes that when a population is unknown, it is necessary to modify the usual canons of sampling theory and to develop alternative procedures for describing specific observational units, or a combination of these for the sampling. These units are (i) a situation, where an observational unit a sample is drawn from all persons who pass through the setting over a specified period of time; (ii) time, in terms of specified days of a week or month; (iii) a social organisation, in that it is the setting which processes and produces the types of behaviour with which the investigation is concerned, and (iv) interactive relationships.

In the study a combination of the above four units was used for the sampling. By isolating an encounter in the setting, this had the advantage of combining the variables of time, situation and social organisation in a focused observational unit. Although interactive relationships were not sampled as such, their process in the setting was assumed inasmuch as they are an intrinsic part of medical encounters.

Briefly, the sampling was effected in the following way:[14] On specific days at specific times over two periods of three weeks each, the researcher took up position at strategic sites in the setting. These sites were identified during field work and participant observation as hosting critical activities in the encounter process. Every tenth patient who appeared to be 65 years and older who passed through a site was approached and requested to participate in the research. It was explained to the patient what the nature of the research was and that confidentiality and anonymity were assured. On consenting, a patient was drawn into the sample. There were no refusals.

A sample of 50 subjects was drawn in this way. Eighty per cent were female. The median age of the subjects was 76 years.

4. DATA COLLECTION

In terms of the qualitative theoretical framework, a survey procedure would have been inappropriate for the empirical investigation. In addition, surveys are generally unsuitable for elderly populations, and for analyzing complex forms of human interaction. A survey would have also failed to tap the singular in the symbolic worlds of the subjects.

The qualitative framework and the decision to focus on the entire encounter process required that the process be observed from as many angles as possible. It had therefore been decided to adopt the triangulation strategy proposed by Denzin (1970, 1978), whereby several methods would be used to collect the data.

Denzin (1978: 87-94) provides procedural directives for producing and collecting "behaviour specimens", which he suggests constitute the logic of naturalistic inquiry. As "slices of ongoing interaction", behaviour specimens take particular sequences or flows of behaviour under inspection. These directives constitute a set of methodological directives for implementing a symbolic interactionistic perspective. In the study behaviour specimens were collected through observations made in a temporal sequence, which followed the order in which the methods were employed for the collection of data in different subsettings.

In the first phase of observation, the researcher sought to gain orientation of the total setting and dynamics. These observations constituted field work activity. Access was gained to health care professionals, administrators of, and lower work participants in the organisation, and to documents and statistics. The observations were recorded in much the same way as the traditional field notes of an ethnographer but in more detail and specificity. In the second phase, while having some orientation in the setting and continuing fieldwork, the researcher became immersed in the setting, outside of actual consultations, as a participant observer. This enabled the compilation of an account of interactions that were observed to take place. In the third phase, an interview guide was drawn up in order to broadly structure the interviews conducted with the subjects in their homes.

4.1 Orientation in the setting

Field work was undertaken for orientation in the setting and its workings by (1) approaching officials, or informants, assumed to be knowledgeable through continuous exposure to situations and topics central to the study and who could provide information, and (2) by becoming personally acquainted with concrete features of and procedures at the setting.

The outpatient centre where the study was located is attached to a general hospital. It is a relatively specialised setting, serving a large, metropolitan White population of, for the main part, fairly indigent persons. About four-fifths of the patients who attend the day clinic at the centre are 65 years and older.[15] At the time of the investigation[17] the centre provided health care to an estimated 14 000 ambulant patients per month, or 700 patients on each weekday. The day clinic operates from 07h00 until 16h00. Morning sessions are mostly taken up with patients' visits for regular consultations with doctors and certain specialists. Afternoon sessions are directed at specialist clinic consultations. The study was confined to the family medicine clinic, which is the normal "general practice" service, where the majority of chronic diseases are primarily treated.

Approaching informants and subsequent interaction took place over several months. Permission for access to undertake the investigation was first secured from the Director of Hospital Services. The researcher was then referred to the Superintendent of the hospital who on granting his approval referred her to the Deputy Superintendent and the First Matron of the Outpatient Department and the Head of the Social Work Department of the hospital. It was explained to officials that the aim of the research was primarily to study an instance of client-agency interface in a medical setting, and that the focus would be on the elderly persons' perceptions of medical encounters at the centre.

Interviews were also conducted with the Chief Administrative Officer and his personnel on difficulties and problems connected with the administration and provision of the service to aged persons. Officials were able to provide inside perspectives of events and problems that the researcher was not yet familiar with. These interviews served as a sounding-board for developing insights, propositions and hypotheses, and more broadly gaining entry to situations and persons.

Access to the organisational setting and most of its subsettings was readily achieved. The researcher then interviewed clerks, cashiers, nursing-sisters, trainee nurses, orderlies, porters and voluntary workers. Records were kept of all conversations with informants, by jotting down notes during interviews and writing these up more comprehensively immediately afterwards. Wherever possible and where these were available, statistics were scrutinised and copies of documents and statistical records were secured.

Denzin (1978: 97) states that in naturalistic observation it is necessary to pay attention to the spatial, temporal, ritualistic and interactional features of a social organisation. If an investigator has successfully entered the subjects' world, it is possible to know where the critical observational and sampling sites are that are representative of the organisation. Denzin (*ibid.*) suggests that a representational map be used to graphically and pictorially display the recurrent and stable features of the social world — that is, the spatial and physical layout of the concrete social setting. He sees a map as an aid in revealing the extent to which the researcher gained familiarity with the phenomenon under study and for justifying the observational and sampling strategies.

FIGURE 1

A REPRESENTATIONAL MAP OF THE LAYOUT OF THE OUTPATIENT CENTRE

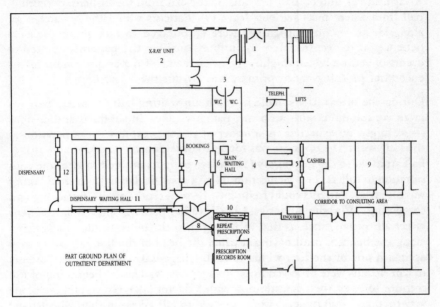

4.2 Participant observation

Participant observation was undertaken by the researcher in the setting to observe the everyday actions and interaction of the participants. This observational method is based on the assumption that understanding (verstehen) of the inner perspectives of actors can only be achieved by actively participating in the subjects' world and gaining insight by means of introspection (Bruyn 1962).

During participant observation the researcher assumed the role of "observer", according to the typology of four participant observation strategies of Denzin (1978: 188) based on Gold (1958: 217-223).[17] Being an observer implies that the investigator and his or her objectives are known to those who are being observed. This is opposed to concealing the scientific role, and

211

attempting to become a full participant in the observation process and an ordinary member of the group or organisation. The researcher was thus able to move about freely, observe participants directly, and engage in casual interviewing of participants. Numerous patients were also observed without their being aware of this.

Participant observation was undertaken over three periods of two weeks each. During these periods the researcher spent several hours daily between 08h00 and 14h00 in the setting. Various observational positions were taken up during these periods: at both entrances to the centre (1, 8) (see Figure 1); in both waiting-halls (4, 11); at the bookings' counter (6); at the cashiers' counter (5); in the corridor between doctors' consulting rooms (9); in front of the X-ray unit (2), and on benches outside the exit from the dispensary waiting-hall from where most patients leave (8). Patients whom the researcher sat alongside in various subsettings were encouraged to talk about their experiences at the centre. Here the impressions that the patients reported of events or actions which might suggest elements of depersonalisation in the encounter process were of primary concern for the researcher.

During the observations made in the main waiting-hall (4) where patients await consultations with a doctor, patients appeared subdued and anxious — as might be expected. A number of patients expressed exasperation at the long wait. The opposite was found in observations made in the waiting-hall attached to the dispensary (11) where patients proceed to after the consultation to collect their medication. Here a good deal of light-hearted banter was observed. Patients could frequently be seen reporting on, discussing and comparing "Wat die dokter gesê het". Other patients showed amusement at certain rituals, such as that of falling in with the crocodile-line shifting along the benches until having reached the head of the line, a patient may approach one of the four windows at the dispensary counter (12). Patients in wheelchairs were observed lined up against a wall at the beginning of the corridor to await their consultation with a doctor (10). On certain occasions very tired and frail patients were observed to fall asleep in their wheelchairs with their heads in their laps.

Observations made during participant observation were recorded by jotting down notes during observation; keeping mental notes of conversations with patients and jotting these down immediately afterwards, and writing up comprehensive field notes later in the day. For the most part these notes consisted of running descriptions of the people and events that were observed or reported on, and of things heard and overheard in conversations.

4.3 The in-depth interviewing

The aim in qualitative interviewing is to provide a framework for a subject to speak freely and in his or her own terms about a set of concerns which the researcher brings to the interaction and whatever else the subject may introduce. Generally, a researcher has an idea of what basic issues he or she wishes to cover in interviews. A researcher derives these notions from the formulation of the research problem; analysis of observations in the setting and experiences reported by participants, and hypotheses based on theory. Although free narration by the subjects is encouraged, such narration must be guided if the interviews and the data that are collected are to contribute to the research objectives.

An interview guide is a list of topics and sub-topics within an area of inquiry about which a researcher wishes to gather information. It provides a framework for the interviewer to develop questions, sequence those questions, and make decisions about which information to pursue in greater depth. It also serves as a checklist on which sub-topics may be ticked off as they are covered.

The interview guide that was used in the study was compiled in the following way: An analysis of the observations made during field work and participant observation, and a study of related literature, helped to delineate the problem and to provide topics and subtopics to be covered in the investigation. The topics provided the main division for the guide and a structure for later analysis and interpretation. The ordering of the topics and subtopics on the guide followed the schema of Stimson, Webb (1975) who, in their study *Going to see the doctor*, divided the process into three phases: prior to seeing the doctor (travelling to the facility, clerking in, waiting for the consultation with the doctor); the consultation with the doctor (the face-to-face interaction), and after the consultation (collecting prescribed medication, returning home, evaluating the medical encounter). The guide was also designed to gather general demographic information; data regarding health status; data concerning patterns of seeking medical care at the centre, and information on problems connected with obtaining health care at the centre.

Subjects were interviewed in their homes by the researcher within three weeks of being sampled at the centre. During the interview the researcher endeavoured to assume a non-argumentative, supportive and sympathetically understanding attitude. In terms of Weber's formal and empathic understanding, the procedure was first to establish rapport with the subject and create a warm and accepting atmosphere. It was again pointed out to subjects what the purpose of the interviews was and in what way the data and findings would be used. It was explained that while factual data of the treatment situation and incidents occurring at the centre were sought, the subjects were also invited to communicate their own attitudes and feelings, and in so doing encouraged to lead the interview and to speak freely on topics and issues which were of most concern to them.

Sub-topics were presented to subjects in the form of loosely worded open-ended questions. These were not necessarily presented in the sequence in which they appeared or were grouped under topics on the guide. The aim was to establish a topic for a subject and to allow him or her to structure the answer. This served the purpose of revealing the subject's attitude toward the doctor, the hospital staff, and the treatment and care; the intensity of the subjects feelings on the sub-topics, and the basis upon which the subject had formed opinions which constituted the frame of reference within which the subject answered the question. It also allowed the topic and sub-topics to be elaborated upon and expanded.

The starting-point of the interviews was the subject's self-reports. Regardless of their interpretations of events and situations, these were accepted inasmuch as they were the subjects' own perceptions and therefore subjectively real. In terms of Weber's formal understanding of accounts of experiences which requires an intellectual, logical and rational sequence of thought and action, the rational actions of the subjects were understood by relating the purpose of the reported behaviour to the personal experience of the actions: why the subject did not complain; why he or she did not take the medication, and so on.

Throughout the interviewing it was endeavoured to probe the sentiments underlying the subjects' accounts of their experiences. The researcher was thus alert to the meanings of the information given and consequently posed questions to clarify these meanings. Different questions, or posing questions differently, were also used to cover the same area with subjects. Generalities were analyzed by formulating questions which reduced the generalities to more concrete experiences: *You say that the doctor never listens to you. What did he say when you told him that the pills do not agree with you?.*

The duration of the interviews ranged from 90 to 120 minutes. All fifty interviews were tape-recorded. This was done with the permission of each of the subjects. Patton (1980: 246) points to the necessity in qualitative interviewing of capturing the actual words of the interviewee, there being no substitute for the raw data of actual quotations spoken by interviewees. In addition sparse notes were made during interviews of key sentences and words on spaces provided below each sub-topic on the interview guide. This served as a kind of non-verbal feedback for the researcher. Each space was later fully written up, after replaying the recording and the researcher having sufficient time to note the responses in full. After the replaying of a recording, notes were written on the researcher's impressions of the subject and tentative interpretations of the experiences and events that were recounted. These notes were filed together with the completed interview guide and its face-sheet for later analysis.

On studying and comparing the contents of the completed guides and notes, distinctions, concepts, ideas and patterns were recorded as these became apparent. This provided for an emergent analysis of the situation and strategies in a qualitative, grounded and disciplined manner. The situation could be depicted analytically, in terms of a summing up of its salient features as perceived by the elderly patients, while strategies could be described in terms of flexibility and inventiveness as keynotes in "action options". Recurrences in the ongoing flow of social life in the setting could then be crystallised and articulated for ordered appreciation.

5. FINDINGS

The purpose of analysis in qualitative research is to organise the description of observations so that it becomes manageable. Description is balanced by analysis and leads into interpretation (Patton 1980: 343).

5.1 Analysis of the data

An analysis of the data was made on the basis of the selected analytical units of Lofland (1971), namely acts, activities, meanings, participation, relationships and setting. According to the schema of Stimson, Webb (1975), the analysis was undertaken in three parts, corresponding to the phases of the encounter process: prior to, during, and after the consultation with the doctor. For a proper understanding of the subjects' accounts of their experiences during each of the phases, the reports of the subjects were analysed against the background of the organisational structure of the centre, as this was established during field work and participant observation. This provided a context for the analysis, as the subjects could be viewed in their componental positions within the contextual setting, and facilitated interpretation and evaluation.

It thus became possible to determine which areas of the treatment-seeking process and aspects of the care held the potential for conflict and depersonalisation of elderly patients. Dysfunctional consequences of depersonalising elements of the service could then be connected to deficiencies in the structural and human relations aspects of the organisation.

(i) Prior to the consultation

After individuals decided to seek treatment at an outpatient centre, they need to mobilise themselves. This entails getting to the agency, clerking in, and psychologically preparing for the face-to-face encounter with the doctor. Problems that subjects reported that they experience during this phase were the following: each mode of travel (ambulance, private car, bus) entailed some inconvenience or difficulty; some subjects needed an escort to accompany them through the procedures at the centre; there was frequently confusion about appointments and with clerking in, during which time administrative staff were often impatient or abrupt; patients' files were often "lost", causing delays and resulting in long waits ("Die lêer is ewig en altoos weg"; "They lost my file ... I waited for hours to see the doctor"). The research did not succeed in retrospectively tapping the pre-consultation feelings and expec-

215

tations of the subjects; it is conceivable, though, that the subjects made mental preparations and had notions of strategies that they planned to adopt in order to achieve what they wanted.

(ii) During the consultation

As access was not had to consultations, it could not be observed firsthand what transpired during encounters between subjects and doctors. It was necessary to analyse subjects' reports of consultations and the extent to which they perceived that their expectations had been met. The nature of the consultations and the patients' expectations appeared to differ according to whether a consultation was for an initial diagnosis, monitoring of a condition, or appraising a change in symptoms. What subjects reported took place in the doctors' room was sketchy: Nurses did routine checks, such as taking patients' blood pressure and testing urine, and the time spent with the doctor seemed to be minimal. Some subjects were satisfied with this arrangement while others were less satisfied, depending on how strongly they wished to communicate with the doctor or discuss their conditions ("As jy by dr. ... kom, sê sy net 'trek uit'"; "The doctor sits and smokes all the time, the nurses do the tests"; "The doctor looks, listens, and then does not hesitate to refer you to a specialist, even if it doesn't appear serious"; "The doctor says nothing, asks nothing, tells nothing"; The doctor just changes the pills, that's all") . Generally, communication appeared to be minimal, and it did not seem that the doctors explained the chronic, and thus irreversible, nature of the illnesses to the patients.

In the analysis of the data related to this phase, it became clear that it was necessary to focus on the interaction that subjects reported took place with their doctors. Satisfaction with and effective outcomes of consultations appeared to depend on the nature of the communication that was expected and achieved from doctors during consultations. Within the context of the communication, subjects negotiated and bargained with their doctors for information on their condition and for attaining a desired prescription. Satisfaction with the communication was, for some subjects, dependent on whether the doctor "took his time" with the patient ("She doesn't hurry me"; "She takes all the time in the world to reassure me") ; whether they were able to ask everything they wanted to ("Yes, and then the doctor asks whether there are any other problems"; "Yes, but he doesn't really listen") ; and whether the doctor imparted satisfactory information ("She tells me everything"; Die dokter sê niks"; They don't tell you the diagnosis, what they found in the X-ray, what the bloodsmear showed, what the pills are for"; "Jy weet niks")

Subjects were questioned on their feelings about the doctors who attended them. Liking for a doctor seemed to depend on the subjects' perception of the doctor's concern for them and being prepared to listen to them. Disliking a doctor was influenced by any abruptness of manner and the doctor not prescribing the pills for which the subject had bargained. Some subjects who saw the same doctor regularly had "confidence" in their doctors ("Hy gee wonderlike behandelings"; Sy's altyd dieselfde — dierbaar"), while subjects who saw different doctors on each occasion had less confidence ("I feel you're no-one's patient"; "Jy ken skaars 'n dokter, is daar weer 'n ander een").

(iii) After the consultation

During this phase patients appraise what happened during the consultation, in terms of satisfaction or dissatisfaction with the event, and they come to decisions about using the prescribed treatment. It is paradoxical that while the ability of patients to control the outcomes of consultations is limited, they have considerable ability to control what happens after they leave the centre. Compliance with prescribed treatments thus depends on evaluations of the encounter once patients return to their homes.

A large majority of the subjects were found to be generally satisfied with their consultations ("Am quite satisfied afterwards ... as I expected"). A few subjects expressed dissatisfaction; this was invariably linked to the subjects' expectations not being met ("I'm dissatisfied ... the doctor must look at my legs"; "I didn't get a script"; "Wat hy voorskryf help niks"). Less than half of the subjects reported that they were normally happy with the medicines that they are prescribed ("They give you the best pills ... never try and give you second best"). Subjects who were dissatisfied were often cynical abut the medicines provided by the centre ("Pills from outpatients aren't any good"; "I collect the medicine but I don't take it ... no good").

In addition subjects were questioned on what advantages they perceived in attending the outpatient centre and what they disliked about the centre. The majority stated that the most important advantage for them was that the treatment was free. They often added that because of financial circumstances they had no option but to seek health care at the centre. Some subjects expressed satisfaction with the medical treatment that they receive. Others enjoyed the opportunity for social contact ("Its an outing"). What the majority disliked most about their visits was the long waiting. Many subjects felt frustrated about the frequency with which files were "lost". A substantial proportion experienced transportation difficulties. Some subjects cited the impersonal treatment that they receive from administrative staff and sometimes from doctors. A large number of subjects conceded that they simply "accept" the service as it is.

5.2 Interpretation

Although the focus of the study was on the patients' perceptions of their medical encounters, it remains incumbent upon the qualitative researcher to stand back from his subject and the data and to sociologically interpret their viewpoints. Through the investigation it was possible to develop a holistic picture of how the subjects perceived their medical encounters and the meanings that these held for them. These perceptions and meanings constituted a perspective of the patient world at the setting.

During the analysis of the data definite patterns and dimensions emerged. Their visibility was largely a function of the multiple methods used to collect the data. Certain critical factors in the treatment and situation of elderly patients at the centre appeared which are important in an evaluation. The most prominent of these critical factors were the following: (1) Certain aspects of the procedures at the centre do hold the potential for the depersonalisation of elderly patients. (2) Many elderly patients do not have insight into the chronic nature of their illnesses and hold unreasonable expectations of a cure. In regard to the first critical factor, most subjects did not appear to recognise dehumanising aspects of the care and accepted these as part of the service and the setting. In regard to the second factor, lack of insight and unfulfilled expectations of a cure probably led to the subjects' nonadherence to therapeutic regimens, the failure of the condition to respond, and the consequent dissatisfaction of the subjects with the medical treatments that they receive at the centre.

Where satisfaction with entire encounters or aspects of care was indicated, it is possible that behind much of this lay an uncritical acceptance or lack of discrimination of the treatment stemming from apathy and acquiescence. In this event, states of apathy or resignation could be indicative of extreme alienation of these subjects. It could thus be asserted tentatively that much of the treatment and many aspects of the care that elderly persons receive at the centre do hold the potential for depersonalisation and alienation but are institutionalised and pass unquestioned as outpatient centre "culture". Thus, elderly persons are shaped by and in turn create this social structure.

6. CONCLUSIONS

The conclusions of the study pertain to both the treatment situation at the centre and the appropriateness of the qualitative framework and methodology that was employed.

6.1 Evaluation of the treatment situation

In terms of the qualitative framework used for the investigation, the "evidence" could not be used to substantiate the hypotheses, although the hypotheses did lend guidance to the investigation and certain findings do suggest some support for the hypotheses and in turn call for further theorising.

Certain major difficulties and inconveniences, as perceived by the subjects, were identified in the service for elderly persons. The most important of these were transportation to and from the centre; lengthy waits; interchangeability of doctors; dissatisfaction with prescribed treatments, and abruptness or rudeness from administrative staff. Each of these problems holds the potential for degradation to the self-concepts of these patients. However, aspects of the care and service which were potentially depersonalising for these persons appeared to be overridden by the economic advantages of receiving medical treatment free or at minimal cost.

General passive acceptance and a largely uncritical approach of elderly patients may discourage and even inhibit improvements at the centre. This has serious practical consequences. It was argued thus, that from a humanistic perspective, the system at the centre could be different for elderly persons who as a result of the institutionalised setting, and a combination of advanced age and medical indigence, have fallen into a state of apathy. This could be effected through attention on the part of health professionals and the organisation to the psychosocial needs of elderly patients; through the operation of a rehabilitative model of patient care; through socialisation of patients by doctors in the chronic nature of their illnesses; through a reduction in insensitivity to elderly patients on the part of centre personnel, and through improvements to the physical and social environment at the settings.

6.2 Evaluation of the qualitative research framework

The qualitative research approach employed in the study succeeded in capturing the essence of the patient world at the setting and depicting the real life-world situation of medical encounters for elderly patients at the centre. The approach and the findings of the study were thus found to offer propositions for mitigating some of the shortcomings of earlier, largely quantitative studies on this subject. Inasmuch as the approach achieved a breadth and depth in coverage of the total experiences of the subjects during their medical encounters, it also had an exploratory function in identifying areas that could benefit from both quantitative and qualitative investigation.

One important limitation of the study was the lack of access to consultations which restricted the area of investigation and excluded important interaction from the research. The study of Stimson, Webb (1975) has shown that provided the necessary co-operation can be secured from medical authorities, most patients are willing to allow a researcher to be present during consultations and observe interactions between patient and doctor firsthand.

The perceptions and interpretations of the researchers may have been biased by preconceptions. An expanded triangulation strategy could have involved several observers and interviewers which would have served to reduce or eliminate such personal biases.

Although costly, videotaping of the social action in the setting would have been a useful observational and analytical tool, especially for retrospectively rating interactions to check out hypotheses not formulated initially.

QUESTIONS

1. What are the author's main points of criticism of positivism?

2. It is sometimes claimed that qualitative research does not involve the formulation of hypotheses. Is this true of this study? Discuss.

3. Describe how the author integrated a theoretical approach with her empirical study.

4. How did the author implement Denzin's guidelines regarding triangulation?

5. Qualitative research usually involves taking an insider's point of view. Discuss in what way this is true of Ferreira's study.

6. Describe briefly how participant observation was employed in the study.

7. Discuss the process by which an interview guide was developed to suit the purposes of this study.

8. The overall aim of data-collection is to obtain reliable data. List the precautions taken by the author in this study in order to ensure a high degree of reliability.

NOTES

1. This chapter is based on an unpublished dissertation for the MA degree in Sociology, entitled "A sociological analysis of medical encounters of aged persons at an outpatient centre", submitted to the University of South Africa in 1982.

2. The term "humanistic" is used here to differentiate between "qualitative" and "quantitative" modes of knowing, emphasising the researcher's attempt to understand the subjects in terms of their own construction of social reality. This implies a different anthropological position to that of positivism. See Hughes (1980).

3. References are given as representative examples.

4. According to the traditional trilogy, there are three models of patient care: custodial, classical and rehabilitative. Each model involves a set of assumptions regarding the disease process, goals for caring for patients and some expectations for the role of the patient (cf. Coe 1978: 311-316).

5. According to Mead (1934), society is made up of individuals who have selves. Society shapes the formation of the individual self and the individual is also the creator of society. For Mead, the essence of the self is reflexive; the individual is only such in relation to others.

6. Cooley (1902) sees the development of the self deriving from interaction of the individual with others. An individual's consciousness of himself is a reflection of the ideas that others have of him which the individual ascribes to the thoughts of others. Cooley uses the concept of the "looking-glass self" to illustrate the reflexive nature of the self.

7. W.I. Thomas (1931) sees action in a situation as consisting of three interrelated elements: (i) objective conditions which include socially enforced rules of behaviour; (ii) pre-existing attitudes of the individual and the group, and (iii) the definition of the situation by the actor, influenced by the cultural and social definitions of the group.

8. Thomas (in Thomas, Znaniecki 1928: 578) states that this subjective factor can never be discounted in social analysis for "... If men define situations as real they are real in their consequences".

9. In his dramaturgical approach, Goffman (1959, 1961, 1962, 1963, 1967, 1971) focuses on descriptions of face-to-face interaction in ordinary situations, and analyses the protection and destruction of self-images.

10. See Ferreira (1982: 47-75) for a full exposition of the development of the theoretical perspective for the investigation.

11. "Patient world" as opposed to "provider world". "World" in this sense refers to the background, attitudes and social support systems of each group. See Weinberger et al. (1982).

12. See Ferreira (1982: 76-78, 84-91) for a fuller exposition of the development of the methodological base for the investigation.

13. Ideas put forward on the nature of the qualitative research paradigm derive from those of Filstead (ed.) 1970; Fletcher 1971; Douglas (ed.) 1974; Filstead, in Cook, Reichardt (eds.) 1979: 33-48; Reichard, Cook, in Cook, Reichardt (eds.) 1979: 7-32, and Patton 1980.

14. See Ferreira (1982: 111-115) for a complete description of the sampling procedure.

15. Evening clinics are attended more by working persons and their families, and were thus excluded from the study.

16. First half of 1981.

17. Gold (1958: 217-233) formulated a typology of four types of participant observation, ranging from full disclosure of the identity and purpose of the researcher to those he is observing to total concealment of his role. The role of "observer" refers to full knowledge of the participants of the role of the researcher and that they are being observed by him.

REFERENCES

BRUYN, S. 1962. The methodology of participant observation. *Human Organizations* 21: 224-235.

DENZIN, N.K. 1970. *Sociological methods: A sourcebook.* Chicago: Aldine.

DENZIN, N.K. 1978. *The research act: A theoretical introduction to sociological methods.* New York: McGraw-Hill.

GLASER, B.G. and STRAUSS, A.L. 1967. *The discovery of grounded theory: Strategies for qualitative research.* London: Weidenfeld and Nicolson.

GOLD, R.L. 1958. Roles in sociological field observations. *Social Forces,* 36: 217-223.

LOFLAND, J. 1971. *Analyzing social settings: A guide to qualitative observation and analysis.* Belmont: Wadsworth.

PATTON, M.Q. 1980. *Qualitative evaluation methods.* Beverley Hills: Sage.

STIMSON, G. and WEBB, B. 1975. *Going to see the doctor.* London: Routledge and Kegan Paul.

WEBER, M. 1949. *The methodology of the social sciences.* New York: Free Press. (Shils, E.A., Finch, M.A., trans. and eds.)

APPENDIX 2

A TYPOLOGY OF VALUE ORIENTATIONS

Dian Joubert

1. The study of values

In clarifying the specific concern of this paper, it may be helpful to start with an indication of sociologists' various interests in regard to values and to give examples of some of the more recent work that has been done on these various aspects. The contributions by Rose (1), von Mering (2) and Kelman (3) are relevant to such an ordering of the field, but they are not definitive. Adapting some of the distinctions of these writers, I would suggest that sociological work on values can be classified as belonging to one or more of the following six concerns or categories:

(i) Attention is given in almost all writings on values to the clarification of the conceptual content of the term, also in distinction of related concepts such as attitude, interest, goal, belief and ideology. The nature and function of values was made the specific concern of analyses by, amongst others, Kluckhohn (4), Kluckhohn and Strodtbeck (5), and Joubert (6).

(ii) Accepting the existence of phenomena called *values*, quite a number of social scientists have constructed lists, fields, classifications, categories or typologies of possible values. All these classifications spell out, as von Mering (7) says of his own classification, 'the possible content of the world of open values within which valuing takes place'. Among the better known classifications, or analytical principles used for the classification of values, are: the pattern alternatives of Parsons (8), F. Kluckhohn's variant value orientations (9), C. Kluckhohn's value emphases (10), Sorokin's culture mentalities (11), Riesmans's conformity types (12), Morris's *Paths of life* (13), Allport-Vernon-Lindsey's *Study of values* (14), Dodd's classification (15), White's *Value anal-*

ysis (16), Lipset's value patterns of democracies (17), Fallding's five types of values (18), and Von Mering's four realms (19).

(iii) The logical postulation of possible values should not be confused with the empirical identification of such values among selected populations. The great variety of research procedures and techniques developed and applied to ascertain the values really held by people is aptly demonstrated by the fact that the well-known Comparative Study of Values in Five Cultures conducted by Harvard's Laboratory of Social Relations did not demand commitment on the part of its field workers to a single research design (20). An analysis (21) of the application in empirical research of the classifications mentioned in (ii) above justifies the generalization that the two techniques most generally utilized are content analysis and questionnaires in which respondents have to react to value-statements or value-situations.

(iv) In the theoretical explanation of social phenomena sociologists have repeatedly argued, and proved empirically, that values are decisive variables. All sociological interpretations correlating values with other variables in the explanation of social patterns are of course relevant here. But so is the entire Weber-Parsons-Dahrendorf (22) debate. An intriguing study subjecting this century-old theoretical question about the relative importance and functionality of values and interests to empirical research was published in 1965 by Sister Marie Augusta Neal (23).

(v) A fifth concern of sociologists with values antedates even the values versus interests debate: it is the discussion about the influence of the sociologist's social values on his theorizing and research. If methodological sophistication has done much to bring greater clarity to this turbid area, recent publications such as Gouldner's *The coming crisis of western sociology* (24) and Friedrich's *A sociology of sociology* (25) may well succeed in reopening the debate.

(vi) A last area concerning values in which sociologists are involved and in which discussion needs no revitalizing by Gouldners, is the sociologist's role in social policy and social action. For sociologists who read Afrikaans, Roode (26) has written a substantial summary of relevant viewpoints and it is of some sociological significance that the South African Sociological Society has chosen as the theme of its 1973 congress: The Professionalization of Sociology (27).

These being the areas of interest of values that sociologists have cultivated with varying degrees of productivity, the present paper boldly offers itself as a contribution to concern no. (ii) It is a proposal for a new typology of values or as I prefer to call them, value orientations. In answer to the valid, though somewhat spoil-sporting, question of *why another classification* of value orientations, I would submit the following considerations: new typologies, like new theories and new car models cannot be rejected solely because we already have so many typologies, theories and makes of cars. Again like theories and cars, the worth of typologies must in the end be determined by their functionality — which means that a final appraisal of the proposed typology must await the presentation of empirical data. More important are the objections that some of the existing classifications of value orientations are either mere lists of items referring to value contents not generally applicable outside the population or situation for which it was designed, or presuppose a conception of value orientations which differs from my own. I have elsewhere (21) analyzed and criticized the first 9 classifications mentioned in (ii) above. I can here but generalize : (a) that some of these classifications relate to attitudes or interests or other behavioural components which I do not conceive of as being value orientations; (b) that, with the exception of the Parsonian pattern-alternatives, these classifications were not derived from explicit theoretical principles; and (c) that the majority of them are mere classifications and not typologies which I understand to be logically integrated and logically exhausting classifications.

It follows from these remarks that I must make my own conception of value orientations explicit before a typology is developed.

2. The nature of value orientations

Value orientations may be defined as conceptions of what is generally desirable in social action and relations. Such a definition allows for the distinction of (a) *value* statements from (b) *existential* statements such as 'I am wealthy' and (c) *cathectic* statements such as 'I should like to be rich'. Statements such as 'Striving after wealth should be discouraged' or 'People should be encouraged to become capitalists' clearly belong to a different logical category. In both these sentences the element of desirability is explicit and dominant. This makes them statements or expressions of value orientation.

Given desirability as the primal quality of value orientations, the specification in social action and relations relates a value orientation in the most ordinary instance to a situation where two people are involved in a social relationship or the one (merely) reacts to the other. The specification thus confirms the essentially social nature and social implications of value orientations and also allows for a distinction between value orientations and attitudes. I would suggest that the term *attitude* be reserved for orientations which are primarily cathectic in nature, which do not necessarily or primarily affect a person's action or relations vis-a-vis others; orientations that do not primarily concern desirability in interpersonal relations. The distinction is disputable and I am well aware of the psychological intricacy of attitudes and value orientations in empirical cases. The distinctive quality of value orientations should, however, become clear when these conceptions of the desirable are given operational content in the developed typology.

225

It is a theoretical assumption that values are general principles, which work directively in people's decisions in, commitment to and justification of social actions and relations.

When a particular mode of action or relationship is considered by a person as desirable, it does not imply that this action or relationship is necessarily the one which he, in terms of his interests or need dispositions, wishes or desires. Also it is not assumed that he will consistently want to or be able to act according to this principle; nor that the intensity of his commitment to the directive principle is constant. It is assumed, however, that adults hold single and patterns of general directive principles that can be identified; that these principles are basic to the normative orientations and actions of the personalities concerned; and that these principles can be so specified and identified that they can be used as strategic sociological and social-psychological variables in the description and explanation of social behaviour.

Again, it is not claimed that value orientations are the most important single consideration in decisions, commitments and/or justifications in social behaviour. But value orientations are conceptualized as being the most general normative considerations. The qualification that value orientations only form one component of a person's total orientation to situations, suggests three different research objectives and designs: (a) The determination of what people's value orientations in fact are; (b) Process analysis in which the role of value orientations in a person's total orientation, his decisions, commitments and justifications is determined; (c) The correlation of value orientations with other variables. It should be obvious that process analysis (b) is the most exacting of the three types of research.

The question: which value orientations are possible? is a theoretical question which has to be answered theoretically. The question: which value orientations are present in particular individuals or collectivities? is, on the contrary, an empirical question which has to be answered by empirical research. If any of the value orientations postulated in a typology developed on theoretical assumptions and logical argument, do not empirically appear in a particular universe, this does not invalidate the typology. It does, however, mean that at least part of the typology is not meaningful to the particular universe. Here again the difference but also the interdependence of logical and empirical considerations must be borne in mind.

3. Theoretical assumptions in the construction of a field of value orientations

The construction of a typology of value orientations as conceptualized above requires (a) the explication of definite theoretical assumptions or principles relevant to the plotting of the *field* of (possible) value orientations, and (b) a specification of the *level of abstraction* of the value orientations concerned. Our definition speaks of conceptions of what is *generally* desirable, but *generally* is of course a relative concept. The content given to *value orienta-tions* in the previous paragraph does not by itself answer the question whether these conceptions of the desirable are formulated for application to the whole of humanity, total societies, ethnic groupings, institutional spheres or roles complexes. Obviously such specification of the level of abstraction relates log-ically to the theoretical principles used in the construction of the field and any decision concerning (a) above has implications for (b). We shall, however, leave problem (b) until the next paragraph.

The first theoretical assumption or principle used in the typology can now be explained: as value orientations are conceptions of the desirable within the total area of social action and relations, the specification of particular value orientations can be achieved by ordering this total area into subareas. A meaningful theoretical principle for such a division or differentiation is the four system problems or basic functional categories developed by T. Parsons. Without necessarily committing ourselves to all the intricacies that Parsons has evolved around these categories, we accept that *Integration, Pattern Main-tenance, Adaptation and Goal Achievement* are the most important and general problem complexes in the total field of social action and relations. These four complexes, then, represent the first principle in the ordering of the field and thus the categorization of value orientations. The four func-tional categories give us four main categories of value orientations.

Our argument for this linkage is relatively simple: value orientations being directive principles in people's social decisions, commitments and justifica-tions, it can be accepted that these processes will be maximally activated when behaviour and relations become problematic. Put differently, it seems logi-cal to assume that problems in social relations activate value orientations and therefore to categorize value orientations in terms of these basic problems. It is perhaps necessary to emphasize that we consciously use a theoretical prin-ciple for the first or horizontal structuring of the field of value orientations and that our focus on the problematic aspect of relations rather than on the content or structural aspect, distinguishes our typology from all those more conventional ones which differentiate value orientations in terms of institu-tional content, postulating economic, religious, kinship, educational, politi-cal and other such values. We submit that the lists of such institutional values can hardly ever be closed and that such classifications have a more limited applicability.

The content which we, for our purposes, give to the four problem complex-es, can be stated as follows: *Integration* refers to problems of solidarity amongst people, problems concerning the establishment, maintenance and discon-tinuation of interpersonal relations. In this problem area tension and strain are occasioned by confrontations among personalities and between personal-ities and collectivities. *Pattern Maintenance* refers to problems of maintain-ing, changing and abandoning of normative patterns. In this area tension

227

and strain come about because of the non-mechanical nature of committed-ness and conformity to normative patterns and the relative degree of freedom in the interpretation of these patterns. *Adaptation* refers to the problem of adaptation to external conditions. Here tension and strain originate because there is no easy adjustment to environments and because man can decide to change his orientation or need dispositions, the environment, or both, to ensure a better 'fit'. *Goal achievement* is self-explanatory. Here tension and strain develop because of a break in time and/or means between what people want and what they have.

The introduction of a second theoretical assumption makes possible the 'vertical' division of the four 'horizontal' subareas. We assume, theoretically, that social engagement allows for the differentiation of four dimensions: social *Time*, social *Space*, social *Movement* and social *Involvement*. It is accepted that in decisions, commitment and — justification relevant to what is considered desirable in all four *problem areas*, value orientations relating to all four *dimensions* are necessary and that each of the areas of Integration, Pattern Maintenance, Adaptation and Goal Achievement therefore have to be subcategorized to provide for orientations relevant to social Time, Space, Movement and Involvement.

Before further explication of the four dimensions, it is convenient to state the third and last theoretical principle in the construction of the typology: the formulation of value orientations as *dichotomous choices*. Irrespective of the meaning that can be attached to the terms chosen to indicate the extreme positions, we conceptualize them as opposites and for the purposes of the application of the typology as mutually exclusive.

The substance of social *Time* as a basic dimension of social engagement is given in the possibilities of past, present or future emphases or orientations in interpersonal relations. If we take into account only two possibilities at a time (past or present, present or future) 4 dichotomies of value orientations and 8 unitary value orientations relevant to social *Time* can be distinguished:

EXCLUSIVENESS (ITa) vs. INCLUSIVENESS (ITz)
TRADITIONALISM (PTa) vs. SITUATIONISM (PTz)
ACQUIESCENCE (ATa) vs. REFORM (ATz)
SHORT-TERM-OBJECTIVES (GTa) vs. LONG-TERM-OBJECTIVES (GTz)

The dimension of social *Space* refers to the range of social engagement. Relevant to this range are decisions on the degree of committedness to collectivities, the homogeneity/heterogeneity of social solidarity, autonomy/independence of other people. Provision must also be made for projections or references to a transcendental space. Four dichotomies and 8 unitary value orientations relevant to social *Space* can be distinguished:

TYPOLOGY OF VALUE ORIENTATIONS

Dimensions of social engagement	Integration	Pattern maintenance	Adaptation	Goal Achievement
Social TIME	(a) Inclusiveness	(a) Traditionalism	(a) Acquiescence	(a) Short-term-objectives
	vs.	vs.	vs.	vs.
T	(z) Exclusiveness IT	(z) Situationism PT	(z) Reform AT	(z) Long-term-objectives GT
Social SPACE	(a) Individualism	(a) Pluralism	(a) Transcendentalism	(a) Interdependence
	vs.	vs.	vs.	vs
S	(z) Collectivism IS	(z) Uniformity PS	(z) Secularism AS	(z) Autonomy GS
Social MOVEMENT	(a) Ascription	(a) Tolerance	(a) Particularism	(a) Idealism
	vs.	vs.	vs.	vs.
M	(z) Achievement IM	(z) Conformity PM	(z) Universalism AM	(z) Pragmatism GM
Social INVOLVEMENT	(a) Discipline	(a) Perfectionism	(a) Dilligence	(a) Planning
	vs.	vs.	vs.	vs.
In	(z) Satisfaction-of-self IIn	(z) Indifference PIn	(z) Carefreeness AIn	(z) Laissez-faire GIn

INDIVIDUALISM (ISa) vs. COLLECTIVISM (ISz)
PLURALISM (PSa) vs. UNIFORMITY (PSz)
TRANSCENDENTALISM (ASa) vs. SECULARISM (ASz)
INTERDEPENDENCE (GSa) vs. AUTONOMY (GSz)

The dimension of social *Movement* refers to people's mutual acceptance/ non-acceptance. Transposed to the level of value orientations, this dimension demands principles or conceptions of desirability to give direction in these, essentially, sociometric choices. Four dichotomies and 8 unitary value orientations relevant to social *Movement* can be distinguished:

ASCRIPTION (IMa) vs. ACHIEVEMENT (IMz)
TOLERANCE (PMa) vs. CONFORMITY (PMz)
PARTICULARISM (AMa) vs. UNIVERSALISM (AMz)
IDEALISM (GMa) vs. PRAGMATISM (GMz)

The dimension of social *Involvement* refers to energy output or a passive/active orientation in social engagements. Four dichotomies and 8 unitary value orientations relevant to social *Involvement* are distinguished:

DISCIPLINE (IIna) vs. SATISFACTION-OF-SELF (IInz)
PERFECTIONISM (PIna) vs. INDIFFERENCE (PInz)
DILIGENCE (AIna) vs. CAREFREENESS (AInz)
PLANNING (GIna) vs. LAISSEZ-FAIRE (GInz)

The paradigm shows the location of 16 dichotomies and 32 unitary value orientations within the entire field, derived by the logical intersection of the four problem complexes and the four dimensions of social engagement.

It must be stated explicitly that we do not make any assumptions about the inter-connectedness of the respective dichotomies or unitary value orientations. Patterns of value orientations have to be determined empirically.

The definitions of value orientations (28) are formulated in strict accordance with the conceptual content given to problem complexes and dimensions of social engagement. Dictionary and conventional definitions of the terms we have chosen are not really relevant. The connotations of the terms remain dependent on the theoretical context based on the three theoretical principles.

4. Levels of abstraction in value orientations

The problem of the level of abstraction stated at the beginning of the previous paragraph, can now be given attention. The question is this: for what range of action and relations is a particular value orientation a generalized conception of what is desirable? The work of Kluckhohn and Strodtbeck (5) and Neil Smelser (29) is not only relevant to this question but of great help. If acquaintance with these publications can be taken for granted, the following generalizations concerning the level of abstraction of the proposed typology, should be intelligible.

We view the 32 unitary value orientations as relevant to all spheres of social action, and the developed typology as applicable to all societies, irrespective of their social and cultural differences — as Kluckhohn and Strodtbeck do with regard to the value orientations that they distinguish. In terms of Smelser's levels of specificity, the proposed typology can be said to represent 'societal values'. Smelser's second level of specificity is that of institutional sectors or spheres. We are aware that T. Parsons has suggested that there is a more direct relation between particular institutional complexes and particular functions, between e.g. politics and Goal Achievement, economy and Adaptation, etc. We would, however, not advise for these correlations to be taken to extremes. Our typology is definitely applicable to a particular institutional complex but we would insist that all four problem complexes and all four dimensions of engagement remain valid and relevant, which means that to any one institutional complex all of the 32 unitary value orientations apply, or, are theoretically possible.

There can, furthermore, be no objection to any attempt to apply the developed typology to the more specific levels differentiated within the value component of action as given by Smelser. The validity and meaningfulness of the typology for collectivities of varying range (societies, communities, groups, etc.) are not problematical, at least not logically or theoretically so, if the unitary value orientations are indexed or operationalized in the form of *value statements* to which *individuals* have to react. I have developed such a test containing 64 value statements and first results have brought relative assurance on the meaningfulness of the typology as well as the practicality of using value statements in questionnaires.

Further remarks on the empirical identification or measurement of value orientations would take us beyond the intended scope of this paper. One last point is, however, in order: if the technique of reaction to value statements is used, the *content* of these statements obviously have to be adjusted to (i) the level of specificity (society, institutional complex, etc.), (ii) the range of the collectivities in which individuals are questioned (society, community, group, organization), (iii) the sociocultural patterns — it would obviously not do to have statements referring to social situations and cultural items that none or few of the respondents have experienced, and (iv) the educational status of the respondents.

QUESTIONS

1. How does the author justify his attempt at constructing yet another typology of value-orientations?

2. How is value-orientation defined?

3. The author lists a number of theoretical assumptions or postulates which underlie his analysis. Discuss them briefly.

4. The author identifies two important issues in the construction of a typology of value-orientations: the explication of definite theoretical principles and a specification of the level of abstraction of the value orientations. With regard to the first issue, Joubert discusses three such principles. Discuss how the construction of the typology on the basis of these principles constitutes a deductive research strategy.

5. What claims regarding the external validity of the typology are made?

6. A typology such as this provides an explicit frame of reference for empirical research. Discuss.

7. Discuss how Joubert's typology meets the criterion of a good typology, viz mutually exclusive and exhaustive classification.

NOTES

1. Rose, A.M. 1956. Sociology and the study of values. *The British Journal of Sociology*, 7/1, pp. 1-17.

2. Von Mering, O. 1961. *A grammar of human values*, Pittsburg.

3. Kelman, H.C. 1968. *Time to speak — On human values and social research*, San Francisco.

4. Kluckhohn, Clyde. 1954. Values and value orientations in the theory of action, in: Parsons & Shils (Eds.), *Toward a general theory of action*, Cambridge, Mass.

5. Kluckhohn, F. & Strodtbeck, F.I. 1961. *Variations in value orientations*, Evanston.

6. Joubert, Dian D. 1964. *Die waardekonsep in die sosiologiese teorie*, Cape Town.

7. Von Mering, O., *Op. cit.*, p. 90.

8. Parsons, T. & Shils, E.A. (Eds.) *Op. cit.*

9. Kluckhohn, F. & Strodtbeck, F.I., *Op. cit.*

10. Kluckhohn, Clyde. 1958. *The scientific study of values*, University of Toronto Installation Lectures.

11. Sorokin, P.A. 1957. *Social and cultural dynamics*, New York.

12. Riesman, D. *et al.* 1955. *The lonely crowd*, New York.

13. Morris, Charles. 1956. *Paths of life*, New York. Also: *Varieties of human value*, Chicago.

14. Allport-Vernon-Lindzey. 1951. *Study of values*, Boston.

15. Dodd, S.C. 1951. On classifying human values: A step in the prediction of valuing, in: *American Sociological Review*, 16/5, pp. 645-653.

16. White, R.K. 1951. *Value-analysis — The nature and use of the method*, Society for the Psychological Study of Social Issues

17. Lipset, S.M. 1963. The value patterns of democracy. *American Sociological Review*, 28/4, pp. 515-531.

18. Fallding, H. 1965. A proposal for the empirical study of values. *American Sociological Review*, 30/2, pp. 223-233.

19. Von Mering, O., *Op. cit.*

20. *Ibid.*, p. xix.

21. Joubert, D.D. 1965. *Waarde-navorsing: 'n Oriëntasie ten opsigte van teoretiese konsepsie, metodologiese beginsels, tipologieë en ondersoek metodes in navorsing oor waardestelsels van samelewings.* Unpublished report completed for National Council for Social Research, 1962. See also Dian D. Joubert, Die waardes van samelewings, *Journal for Social Research*, 14/1, pp. 83-88.

22. Dahrendorf, R. 1959. *Class and class conflict in industrial society*, London.

23. Neal, M.A. 1965. *Values and interests in social change*, Englewood Cliffs, N.J.

24. Gouldner, A.W. 1970. *The coming crisis of western sociology*, London.

25. Friedrichs, R.W. 1970. *A sociology of sociology*, New York.

26. Roode, C.D. 1972. Waardebetrokkenheid, die sosiologie en die sosioloog, in: *Suid-Afrikaanse Tydskrif vir Sosiologie*, no. 4, pp. 4-13.

27. *Ibid.*

28. *Definitions of Value Orientations*

   I. *Exclusiveness — Inclusiveness* (Integration/Time)
   Exclusiveness places the emphasis on the maintenance of identity, homogeneity, and solidarity established over time. Inclusiveness refers to a readiness to enter into new solidarities, a readiness to associate with people who are 'different'.

II. *Individualism — Collectivism* (Integration/Space)
Individualism indicates the placing of the interests of the individual above those of the collectivity. Collectivism indicates the placing of the interests of the collectivity above those of the individual.

III. *Ascription — Achievement* (Integration/Movement)
Ascription indicates respect for and acceptance of other people because of what they are, rather than because of what they have achieved. It means that someone's sex, age, race, ethnic group and kinship or family connections count more than his personal achievements in decisions on the degree of respect or acknowledgement accorded him or readiness to interact with him in kinship, occupational and associative roles. Achievement indicates respect for and acceptance of other people primarily because of the positions, qualities and achievements they have attained through their own efforts, application and abilities.

IV. *Discipline — Satisfaction-of-Self* (Integration/Involvement)
Discipline indicates an emphasis on self-control and a subordination of self-satisfaction because this, when indulged, can disturb the more important group order. Discipline would also more often approve than disapprove of the use of punishment/control/regimentation. Satisfaction-of-Self indicates a giving of priority to own satisfaction/ indulgence/expression above discipline for the sake of others.

V. *Traditionalism — Situationism* (Pattern Maintenance/Time)
Traditionalism indicates the granting of priority to old-established patterns of behaviour. It is conservative and bent on maintaining the pattern. The emphasis is always on the past. Situationism indicates a readiness to subject the applicability of patterns of behaviour to the demands set by a specific situation. It includes a preparedness to apply the principles of expedience and efficacy.

VI. *Pluralism — Uniformity* (Pattern Maintenance/Space)
Pluralism indicates a readiness to live with people who have other views and patterns of behaviour without attempting to standardise everything. Uniformity indicates a stress on uniformity/homogeneity/standardisation in patterns of behaviour within defined groups.

VII. *Tolerance — Conformity* (Pattern Maintenance/Movement)
The question here is about tolerance/intolerance of 'different' patterns of behaviour of other people who in any case have to be lived with. This differs from Pluralism — Uniformity in that the emphasis does not fall on the desirability of variety/standardisation of patterns of behaviour within particular collectivities. The stress is on acceptance of other people and patience with them in spite of their 'otherness', or otherwise impatience and emphasis that others are acceptable only if they conform to 'our' patterns.

234

VII. *Perfectionism — Indifference* (Pattern Maintenance/Involvement)
Perfectionism — Indifference refers to differences that can exist with regard to the degree to which accepted patterns of behaviour must be complied with. It touches upon freedom of movement in one's commitment to accepted rules of conduct.

IX. *Acquiescence — Reform* (Adaptation/Time)
Acquiescence indicates readiness to rest in circumstances rather than to try to affect them in some way. Reform indicates the attitude that man can usually do something about his circumstances, that he ought to do it, and that he can thereby improve his adjustment.

X. *Transcendentalism — Secularism* (Adaptation/Space)
Transcendentalism indicates the projection of problems of adjustment to an other-worldly or supernatural space. It includes religious interpretations of problemsituations; a rejection of 'worldliness'. Secularism indicates an acceptance and activation of the given perceived world as the only space within which can be sought and found meaningfulness.

XI. *Particularism — Universalism* (Adaptation/Movement)
Particularism implies that one's treatment of and interaction with other people is dependent upon one's particular personal relationships to them. Universalism implies that when other people fall into a specific category, one treats them all in exactly the same way and does not allow personal preferences or personal relationships outside the particular role in which the action takes place to have an influence. Universalism is connected with the ability and readiness to make role distinctions. Particularism represents a lesser inclination to keep roles separate.

XII. *Diligence — Carefreeness* (Adaptation/Involvement)
Diligence indicates a belief in action and zeal in order to ensure satisfactory adjustment. Carefreeness indicates an attitude of un-worriedness, passivity and disinclination to accept responsibility.

XIII. *Short-term Objectives — Long term Objectives* (Goal Achievement/Time)
Short-term objectives indicates a belief that it is sufficient and/or possible to plan in advance for only a limited period, that one must not expect too much of the future. Long-term objectives indicates belief in the meaningfullness of aims which lie in the distant future.

XIV. *Interdependence — Autonomy* (Goal Achievement/Space)
Interdependence recognises that objectives can be achieved only with the cooperation of others. Autonomy stresses independence in goal achievement.

XV. *Idealism — Pragmatism* (Goal Achievement/Movement)
Idealism indicates belief in ideals which are not necessarily attainable

in practice. In contrast, pragmatism elevates practicability to the level of a primary requirement of all objectives.

XVI. *Planning* — *Laissez-faire* (Goal Achievement/Involvement)
Planning emphasises systematic advance arrangements. Laissez-faire denies that matters have to be planned in order to be successful.

29. Smelser, N.J. 1963. *Theory of collective behavior.*

APPENDIX 3

HUMAN FACTORS IN STOPE PRODUCTIVITY — A FIELD EXPERIMENT

KF Mauer and AC Lawrence

SYNOPSIS

An experiment in which three human variables were manipulated in eight stopes was conducted in a gold mine over a period of roughly six months. The three variables, which each had two levels, concerned the degree of movement from gangs, the quality of the black production supervisors, and the extent to which gangs were composed of a single ethnic group (Malawians). Time was included as a variable with three levels in the analysis of the findings. On the average, stable gangs produced 12 per cent more than gangs with a high percentage of transfers, gangs with better production supervisors were more successful by nearly 9 per cent than those with poorer production supervisors, and homogeneous gangs were more productive than heterogeneous ones by as much as 15 per cent. In addition, it was found that a number of the variables exercised a joint influence on stope productivity and that the effects of the variables were accentuated by the length of time they had been in operation.

INTRODUCTION

A good deal of research has revealed the presence of significant correlation between various human factors and work performance. Although such findings are useful in identifying those human factors that play a part in work performance, two considerations limit their practical utility. Firstly, the cause and effect relationship is not always clear. For example, does an authorita-

237

rian style of management result in low production as is often suggested, or does low performance result in an authoritarian style? Secondly, even if the causal direction can be correctly inferred, it is seldom clear to what extent other considerations will interfere with the application of the findings in practice. For example, high turnover of labour may be shown to result in low production, but it does not follow that adequate steps can be taken in practice to reduce turnover and thereby raise production.

The solution to the first problem lies in a research design that experiments with or manipulates, in a controlled manner, those variables thought to cause changes in production (the *independent* variables), and that assesses the effect of these manipulations on some measure of work performance (the *dependent* variable or *criterion*). An experimental design also solves the second problem, provided that the experiment is conducted in a natural setting in the *field*, that is, under actual working conditions rather than artificial or laboratory conditions.

This paper describes a field experiment that examined the effects of three human factors over a period of time on the productivity of eight stoping gangs in a gold mine.

WORK PERFORMANCE CRITERION

The choice of a criterion for the assessment of stope productivity posed certain problems. While it was generally agreed that the most adequate measure of stoping performance would be based on monthly survey measurements, the use of such figures would have required the extension of the experiment over a considerable period of time to ensure sufficient observations for statistical evaluation. A proposal to conduct the experiment over a period of a year or more was likely to have met with resistance from the participants. Even while people might initially have been agreeable, interest in the research might have lagged, and stopes included at the outset might have become worked out before valid conclusions could have been reached.

A measure of stoping productivity that was readily available in the mine was *tons trammed per stope per week*. Although clearly not as reliable as survey measurements, it appeared that these figures would provide an adequate criterion for the purposes of the experiment.

INDEPENDENT VARIABLES

The four independent variables included "time" (with three levels) and three human factors (each with two levels).

The latter were selected from among those that had been shown to be related to gang performance in previous exploratory research similar to that described by Lawrence (1972), and that could be manipulated with compara-

238

tive ease in the mine. The aim of the experiment was to determine the extent to which changes in these four variables resulted in changes in the criterion.

Time

The experiment was conducted over a period of about six months, and for the analysis this was divided into three periods of approximately equal length. These three levels are referred to as *time 1, time 2,* and *time 3.*

Ethnic composition of stoping gangs

The proportion of Malawian workers employed in the mine was considerably greater than that of any other group. To test the hypothesis that ethnic homogeneity was conducive to higher productivity, the ethnic structures of four of the eight gangs involved in the experiment were changed so that Malawians were in the majority. The Malawian content of these gangs was raised from about 35 per cent to more than 50 per cent. These gangs were then referred to as the *homogeneous* gangs and constituted Level 1 of this variable.

The ethnic structure of the other four gangs was changed so that no one tribe exceeded more than 30 per cent of the gang complement. These gangs formed Level 2 and were referred to as the *heterogeneous* gangs.

Mobility of men in stoping gangs

Mobility of mineworkers from one gang to another as the result of transfers was fairly considerable in the mine. Exploratory analysis suggested that movement of less than 4 per cent per week occurred in only 37 per cent of gangs, that in 54 per cent of gangs movement was between 4 and 9 per cent, and that the remaining 9 per cent of gangs had movement in excess of 9 per cent.

To test the hypothesis that excessive mobility had a detrimental effect on productivity, at least 12 per cent of the men in the gangs were transferred every week from four of the experimental gangs. Once a man had been transferred from a gang, he was not allowed to return to that gang. These gangs were called *mobile* and constituted Level 1 of this variable.

To limit the extent to which miners and shift bosses were likely to resent the experimental treatments, these men decided which blacks were to be transferred from the mobile gangs each week. Transfers were not allowed in the other four gangs, and the only movement was that resulting from the expiry of individual contracts. This never amounted to more than 4 per cent per week during the course of the experiment. These gangs were called the *stable* gangs and formed Level 2 of the variable.

In the preceding exploratory study it had been found that a number of variables associated with black production supervisors bore a relationship to stope production. It was therefore decided to include a factor related to the quality of black supervision in gangs. A schedule designed to assess the on-the-job performance of black production supervisors was employed for this purpose. The schedule contained 52 items, which constituted four scales related to job performance. The scales were called *subordinate relations, production and communication, accident prevention, and physical job requirements.*

Miners and shift bosses assessed their black production supervisors by means of the schedule, and for Level 1 of this variable four of the experimental gangs were allowed production supervisors who were graded as at least stanine 6 on the *production and communication* and *the subordinate relations* scales. This meant that the performance of the production supervisors in these gangs was equal to or better than that of the upper 40 per cent of black production supervisors in general.

For Level 2 of this variable, the other four gangs were allocated black production supervisors who were rated at stanine 4 or less in other words, the performance of production supervisors in these gangs was no better than that of the lower 40 per cent of black production supervisors in general.

EXPERIMENTAL DESIGN

To accommodate the four independent variables effectively, the eight stoping gangs were arranged in a conventional 2x2x2x3 factorial design, as shown in Table 1. Each cell of the table represents a different combination of the three human factors split over the three periods of time. For example, the first cell describes conditions $A_1B_1C_1$; which applied to one gang during the three time periods T_1, T_2 and T_3. Hence, the code $A_1B_1C_1T_1$ represents, for time period 1, the gang that was *homogeneous* (A_1), stable (B_1), and that had *production supervisors of better quality* (C_1).

For optimum results, the eight stopes in which the gangs worked should have been identical in all respects. Although the mine had roughly eighty production stopes at the time of the experiment, it was only with considerable difficulty that eight stopes could be found that approximated the experimental requirements. However, with the assistance of mine management, an attempt was made to ensure that the stopes were equivalent in terms of reef (all were situated in the Kimberley reef area), wet-bulb temperature, access time, face length, gang strength, ability of the responsible contractor, and stoping method (largely determined by the dip of the reef). In addition, it was necessary to ensure that the selected stopes had an expected life of at least six months.

TABLE 1

ARRANGEMENT OF THE EXPERIMENTAL TREATMENTS IN THE EIGHT STOPES

Supervision	Time period	Homogeneous (A_1)		Heterogeneous (A_2)	
		Stable (B_1)	Mobile (B_2)	Stable (B_1)	Mobile (B_2)
Better supervision (C_1)	Time 1 (T_1)	$A_1B_1C_1T_1$	$A_1B_2C_1T_1$	$A_2B_1C_1T_1$	$A_2B_2C_1T_1$
	Time 2 (T_2)	$A_1B_1C_1T_2$	$A_1B_2C_1T_2$	$A_2B_1C_1T_2$	$A_2B_2C_1T_2$
	Time 3 (T_3)	$A_1B_1C_1T_3$	$A_1B_2C_1T_3$	$A_2B_1C_1T_3$	$A_2B_2C_1T_3$
Poorer supervision (C_2)	Time 1 (T_1)	$A_1B_1C_2T_1$	$A_1B_2C_2T_1$	$A_2B_1C_2T_1$	$A_2B_2C_2T_1$
	Time 2 (T_2)	$A_1B_1C_2T_2$	$A_1B_2C_2T_2$	$A_2B_1C_2T_2$	$A_2B_2C_2T_2$
	Time 3 (T_3)	$A_1B_1C_2T_3$	$A_1B_2C_2T_3$	$A_2B_1C_2T_3$	$A_2B_2C_2T_3$

TABLE II

DEVIATION (%) IN TONS TRAMMED PER WEEK FROM BASE LEVEL

Supervision	Time period	Homogeneous (A_1)		Heterogeneous (A_2)	
		Stable (B_1)	Mobile (B_2)	Stable (B_1)	Mobile (B_2)
Better supervision (C_1)	T_1	−5,39	18,57	−2,49	−9,22
	T_2	−13,24	38,41	3,91	−26,90
	T_3	11,21	46,53	1,35	−8,38
Poorer supervision (C_2)	T_1	2,29	0,44	11,17	−15,85
	T_2	16,52	−3,45	41,28	−43,89
	T_3	24,25	−21,68	27,99	−44,52

TABLE III

	Source	Sum of squares	df	Variance estimate	F-Value	p
Main effects	A	8 374,44	1	8 374,44	43,46	<0,001
	B	7 663,22	1	7 663,22	39,77	<0,001
	C	1 882,48	1	1 822,48	9,46	<0,003
	T	557,11	2	278,55	1,45	Not sig.
Second-order interactions	AB	21 756,27	1	21 756,27	112,90	<0,001
	AC	4 502,76	1	4 502,76	23,37	<0,001
	AT	921,86	2	460,93	2,39	Not sig.
	BC	25 204,87	1	25 204,87	130,79	<0,001
	BT	2 776,31	2	1 388,15	7,20	<0,001
	CT	2 092,47	2	1 046,24	5,43	<0,005
Third-order interactions	ABC	376,84	1	376,84	1,96	Not sig.
	ABT	3 692,48	2	1 846,24	9,58	<0,001
	ACT	640,23	2	320,12	1,66	Not sig.
	BCT	4 227,48	2	2 113,74	10,97	0,001
Fourth-order interaction	ABCT	78,03	2	39,02	0,20	Not sig.
	Error	24,666,50	128	192,71		

FIGURE 1 — MAIN EFFECTS

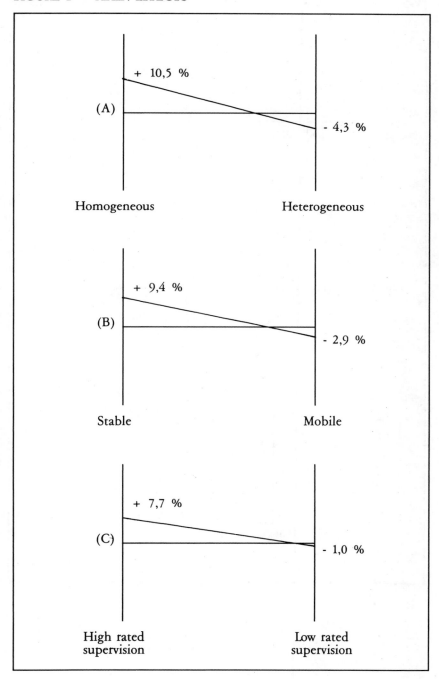

FIGURE 2 — SECOND-ORDER INTERACTIONS

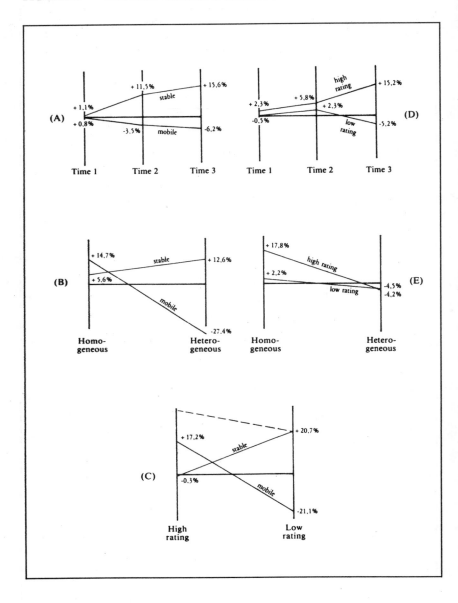

FIGURE 3 — THIRD-ORDER INTERACTIONS

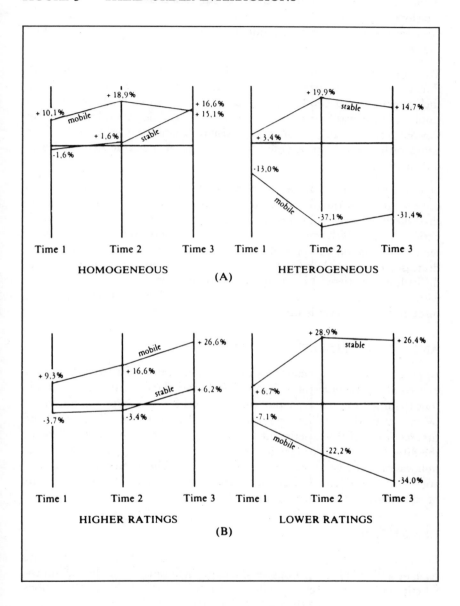

A further consideration in the choice of stopes was that they should not be too close to one another. This was necessary to limit the extent to which various treatments might have contaminated one another, thereby confounding the results.

The stopes were also split across two shafts. To counteract the possible influences of different styles of management, the treatments were allocated in such a manner that two homogeneous gangs were situated at each shaft. A similar strategy was followed with regard to the mobile gangs. However, this was not possible with the black supervision variable and, as a result, three gangs with "better" supervision were situated at the same shaft and only one at the other.

Once the experiment had been set up, it remained necessary to exercise constant control over the treatments imposed upon the various stopes to ensure that conditions were being met. A number of problems arose in the six-month period during which the experiment was being conducted. These problems related to fears on the part of shift bosses that production output would decrease, a pressure burst that occurred in one of the experimental stopes, difficulties experienced in maintaining homogeneous conditions associated with year-end labour intakes, and an observed falling-off of interest among mine personnel towards the end of the experiment.

ANALYSIS OF RESULTS

Approximately twenty weekly measures of tons trammed were obtained for each combination of factors in Table 1. As historical information about weekly tons trammed was not available, the base level for each stope was estimated by the calculation of linear regressions for the performance figures for the first six weeks of the experiment and setting $x = 0$ in $y = mx$ıb. To allow for the different levels of production in the eight stopes, the percentage deviation was calculated each week from the base level. The mean percentage deviations for each of the 24 treatments are shown in Table II, and the results of the analysis of variance in Table III.

DISCUSSION

By means of the analysis-of-variance technique it is possible to evaluate the separate and joint influence of several independent variables on the experimental criterion. As the technique does not rely on a single set of observations but rather on all observations for all treatments in which a condition occurs, the findings are more stable and there is less chance of misinterpretation than with some other techniques.

If the level for rejection of the null hypothesis is set at the $p = 0,005$ level, it can be seen from Table III that the only effects that were not significant were the main effect for time, the second-order interaction between homogeneity and time, the third-order interactions between homogeneity, mobility, and rated quality of black supervision and between homogeneity, supervision and time, and the single interaction between all four factors.

In general, the *p*-values were so small that the differences reflected in Table III could not be attributed to chance.

Where an interaction exists, it indicates that a factor has different effects on the criterion under different conditions of a second factor, and under these conditions it may be misleading to view the main effects of a factorial experiment individually. However, the findings are more readily understood if main effects as well as second- and third-order interactions are reviewed.

MAIN EFFECTS

Ethnic Homogeneity

Figure 1(A) shows that those gangs with more than 50 per cent Malawians had a mean overall improvement of 10,5 per cent per gang in tons trammed per week when interactions with other variables were ignored. In the case of the ethnically heterogeneous gangs, however, weekly production was depressed to the extent of 4,3 per cent per week on the average during the course of the experiment.

The advantage resulting from the creation and maintenance of gangs in which one ethnic group predominated was relatively large, and the apparent loss of production associated with the random allocation of labour makes the introduction of the former condition appear worth while.

Mobility

The difference in productivity between mobile and stable gangs was slightly smaller than the difference in the preceding case. In those gangs in which movement was restricted, production increased by an average of roughly 10 per cent per week. The mean loss, on the other hand, in the four mobile gangs amounted to 3 per cent week per gang — a difference of 13 per cent. This is illustrated clearly in Figure 1(B).

Quality of Black Supervision

Figure 1(C) illustrates the findings regarding the rated quality of production supervisors as assessed by miners and shift bosses in relation to stope productivity.

The four gangs that were assessed as having better-quality production supervisors showed a mean weekly increase of nearly 8 per cent per gang. In the gangs with supervision that was assessed as less adequate, production output dropped by 1 per cent per week.

SECOND-ORDER INTERACTIONS

Mobility in Gangs

The main effect illustrated in Figure 1(B) has shown that, in general, the four mobile gangs suffered a drop in mean production of only about 3 per cent, while the performance of stable gangs increased by 9 per cent. However, the significant second-order interactions listed in Table III showed that the impact of gang mobility could be judged only if other variables were taken into account.

Firstly, these percentages were the mean or average figures for the whole experiment, but the impact of gang mobility was found to have accumulated over time as shown in Figure 2(A). By the end of the third time period, stable gangs had improved by nearly 16 per cent, while the mobile gangs had dropped by more than 6 per cent. In addition, the effects appeared to be continuing; there was no indication that the trends would not have continued if the experiment had been of longer duration.

Secondly, as shown in Figure 2(B), the combination of gang mobility with gang heterogeneity resulted in a drop in production of 27 per cent, whereas stable gangs improved their performance by nearly 13 per cent, even under heterogeneous conditions. Under homogeneous conditions, the difference between mobile and stable gangs was less marked. In fact, the homogeneous gangs functioned somewhat better under mobile conditions, although the reasons for this are not yet fully understood. It seems that the effect of mobility in a homogeneous gang was entirely different from that in a heterogeneous gang. Perhaps, when a gang was essentially of one ethnic group, there was not much disruption as a result of men joining and leaving, and, in fact, the mobility may have served a useful purpose by bringing the men fresh news of their families and homeland and so on.

Thirdly, Figure 2(C) shows how the effect of mobility was dependent also on the quality of black supervision. Poor supervision coupled with gang mobility was associated with a *drop* in production of 21 per cent, whereas gang stability compensated for poor supervision and was associated with an *increase* in production of 21 per cent.

Gang mobility under conditions of "good" supervision seemed to have a beneficial result. It is likely, however, that Figure 2 shows that so-called "good" black production supervisors were those who could cope with the highly mobile conditions that exist in the industry, and that they had not been trained in the leadership skills necessary to capitalize on the benefits inherent in stable gangs. Presumably, the poorer production supervisors had

248

less influence on their gangs and did not interfere with their potential to produce effectively. If this hypothesis is correct, one would expect that, if production supervisors had been trained to benefit from gang stability, the performance of their gangs would have been reflected by a line such as that shown dotted in Figure 2(C).

In general, it is clear that excessive mobility was a serious consideration so far as gang production was concerned.

Quality of Supervision

The effect of black production supervisors of different calibre was also subject to the influence of variables other than mobility. The arrangement of production supervisors did not have an immediate effect on the performance of the gangs but, as time passed, the output of the gangs with the better supervisors improved by 15 per cent, whereas the gangs with poorer supervisors deteriorated by 5 per cent — Figure 2(D).

Also, the better production supervisors were able to achieve more with homogeneous gangs than was possible with heterogeneous gangs — Figure 2(E). Heterogeneity resulted in a fall in output regardless of the quality of the supervisors.

THIRD-ORDER INTERACTIONS

The two significant third-order interactions listed in Table III emphasize further the importance of the time element to the introduction of changes such as those in the experiment. There is sometimes a tendency when organizational changes are made to look for or to be influenced by short-term results and perhaps to discontinue worthwhile innovations before sufficient time has been allowed for the effects to be demonstrated.

The third-order interaction illustrated in Figure 3(A) shows that the second-order interactions between homogeneity and mobility changed over the course of time. Had there been no time effect, the two diagrams in Figure 3(A) would have resembled that in Figure 2(B).

Stable gangs tended to produce superior long-term results irrespective of whether the gangs were composed predominantly of Malawians or of a variety of tribes. The opposite tendency was observed where gangs were mobile. It was evident that mobility combined with heterogeneity produced the largest overall drop in productivity. This effect was magnified by the passage of time with decreases of 37 and 31 per cent during the last two periods. Although there was a slight upward tendency in productivity for these gangs over the last period of time, this appeared to have been attributable to the reluctance on the part of shift bosses to continue transferring men, which resulted in the required percentage of transfers not being maintained during the closing phase.

The interaction shown in Figure 3(B) is rather perplexing. Under stable gang conditions, the gangs under black production supervisors with lower assessments produced better results than the gangs under better supervisors. There was a tendency for gangs with better supervision to show an improvement in the last time period of the experiment, whereas those with poorer supervision dropped off in output. This may have been a result of the rearrangement of black production supervisors, and, if the experiment had been extended and if these trends had continued, the stable gangs with better supervision may have emerged as the higher producers.

Under mobile conditions, the gangs that had better-quality production supervisors showed an increase of nearly 27 per cent per week in tons trammed per gang at the end of the experiment. The combination of inadequate supervision and mobility exerted a strong negative influence on productivity, which increased with time. The mean production loss per week in those gangs with a combination of mobile conditions and supervisors with low ratings amounted to 34 per cent per week at the conclusion of the experiment.

CONCLUSION

Field experiments that involve human beings and their work performance are not always easily designed. The following are some of the more important considerations that were taken into account in the experiment described in this paper.

(a) There are moral and ethical limits to the extent to which human beings can be experimented with.

(b) The level of work performance is influenced not by one human factor but by numerous factors acting and interacting simultaneously. The number of human factors that can be experimented with simultaneously is usually restricted by practical considerations to three or four.

(c) A change in a relevant human factor is unlikely to have an *immediate* effect on work performance. The effect is more likely to be revealed only over a period of time, and the experiment must continue long enough to permit this.

(d) On the other hand, the maintenance of experimental conditions over a lengthy period in a field setting is seldom easy.

Uncontrolled variables that were expected or hoped to remain constant during the experiment might change for reasons beyond the control of the experimenter. Also, the experiment is likely to interfere to at least some extent with the normal work organization, and to require extra involvement for some personnel. It is desirable therefore for the duration of the experiment to be as short as possible.

(e) There is a danger that, unless specific steps are taken to avoid this, the design of the experiment or the presence of researchers may affect the subjects of the experiment in an unknown and uncontrolled manner.

The results of a properly designed field experiment have considerable utility, however. Mobility as the result of transfers between gangs is a common feature of gold mining, and the experiment described here has shown how excessive mobility in stoping gangs can seriously interfere with gang performance. This is particularly the case if mobility is coupled with heterogeneous gangs, as is normally the case, and is continued over a long period of time.

The findings have also suggested that black production supervisors need training in the utilization of the human resources available to them. In particular, there should be considerable advantage in training supervisors to develop "team" concepts in their gangs and to capitalize on gang stability.

It has also been shown that relative ethnic homogeneity (at least for Malawians) was conducive to increased productivity in terms of tons trammed. The reasons for this influence are probably to be sought in the increased extent to which members of the gang were able to communicate with one another, and the greater cultural similarity between members, which would have reduced the need for individuals in gangs to adjust to unfamiliar socio-cultural norms of fellow-workers. If this were the case, benefits should accrue from homogeneous gangs irrespective of the ethnic origin of the men. On the basis of the findings, however, this generalization is unwarranted, and further research is needed on this factor.

QUESTIONS

1. What, according to the authors, is the main problem regarding causality in this kind of study and how does an experiment solve this problem?

2. Describe the difference between independent and dependent variables with reference to this study.

3. Rigid operationalization of the central concepts is a feature of quantitative studies. Discuss this statement with reference to this study.

4. Experimental research is usually regarded as the paradigm case of controlled research. However, no research on human beings can ever control

251

for all the relevant factors. Discuss these statements with regard to the article.

5. Discuss briefly the following statement: the main conclusions draw in this study are adequately supported by the empirical evidence.

REFERENCES

LAWRENCE, A.C. 1972. A new approach to the study of human factors in stope productivity. J.S. *Afr. Inst. Min. Metall.*

MAUER, K.F. 1972. *The African production supervisor in the South African mining industry.* Durban, University of Natal, unpublished M.A. thesis.

EDWARDS, A.L. 1968. *Experimental design in psychological research.* London, Holt, Rinehart and Winston, 3rd edition.

SCHEFFE, H. 1959. *The analysis of variance.* New York, John Wiley and Sons.

BIBLIOGRAPHY

ABRAHAMSON, M. 1983. *Social research methods.* Englewood Cliffs: Prentice-Hall.

ACHINSTEIN, P. 1968. *Concepts of science.* Baltimore: John Hopkins Press.

AGNEW, M. & PYKE, S.W. 1982 . *The science game.* Third edition . Englewood Cliffs: Prentice-Hall .

ALLEN, E.D. & COLBRUNN, E.B. 1976. *A short guide to writing a research paper.* Revised edition. Everett Edwards: De Land.

ALLEN, E.D. & COLBRUNN, E.B. 1976. *Student writer's guide.* 5th edition. Everett-Edwards: De Land.

ANDERSON, G. (ed.). 1984. *Rationality in science and politics.* Dordrecht: D. Reidel Publ. Co.

ANDERSON, K.E. & HOUGH, O.M.A. 1978. *Handbook for the preparation of research reports and theses.* Lonham: University Press of America.

ASQUITH, P.D. & KYBURG, H.E. (eds.). 1979. *Current research in philosophy of science.* Ann Arbor: Edwards Brothers

ATKIN, C & CHAFFEE, S.H. 1972. Instrumental response strategies in opinion intetviews. *Public Opinion Quarterly 36*: 69-79.

BABBIE, E. 1979. *The practice of social research.* Second edition. Belmont: Wadswotth Publ. Co.

BAILEY, E.P. Jr., et al. 1981. *Writing research papers: a practical guide.* New York: Holt, Rinehart and Winston.

BAIRD, J.C. & NOMA, E. 1978. *Fundamentals of scaling and psychophysics.* New York: John Wiley and Sons.

BALES, R.F. 1950. *Interaction process analysis.* Reading: Addison-Wesley.

BALIAN, E.S. 1983. *How to design, analyze and write doctoral research: the practical guidebook.* Lonham: University Press of America.

BANKS, J.A. 1979. Sociological theories, methods and research techniques - a personal viewpoint. *The Sociological Review 27* (3): 561-577.

BARBER, T.X. 1976. *Pitfalls in human research.* New York: Pergamon Press.

BARNES, B. 1972. *Sociology of science.* Harmondsworth: Penguin Books.

BARNES, B. 1982. *T.S. Kuhn and social science.* London: The MacMillan Press.

BATESON, N. 1984. *Data construction in social surveys.* London: George Allen and Unwin .

BEASLEY, K.L. 1982. *Administration of sponsored programs: handbook for developing and managing research activities and other projects.* San Francisco: Jossey-Bass .

BECKER, H. 1963. *Outsiders.* New York: The Free Press.

BEHLING, J.H. 1978. *Guidelines for preparing the research proposal.* Lonham: University Press of America.

BELSON, W.A. 1981. *The design and understanding of survey questions.* Aldershot: Gower.

BENTON, T. 1977. *Philosophical foundations of the three sociologies.* London: Routledge and Kegan Paul.

BERELSON, B. 1952. *Content analysis in communications research.* New York: Free Press.

BERMONT, H. 1979. *The successful consultant's guide to writing proposals and reports.* Washington: Bermont Books.

BERNSTEIN, J. 1976. *The restructuring of social and political theory.* New York: Harcourt.

BERNSTEIN, J. 1983. *Beyond objectivism and relativism.* Philadelphia: University of Pennsylvania Press.

BHASKAR, R. 1979. *The possibility of naturalism.* Brighton: The Harvester Press.

BLUSTEIN, L. & GEARY, R.J. 1981. *Writing the research paper.* Revised edition. Waltham: Bluestein - Geary.

BOGDAN, R. 1974. *Being different - The autobiography of Jane Fry.* London: John Wiley & Sons.

BOGDAN, R. & TAYLOR, S.J. 1975. *Introduction to qualitative research.* New York: Wiley & Sons.

BOGUE, G. 1981. *Basic sociological research design.* Glenview: Scott Foresman.

BOHME, G. 1975. The social function of cognitive structures: a concept of the scientific community within a theory of action. In: Knorr, K.D. *et al. Determinants and controls of scientifc development.* Dodrecht: D. Reidel. Pp. 205-225.

BOTHA, L. 1983. *'n Analise van rasionaliteit, waarheid en konseptuele raamwerke.* M.A. Verhandeling. RAU.

BOTHA, M.E. 1984. *Metaforiese perspektief en fokus in die wetenskap.* Potchefstroom: PU vir CHO.

BRISLIN, R., LONNER, W.J. & THORNDIKE, R.M. 1973. *Cross-cultural research methods.* New York: Wiley.

BROWN, H.I. 1977. *Perception, theory and commitment.* Chicago: Precedent Publishing Co.

BRUYN, S.T. 1966. *The human perspective in sociology: The methodology of participant observation.* Englewood Cliffs: Prentice-Hall.

BULMER, M. (ed.). 1981. *Social research ethics.* London: The MacMillan Press.

BURGESS, R.G. (ed.). 1982. *Field research: A sourcebook and field manual.* London: Allen & Unwin.

BURGESS, R.G. 1984. *In the field.* London: George Allen & Unwin.

CAMPBELL, B. 1981. *Race-of-interviewer effects among southern adolescents.* Public Opinion Quarterly 4S: 2 31-244

CAMPBELL, D.T. 1957. Factors relevant to the validity of experiments in social settings. *Psychological Bulletin S4*: 297-312.

CAMPBELL, D.T. & FISKE, D.W. 1958. Convergent and discriminant validation by the multitrait - multimethod matrix. *Psychological Bulletin 56*: 81-105.

CAMPBELL, D.T. 1969. Prospective: artifact and control. In: Rosenthal, R. & Rosnow, R.L 1969a. *Artifact in behavioural research.* New York: Academic Press. Pp. 351-382.

CAMPBELL, D.T. & STANLEY, J.C. 1963. Experimental and quasi-experimental designs for research on teaching. In: N. L. Cage, (ed.), *Handbook of research on teaching.* Chicago: Rand McNally.

CANNELL, C.F. & KAHN, R.G. 1968. Interviewing. In: Lindsey & Aranson, (eds.): *Handbook of Social Psychology, vol 11.* Reading: Addison--Wesley. Pp. 526-595.

CANNELL, C.F., MILLER, P.V. & OKSENBERG, L. 1981. Research on interviewing techniques. *Sociological Methodology* Vol. 12: 389-437.

CARMINES, E.G. & ZELLER, R.A. 1979. *Reliability and validity assessment.* Beverley Hills: Sage Publications.

CARNAP, R. 1962. *Logical foundations of probability.* Second edition. Chicago: University of Chicago Press.

CARNAP, R. & JEFFREY, R.C. (eds.) 1971. *Studies in inductive logic and probability.* Vol 1. Berkeley: UCLA Press.

CEELY, J. et al. 1978. *Writing a research paper.* New edition. Wellesley Hills: Independent School Press.

CHALMERS, A.F. 1982. *What is this thing called science?* Second edition. Milton Keynes: The Open University Press.

CHAPIN, F.S. 1974. *Experimental designs in sociological research.* Westport: Greenwood.

CHRISTENSEN, L.B. 1980. *Experimental methodology.* Second edition. Boston: Allyn and Bacon.

COGGINS, G. 1977. *A guide to writing essays and research papers*. New York: Van Nostrand Reinhold.

COLEMAN, W.E. 1980. *Grants in the humanities*. New York: Neal-Schuman.

COLLINS, H.M. (ed.). 1982. *Sociology of scientific knowledge: a sourcebook*. Bath University Press.

COLLINS, H.M. 1983. The sociology of scientific knowledge: studies of contemporary science. *Annual Review of Sociology 9*: 265-285.

COOK, T.D. & CAMPBELL, D.T. 1979. *Quasi-experimentation*. Boston: Houghton Mifflin Company.

COPI, I.M. 1972. *Introduction to logic*. Fourth edition. New York: The MacMillan Co.

CRANE, D. 1972. *Invisible colleges*. Chicago: University of Chicago Press.

CRONBACH, C.J. 1946. Response sets and test validity. *Educational and Psychological Measurement 6*: 475-94.

DAS, M.A. & GIRI, N.C. 1979. *Design and analysis of experiments*. New York: Wiley.

DAVIS, K. 1971. Sexual behaviour. In: Merton, R.K. & Nisbet, R., *Contemporary social problems*. Third edition. New York: Harcourt. Pp. 313-360.

DAVITZ, J.R. & DAVITZ, L.L. 1977. *Evaluating research proposals in the behavioral sciences: a guide*. New York: Teachers College Press.

DAWES, R.M. 1972. *Fundamentals of attitude measurements*. New York: John Wiley & Sons.

DEAN, D.G. 1961. Alienation: its meaning and measurement. *American Sociological Review 26*: 753-758.

DENZIN, N.K. 1978. *The research act*. Second edition. New York: McGraw-Hill Book Co.

DOBY, J.T (ed)1954. *An introduction to social research*. Harrisburg: The Stackpole Company.

DOUGLAS, J.D. 1976. *Investigative social research*. Beverley Hills: Sage Publications.

DRAPER, S. 1978. *Simple guide to research papers*. Revised edition. New York: Avery Publication group.

DRAY, W. 1964. *Philosophy of history*. Englewood Cliffs: Prentice-Hall.

DREW, C.J. 1980. *Introduction to designing and conducting research*. Second edition. St. Louis: Mosby.

DU PLESSIS, P.G.W. & SNYMAN, J.J. (reds.) 1987 *Wetenskapbeelde in die geesteswetenskappe*. Pretoria: HSRC Press

DUREN, D. & ANDREANI, J. 1979. *Writing successful proposals*. Lynwood: Durand International.

EDWARDS, A.L. 1957. *Techniques of attitude scale construction*. New York: Appleton Century Crofts.

FEIGL, H. 1970. The orthodox view of theories: remarks in defence as well as critique. In: Radner, M. & Winokur, S. (eds.) *Analyses of Theories and methods of physics and psychology*. Minneapolis: Univ. of Minnesota Press. Pp. 33-16.

FILMER, P. , PHILLIPSON, M., SILVERMAN, D. & WALSH, D. 1972. *New directions in sociological theory*. London: Collier-MacMillan.

FILSTEAD, W.H. 1970. *Qualitative methodology*. Chicago: Rand McNally.

FINNEY, D.J. 1974. *Experimental design and its statistical basis*. Chicago: University of Chicago Press.

FISHBEIN, M. (ed.). 1967. *Readings in attitude theory and measurement*. New York: John Wiley & Sons.

FRIEDMAN, N. 1967. *The social nature of psychological research*. New York: Basic Books

GIDDENS, A. 1976. *New rules of sociological method*. London: Hutchinson.

GIDDENS, A. 1979. *Central problems in social theory*. London: The MacMillan Press.

GIERE, R.N. 1979. *Understanding scientific reasoning*. New York: Holt, Rinehart & Winston.

GILES, H. & CHAVASSE, W. 1975. Communication length as a function of dress style and social status. *Perceptual and Motor skills 40*: 961-62.

GLASER, B. & STRAUSS, A.L. 1967. *The discovery of grounded theory.* Chicago: Aldine.

GOLDEN, M.P. (ed.). 1976. *The research experience.* Itasca: F.E. Peacock Publ.

GORDEN, R.L. 1980. *Interviewing: Strategy, techniques and tactics.* Third edition. Homewood, Illinois: Dorsey Press.

GORRELL, J.M. 1981. *The explanatory, heuristic and meaning-constituring functions of theoretical models.* Ph.D., Brown University.

GRAVES, H.F. & HOFFMAN, L. 1965. *Report writing.* 4th edition. Englewood Cliffs: Prentice-Hall.

GROENEWALD, J.P. 1981. *Maatskaplike navorsing: ontwerp en ontleding.* Pretoria: Academica.

GUTTING, G. (ed.). 1980. *Paradigms and revolutions.* Notre Dame: University of Notre Dame Press.

HAGSTROM, W.O. 1965. *The scientifc community.* New York: Basic Books.

HAKIM, C. 1982. *Secondary analysis in social research.* London: Allen & Unwin.

HATCHET, S. & SCHUMAN, H. 1975. White respondents and race of interviewes effects. *Public Opinion Quarterly 39*: 523-528.

HEMPEL, C.G. 1958. The theoretician's dilemma: a study in the logic of theory construction. In: Hempel C.G. 1965. *Aspects of scientifc explanation.* New York: The Free Press. Pp. 173-226.

HEMPEL, C.G. 1965. *Aspects of scientific explanation.* New York: The Free Press.

HENERSON, M.E. 1978. *How to measure attitudes.* Beverley Hills: Sage.

HIMES, J.S. 1980. *Conflict and conflict management.* Athens, Georgia: Univ. of Georgia Press.

HOLDOWAY, S. 1982. An inside job; a case study of covert research on the police. In: Bulmer, M. (ed.) *Social research ethics.* London: MacMillan. Pp. 59-79.

HOLLIS, M.& LUKES, S. (eds.)1983. *Rationality and relativism.* Cambridge: MIT Press.

HOLSTI, O.R. 1962. *Content analysis for the social sciences and humanities.* Reading: Addision-Wesley.

HUGHES, J. 1980. *The philosophy of social research.* London: Longman.

HYMAN, H.H. 1954. *Interviewing in social research.* Chicago: The University of Chicago Press.

JOHNSON, J.M. 1975. *Doing field research.* New York: The Free Press.

KAPLAN, A. 1964. *The conduct of inquiry.* San Francisco: Chandler Publ. Co.

KAUFMAN, F. 1944. *Methodology of the social sciences.* New Jersey: Humanities Press.

KAZDIN, A.E. 1980. *Research design in clinical psychology.* New York: Harper & Row.

KEAT, R. & URRY, J. 1975. *Social theory as science.* London: Routledge & Kegan Paul.

KEKES, J. 1976. *Justification of rationality.* New York: SUNY Press.

KENISTON, K. 1960. Alienation and the decline of utopia. *The American Scholar 29*:163-168.

KEPPEL, G. 1973. *Design and analysis: a researcher's handbook.* Englewood Cliffs: Prentice-Hall.

KERLINGER, F. 1973. *Foundations of behavioral research.* Second edition. New York: Holt, Rinehart & Winston.

KNORR-CETINA, K.D. 1981. *The manufacture of knowledge.* Oxford: Pergamon Press.

KOLSON, K.L. & GREEN, J.J. 1970. Response set bias and political socialization research. *Social Science Quarterly 51*: 527-538.

KONINGSVELD, H. 1980. *Het verschijnsel wetenschap.* Amsterdam: Boom Meppel.

KRAUSZ, E. & MILLER, S.H. 1974. *Social research design.* London: Longman.

KRIPPENDORF, K. 1981. *Content analysis.* Beverley Hills: Sage publications.

KRUGER, D. 1979. *An introduction to phenomenological psychology.* Cape Town: Juta.

KUHN, T.S. 1970. *The structure of scientific revolutions*. 2nd enlarged edition. Chicago: The University of Chicago Press.

LAKATOS, 1. 1970. Falsification and the methodology of scientific research programmes. In: Lakatos, I. & Musgrave, A. , (eds.) *Criticism and the growth of knowledge*. Cambridge: Cambridge University Press. Pp. 99-196.

LAKATOS, I. & MUSGRAVE, A. (eds.) 1970. *Criticism and the growth of knowledge*. Cambridge: Cambridge University Press.

LAUDAN, L. 1977. *Progress and its problems*. London: RKP.

LEEDY, P.D. 1980. *Practical research, planning and design*. New York: MacMillan Publ. Co.

LESTER, J.D. 1983. *Writing research papers: a complete guide*. 4th edition Glenview: Scott Foresman.

LOFLAND, J. 1971. *Analyzing social settings*. New York: Wadsworth.

LUTYNSKA, K. 1970. The place of interviewing in Polish sociological research and its influence on the results obtained. *Polish Sociological Bulletin* 2: 121-129.

LYKKEN, D.T. 1968. Statistical significance in psychological research. *Psychological Bulletin 70*: 151-159.

McCALL, G.J. & SIMMONS, J.L. (eds.)1969. *Issues in participant observation*. Reading: Addison-Wesley.

MANHEIM, H.L. 1977. *Sociological research: philosophy and methods*. Homewood: The Dorsey Press.

MARAIS, H.C. 1979. *Kommunikasiekunde: 'n Navorsingsperspektief*. Intreerede, UOVS.

MARGOLIN, J.B. 1983. *The individual's guide to grants*. New York: Plenum.

MARSH, C. 1982. *The survey method*. London: George Allen & Unwin.

MARX, M.H. 1963. *Theories in contemporary psychology*. London: The MacMillan Co.

MASTERMAN, M. 1970. The nature of a paradigm. In: Lakatos, I. & Musgrave, A. (eds.) *Criticism and the growth of knowledge*. Cambridge: CUP. Pp. 59-89.

MENDRAS, H. 1969. Problems of enquiries in rural communities. *Sociological Sela* 7: 23-24, 41-52.

MERTON, R. 1973. *The sociology of science: theoretical and empirical investigations*. Chicago: Chicago Univ. Press.

MILGRAM, S. 1963. Behavioral study of obedience. *Journal of Abnormal and Social Psychology* 67: 371-378.

MILLER, D.C. 1970. *Handbook of research design and social measurement*. New York: David McKay Co.

MITROFF, I.I. 1974. *The subjective side of science*. Amsterdam: Elsevier.

MITROFF, I.I. & KILMANN, R.H. 1978. *Methodological approaches to social science*. San Francisco: Jossey Bass.

MOSER, C.A. & KALTON, G. 1971. *Survey methods in social investigation*. Second edition. London: Heinemann Educational.

MOUTON, J. 1977. Paradigma: Ideologie of nie? *Perspektief 16(1):* 38-53.

MOUTON, J. 1979. Wetenskaplikes: Miere, spinnekoppe of bye? *Bulletin vir dosente (RAU)* 11(3): 14-38.

MOUTON, J. 1980. Naturalism and anti-naturalism in contemporary philosophy of science. *Koers* 45(4): 270-279.

MOUTON, J. 1983a. Kwantitatiewe en kwalitatiewe metodologiee in die geesteswetenskappe. *Suid-Afrikaanse Tydskrif vir Sosiologie 14(4)*: 124-131.

MOUTON, J. 1983b. On the meaning of "philosophy of science", "research methodology" and "research technology." *Research Bulletin* 13(3): 33-37.

257

MOUTON, J. 1984a. *Philosophy of social science and the qualitative paradigm.* Paper given at The International Conference on Research Methodology in the Social Sciences, University of Durban-Westville, 16-18 July 1984.

MOUTON, J. 1984b. 'n Topologie van die wetenskapsfilosofie. In: *Wetenskap en Woord.* Potchefstroom, PU vir CHO. Pp. 132-169.

MOUTON, J. 1984c. *Wetenskap as terapie.* D. Litt. et Phil. RAU.

MYERS, J.L. 1979. *Fundamentals of experimental design.* Third edition. Newton: Allyn & Bacon.

NESSELROADE, J.R. & BALTES, P.B. 1979. *Longitudinal research in the study of behavior of development.* New York: Academic Press.

NEWTON-SMITH, W.H. 1981. *The rationality of science.* London: Routledge & Kegan Paul.

NICHOLSON, M. 1983. *The scientifc analysis of social behavior.* London: Frances Pinter Publ.

NISBET, R. 1974. *The social philosophers.* London: Heinemann Books.

NOLAND, R.L. 1970. *Research and report writing in the behavioral sciences: psychiatry, psychology, sociology, educational psychology, cultural anthropology managerial psychology.* Springfield: C. C. Thomas.

NOWAK, S. 1976. *Understanding and prediction.* Dordrect: D. Reidel.

NUNNALY, J.C. 1964. *Educational measurement and theory.* New York: McGraw-hill.

NUNNALY, J.C. 1978. *Psychometric theory.* New York: McGraw-Hill.

ODENDAL, F.F. 1976. Oor die aanspreekvorme in Afrikaans. In: De Klerk, W.J. & Ponelis, F.A. (reds.) *Gedenkbundel H.J.J.M. van der Merwe.* Pretoria: Van Schaik. Pp. 105-113.

OPPENHEIM, A.N. 1966. *Questionnaire design and attitude measurement.* London: Heinemann.

PAREEK, U. & RAO, T.V. 1980. Cross-cultural surveys and interviewing. In: Triandis, H.C. & Berry, J.W. (eds.) *Handbook of cross-cultural psychology,* vol. 2. Pp. 127-179.

PAPINEAU, D. 1979. *Theory and meaning.* New York: Oxford U.P. Inc.

PHILLIBER, S., SCHWAB, H.R. & SLOSS, G.S. 1980. *Social research.* Itasca: F.E. Peacock Publishers.

PHILLIPS, B.S. 1966. *Social research: Strategy and tactics.* New York: MacMillan.

PHILLIPS, G.R. & HUNT, L.J. 1976. *Writing essays and dissertations: a guide to the preparation of written assignments in colleges and universities.* Beaverton: International Scholarly Book Services.

PLUMMER, K. 1983. *Documents of life: An introduction to the problems and literature of a humanistic method.* London: Allen & Unwin.

POPPER, K.R. 1959. *The logic of scientifc discovery.* London: Hutchinson.

POPPER, K.R. 1963. *Conjectures and refutarions.* London: Routledge & Kegan Paul.

POPPER, K.R. 1973. The rationality of scientific revolutions. In: Hacking, I. (ed.) *Scientific revolutions.* Oxford: OUP. 1981. Pp. 80-106.

PUTNAM, H. 1975. *Mind, language and reality.* Cambridge: Cambridge University Press.

RADNITZKY, G. 1970. *Contemporary schools of merascience.* 2nd edition. New York: Humanities Press.

RADNITZKY, G. 1974. From logic of science to theory of research. *Communication and Cognition* 7(1): 61-124.

RADNITZKY, G. 1980. Progress and rationality in research. In: Grmek, Cohen & Cimino, (eds.), *On scientific discovery.* Dordrecth: D. Reidel Publ. Co. Pp. 43-102.

RAVETZ, J.R. 1971. *Scientific knowledge and its social problems.* Oxford: OUP.

RANGONETTI, T.J.A. 1970. A social psychology of survey techniques. *Cornell Journal of Social Relations* 5: 41-50.

ROETHLISBERGER, F.L. & DICKSON, W.J. 1939. *Management and the worker.* Cambridge: Harvard Universities Press.

ROSE, G. 1982. *Deciphering sociological research*. London: The MacMillan Press.

ROSENBERG, M. 1968. *The logic of survey analysis*. New York: Basic Books.

ROSENTHAL, R.E. & FODE, K.L. 1963. Three experiments in experimenter bias. *Psychological Reports* 12: 491-511.

ROSENTHAL, R. & ROSNOW, R.L. 1969a. *Artifact in behavioral research*. New York: Academic Press.

ROSENTHAL, R. & ROSNOW, R. L. 1969b. The volunteer subject. In: Rosenthal & Rosnow, 1969a, *Artifact in behavioral research*. New York: Academic Press. Pp. 61-118.

ROSSI, P. 1957. - *Francis Bacon - From magic to science*. London: Routledge & Kegan Paul.

RUDNER, R.S. 1966. *Philosophy of social science*. Englewood Cliffs: Prentice Hall.

RUSSO, W. 1980. *Secrets of the research paper: an easy guide to success*. Needham: Oman.

RYAN, A. 1970. *The philosophy of the social sciences*. London: The MacMillan Press.

SALMON, W.C. 1970. Statistical explanation. In: Colodny. R.G. (ed.) *The nature and function of scientific theories*. Pittsburg: University of Pittsburgh Press. pp. 1 73-23 1.

SALMON, W.C. 1973. *Logic*. Second edition. Englewood Cliffs: Prentice-Hall.

SANDERLIN, D. 1983. *Writing The history paper: the student research guide*. Revised edition. New York: Barron.

SCHEFFLER, I. 1967. *Science and subjectivity*. Indianapolis: Bobbs-Merril Co.

SCHUMAN, H. & PRESSER, S. 1981. *Questions and answers in attitude surveys*. New York: Academic Press.

SCHUTTE, De W., & VAN WYK, M.J. 1982. *'n Ontleding van die Reigerpark-onrus op 9 Mei 1981 aan die hand van Smelser se teorie van kollektiewe optrede*. Verslag K-10. Pretoria: RGN.

SCHUTTE, G. 1982. *Familiars and strangers: empirical social research as social relationship*. Johannesburg: Witwatersrand University Press.

SCHWARTZ, H. & JACOBS, J. 1979. *Qualitative sociology: A method to the madness*. New York: The Free Press.

SCHWARTZ, R.D. & SKOLNICK, J. H. 1962. Two studies of legal stigma. *Social Problems 10*: 133-142.

SCRIVEN, M. 1976. *Reasoning*. London: McGraw-Hill Book Co.

SEEMAN, M. 1959. On the meaning of alienation. *American Sociological Review* 24:783-819.

SELLTIZ, C., JAHODA, M., DEUTSCH, M. & COOK, S. W. 1965. *Research methods in social relations*. Revised edition. New York: Holt, Rinehart & Winston.

SHANNON, C.E. & WEAVER, W. 1948. *The mathematical Theory of communication*. Urbana: Univ. of Illinois Press.

SIMON, M.A. 1982. *Understanding human action*. Albany: SUNY Press.

SLETTO, R.F. 1973. *A construction of personality scales by the criterion of interval consistency*. Hanover: Sociological Press.

SMITH, H.W 1975. *Strategies of social research*. Englewood Cliffs: Prentice Hall.

SMITH, R.B. & MANNING, P.K. (eds.) 1982. *Qualitative methods*. Vol. 11. Cambridge: Ballinger Publ. Co.

SPECTOR, P.E. 1981. *Research designs*. Beverley Hills: Sage.

SPRADLEY, J. 1979. *The ethnographic interview*. New York: Holt, Rinehart & Winston.

SPRADLEY, J. 1980. *Participant observation*. New York: Holt, Rinehart & Winston.

STERN, P. 1979. *Evaluating social science research*. New York: Oxford University Press.

STERNBERG, R. 1977. *Writing the psychology paper*. New York: Barron.

STOKER, H.G. 1969. *Beginsels en metodes in die wetenskap*. Potchefstroom: Potchefstroom Herald.

STOKER, N.W. 1966. *The social system of science*. New York: Holt, Rinehart & Winston.

STROUP, H. 1961. *A historical explanation of alienation social casework* 42: 107-111.

SUDMAN, S.E. & BRADBURN, N.M. 1982. *Asking questions.* San Francisco: Jossey Bass Publications.

SUPPE, F. 1974. *The structure of scientific theories.* Chicago: University of Illinois Press.

SUSSAMS, J. 1983. *How to write effective reports.* New York: Nichols Publications.

TAYLOR, M.G. 1974. *How to write a research paper.* Paolo Alto: Pacific Books.

TRIGG, R. 1973. *Reason and commitment.* Cambridge: CUP.

VAN DEN BERG, J.H. 1955. *The phenomenological approach to psychiatry.* Springfield: C.C. Thomas .

VAN DER MERWE, N.T. 1975. Paradigm, science and society. *Koers* 40: 328-358.

VAN LEENT, J.A.A. 1965. *Sociale psychologie in drie dimensies.* Utrecht: Anla-Boeken.

VON WRIGHT, G.H. 1971. *Explanation and understanding.* New York: Ithaca.

WARREN, J.E. 1972. *How to write a research paper.* Brookline Village: Branden.

WEBB, E.J., CAMPBELL, D.T., SCHWARTZ, R.D. & SECHREST, L. 1966. *Unobtrusive measures.* Chicago: Rand McNally & Co.

WHITE, V.P. 1975. *Grants: how to find out about them and what to do next.* New York: Plenum.

WHITE, V.P. (ed.). 1983. *Grant proposals that succeeded.* New York: Plenum.

WHYTE, W.F. 1955. *Screen corner society.* Enlarged edition. Chicago: The University of Chicago Press.

WILES, R.M. 1968. *Scholarly reporting in the humanities.* 4th edition. New York: University of Toronto Press.

WILLIAMSON, J.B., KARP, D.A. & DALPHIN, J.R. 1977. *The research craft.* Boston: Little, Brown and Co.

WILSON, B. (ed.). 1970. *Rationality.* Oxford: OUP.

WINCH, P. 1958. *The idea of a social science.* London: Routledge & Kegan Paul.

WINDELBAND, W. 1980. (1894) History and natural science. *History and Theory* 19(2): 165-184.

WRIGHT, L. 1982. *Better reasoning.* New York: Holt, Rinehart & Winston.

ZEHNER, R.B. 1970. Sex effects in the interviewing of young adults. *Sociological Focus* 3: 75-84.

ZELDITCH, M. 1962. Some methodological problems of field studies. *American Journal of Sociology* 67: 566-576.

ZELLER, R. & CARMINES, E. 1980. *Measurement in the social sciences.* Cambridge: CUP.

ZILSEL, E. 1945. The genesis of the concept of scientific progress. *Journal of the History of Ideas* 6: 325-349.

ZNANIECKI, F. 1934. *The method of sociology.* New York: Farrat & Rinehart.

SUBJECT INDEX

connotation 58ff, 126ff
  - conventional 58, 127
  - subjective 58, 126-127
constitutive definition, see theoretical definition
construct 60, 127, 160
construct validity 67ff
constructive replication 96
content analysis 66, 97
context effect 81, 89-90, 92, 120
contextual research strategy 49ff, 121
contextual validity 15
contract research 36-37
control 76ff, 159
control group 93, 94
conventional connotation 127
Cook, TD & Campbell, DT 94
correlational studies 44
covert research 93-94
Crane, D 9
criterion validity 67-68
cross-sectional studies 40, 41

Data sources 76ff, 121, 193
Davis, K 35
Dean's social alienation scale 65ff
deduction 30, 107ff
deductive inference, see deduction
deductive strategy 103, 111ff, 116
definition 125, 131ff
  - see also operational definition, theoretical definition
denotation 58ff, 126ff
Denzin, NK 70, 91
Descartes, R 14
description 44
descriptive research 14
descriptive studies 43-44
determinism 47
diachronic studies, see longitudinal studies
differential reactivity 77
direct observation 77
  - see also participant observation, systematic observation
disciplinary perspective 18

Kuhn, TS 9, 11, 12, 20, 26, 30, 36, 72, 129, 145ff, 151, 189, 192

Language game 4
life documents 97
logical argumentation 106
logical evidence 4
logical positivism 14, 19, 29, 46, 151
logicality 30
longitudinal studies 40

Manheim 77
market of intellectual resources 20, 21ff
Marx, K 60ff, 62, 128
matching of participants 94
meaning 58ff, 126ff
    - see also connotation, denotation
meaning, field of 63ff
meaning, shades of 63ff
measurement effects 89, 242
measurement reliability 95
measurement validity 59, 67ff
measuring instrument effects 81
memory decay 87
metaphysical assumptions 146
metatheoretical assumptions 192
metatheoretical guidelines 192
methodological 15-17
methodological beliefs 23
methodological dimension 15, 19ff
    - participatory action approach 19
    - qualitative approach 19
    - quantitative approach 19
methodological guidelines 192-195
Milgram, S 34-35
Mill, JS 126
Mitroff, II & Kilmann, RH 11
model 60, 125, 137, 138ff, 151
    - precursor model 141ff
mono-operation bias 69
multi operationism 69, 91

Naive inductivism 57
naturalistic research, see qualitative research

Neo-Marxism 21
nomothetic research strategy 48ff, 50
   - **see also** general research strategy
normal science 145-147
normative beings 76

Objectivity 16, 194
observation 158ff
   - qualitative and quantitative 159ff, 164ff
   - **see also** participant observation, systematic observation
observation effects 81ff, 157
   - **see also** context effects, measurement effects,
     researcher effects, participant effects
omniscience syndrome 87
operational definition 60, 132ff, 162
   - **see also** operationalization
operational specificity 158ff
operationalization 22, 25, 64ff, 72

Paradigm 12, 19, 30, 144ff
pardigm programme 125
participant effects 81, 86ff
participant motivation 88
participant observation 92, 93, 96, 160, 164, 165
period effect 120
phenomenology 26, 164, 175
philosophy of science 71-72
philosophy of the social sciences 12, 21
physical sources 77
planning a research project 175
Popper, K 14, 15, 25, 29ff, 31, 57-58, 71, 134
positivism 21, 30
precursive theoretical models 141
predictive research 14, 45
predictive validity 67ff
presupposition 192
probability 15
problem formulation 24, 37ff, 57ff, 192
project perspective 18
project report 189
projective techniques 77
propositions 131ff
   - **see also** definition hypothesis
Putnam, H 15